Instructor's Resource Manual

ABNORMAL PSYCHOLOGY
Fifth Edition

Gerald C. Davison
University of Southern California

John Neale
SUNY at Stony Brook

Prepared by

Marian E. Williams
University of Southern Califonia

WILEY

JOHN WILEY & SONS
New York   Chichester   Brisbane   Toronto   Singapore

ISBN 0-471-51856-5
Printed in the United States of America

10 9 8 7 6 5 4 3 2 1

PREFACE

This manual is designed for those using the Fifth Edition of Davison and Neale's <u>Abnormal Psychology</u>. Its aim is to lighten the instructor's load by providing a convenient resource which summarizes material from the text but also adds substantially to it. It is my hope that the materials contained herein will aid instructors in writing lectures, prompting discussions, using outside resources in the classroom, and summarizing the most important text material for students. There is a chapter in the manual corresponding to each chapter in the book. Each chapter in the Instructor's Resource Manual is organized as follows:

CHAPTER SYNOPSIS: A brief but fairly detailed review of the chapter in the text. This can be used to get a quick review/overview of the entire chapter.

STUDENTS SHOULD KNOW . . . KEY POINTS: A listing of approximately ten major points that are made in each chapter. This list provides the instructor with a convenient listing of key points to highlight or review in a lecture. This material should also provide ideas for writing exam questions, particularly short answer essay questions.

STUDENTS SHOULD KNOW . . . NEW TERMS: A listing of new terms that are introduced in the relevant test chapter. This list also provides material for review in a lecture and will be of help in writing exam items, particularly fill in the blanks or definitions. The text contains a glossary in which most of these terms are defined.

STUDENTS SHOULD KNOW . . . NEW NAMES: A listing of major individuals who are featured in the relevant chapter. Also useful for review and writing test items.

LECTURE LAUNCHERS: For each chapter, four to seven summaries of related research, case histories, or discussion pieces are presented. The material here is related to the chapter content, but it expands on it in various ways. This material can be easily added to a lecture or, in some cases, comprises enough material for a brief lecture in itself. References are provided if the instructor wishes to examine the original source in order to expand on what is contained in the Instructor's Resource Manual. Many of these references would make for suitable supplementary readings for students in the course.

DISCUSSION STIMULATORS: This section contains half a dozen or so suggestions regarding interesting (often controversial) topics for discussion, classroom demonstrations, in-class exercises and role-plays, and questionnaires that could be distributed to students. Many of the suggestions are ideas that have worked successfully for me in the past.

INSTRUCTIONAL FILMS: This is a listing of films that can be used both to convey relevant information to the class and to break up the lecture routine. They are particularly good to use after an exam, when student fatigue is high and attention is low. A list of film distributors is included at the end of the Instructor's Manual.

ADDITIONAL SUPPLEMENTS:

In addition to the Instructor's Resource Manual, there are several other useful auxiliary resources available for the Fifth Edition of Davison/Neale's Abnormal Psychology:

A Test Bank, prepared by Marian Williams, contains 75 to 80 multiple choice questions for each chapter of the text. Questions pertaining to material emphasized in the Study Guide are so marked.

Computerized Test Bank -- Available for IBM and Macintosh computers.

Student Study Guide, 5/E -- Written by Douglas Hindman, Eastern Kentucky University, includes the following per chapter: Chapter Summaries; Key Terms (with space to write in definition); Learning Objectives; Study Questions; Self Test with Answers. Half the Self Test items reappear in the Test Bank in a clearly labeled section.

Case Studies in Abnormal Psychology, 2/E by Oltmans, Neale, and Davison provides a number of interesting and engaging case histories and discussions of the cases. Students particularly enjoy this sort of material.

Readings in Abnormal Psychology -- By Jill Hooley (Harvard University), John Neale and Gerald Davison. A wide-ranging selection of articles not only from scholarly journals but also from the popular media that explore first person accounts of abnormality. Essays by Hooley, Neale and Davison bring the articles into sharp focus. Special discount when packaged with the text.

Video-Cassette Diagnostic Interviews -- Six thirty-minute interviews of representative disorders: Depression, Schizophrenia, Obsessive-compulsive Disorder, Drug Dependence, Mania and Childhood Hyperactivity. $500/set. Gratis to adopters of Davison/Neale; demo tape available.

Computer Tutor -- Unique software game that allows 1-5 students to play against each other while being quizzed on the content of Davison & Neale, 5/E. The fun study aid. All incorrect answers explained. No overlap with the text bank. Items written by Bradley Olsen of Northern Michigan University. Gratis to adopters of Davison/Neale. IBM format only. Demo disk available.

SPECIAL DISCOUNT:

The Study Guide, Case Studies book, or Readings book can be purchased by your students at an attractive discount if you order them in sets from John Wiley & Sons. Contact your local Wiley representative for details. If you don't know your local rep's phone number, contact your bookstore manager, your department secretary or Dorothy Rock at (212) 850-6059.

CONTENTS

CHAPTER 1

Introduction: Historical and Scientific Considerations

CHAPTER SYNOPSIS:

While many people are intrigued by the prospect of finding explanations for the causes of abnormal behavior, explorers in the field must have "great tolerance for ambiguity" in order to be comfortable with the tentative, often conflicting pieces of information available. In fact, it is the kinds of questions asked rather than the specific answers to those questions which constitute the essence of the field. This text focuses on addressing the study of abnormal psychology using objective rules of science, rather than a phenomenological approach.

The Mental Health Professions

A <u>clinical psychologist</u> holds a Ph.D. degree and receives intensive research training in addition to specialized training in diagnosis and psychotherapy.

A <u>psychiatrist</u> holds an M.D. and receives the same medical training as do other physicians, in addition to a residency in psychotherapy. Because of their medical training, psychiatrists are able to prescribe psychoactive medications.

<u>Psychoanalysts</u> have received specialized training at a psychoanalytic institute. Although Freud maintained that a medical degree was not a necessary prerequisite to psychoanalytic training, until recently most psychoanalytic institutes have required an M.D. and psychiatric residency.

A <u>Psy.D.</u> (Doctor of Psychology) is a graduate degree similar to a Ph.D., but doctoral training involves less emphasis on research and more emphasis on clinical work.

A <u>psychiatric social worker</u> has a Masters of Social Work degree. There are also master's and doctoral programs in <u>counseling psychology</u>, somewhat similar to graduate training in clinical psychology but usually with less emphasis on research.

<u>Psychopathologists</u> are a diverse group of people from various disciplines who conduct research into the nature and development of various mental disorders but do not engage in treatment.

In general, the clinical work conducted by different professionals depends more on the theoretical orientation of the school attended than on the type of academic degree obtained.

History of Psychopathology

The doctrine that an evil being may control the behavior of another person is called demonology. Demons were thought to be the cause of abnormal behavior in many ancient societies, and various rituals, sometimes tortuous ones, were performed to exorcise them. Even in these early times, however, priests learned to temper their incantations with kindness, and rest and exercise were often prescribed for the disturbed.

Hippocrates was one of the earliest proponents of the somatogenic hypothesis of psychopathology--the belief that something wrong with the "soma" or physical body causes a disturbance in thought and action. He also recognized that environmental and emotional stress could influence behavior. Although his conception of brain functioning based on the balance of "humors" or fluids in the body was rather crude, Hippocrates' basic premise relating human behavior to bodily functioning foreshadowed modern thinking.

The decline of the Roman empire and the rise of various religious groups eventually led to a return to concern about demonology. In the 16th and 17th centuries thousands of people were tried as witches and subjected to torture and possible execution.

While witch trials in Salem have been taken as examples of mentally ill individuals being denounced as witches, several factors suggest that it may have been ergot (a fungus with hallucinogenic effects), rather than mental illness, which was responsible for the unusual behavior of some of those accused of demonic possession (Caporael, 1976). For some time the prevailing interpretation has been that all the mentally ill of the later Middle Ages were considered witches. More careful analyses reveal that although some accused witches were mentally disturbed, many more sane than insane people were tried. Records of lunacy trials in Britain suggest that the most common explanations for abnormal behavior were physical illness or injury or emotional shock; only one case was attributed to demonic possession (Neugebauer, 1979). In fact, it was during the Middle Ages that the insane asylum first appeared.

When leprosy gradually disappeared from Europe during the 15th century, many former leper hospitals were turned into institutions for the insane. Despite the inclusion of abnormal behavior within the domain of hospitals and medicine, conditions in many of the asylums were deplorable.

"Treatment" for the insane included drawing large quantities of blood and frightening patients by convincing them of their impending death. Phillipe Pinel was among the first to advocate humane treatment of the mentally ill in the late 18th century; he removed the chains of patients imprisoned in his hospital and treated them as sick human beings in need of compassion and understanding, rather than as beasts.

Progress in understanding mental illness was fostered by the discovery in the middle ages that the long accepted presentation of human anatomy by Galen, Hippocrates' disciple, was incorrect. The ensuing emphasis on an empirical approach to classifying mental disorders and studying their etiology marks the beginning of contemporary thought about psychopathology. Emil Kraepelin, a proponent of the somatogenic hypothesis, pointed out that groups of symptoms, called syndromes, appear together regularly in mental illnesses as in physical ones. His classification system became the basis for the present diagnostic categories. The discovery of the connection between <u>general paresis</u>, with its deterioration in mental and physical health, and the medical condition of <u>syphilis</u> greatly promoted the somatogenic hypothesis; if one type of psychopathology had a biological cause, then so could others. The search for somatogenic causes has dominated psychiatry well into the 20th century.

The <u>psychogenic</u> viewpoint--the belief that mental illness is due to psychic malfunction--appeared in the late eighteenth century. Mesmer believed that hysterical disorders, such as physical incapacities that defied anatomical rules, were caused by magnetic fluids in the body that could be influenced by other people; he used hypnotism to cure people of such disorders. While Mesmer viewed hysterical symptoms as purely physical, Charcot became convinced that such phenomena were caused by psychological factors; Breuer developed the <u>cathartic method</u> to relieve the emotional tension presumably underlying the paralysis.

While the term "to mesmerize" is derived from his name, Mesmer was neither the first to practice hypnosis nor the only one to use it in his time. The technique is likely an ancient one which was used by the faith healers of various cultures. Moreover, hypnotism was and continued to be used as a method of blocking pain. James Braid, a physician credited with coining the term hypnosis, avoided Mesmer's mystical approach while experimenting with the phenomenon more objectively. While the discovery of drugs for anesthesia limited the use of hypnosis in medicine, practitioners have continued to use hypnotic procedures for psychotherapeutic purposes, such as relieving combat exhaustion in World War II.

Science: A Human Enterprise

Science is not a completely objective enterprise; rather it is shaped by the limitations of our conceptual frameworks and influenced by subjective factors. Kuhn's concept of _paradigm_--the conceptual framework or model within which a scientist works--suggests that both the kind of concepts that are viewed as legitimate and the methods used to collect data are based on a shared set of assumptions. The paradigms scientists embrace may even affect the interpretation of facts; this "I'll see it when I believe it" feature of science is illustrated in the clash between the psychoanalytic and behavioral paradigms.

In a study exploring the influence of theoretical frameworks on the judgements of clinicians, Langer and Abelson (1974) had behaviorally and psychoanalytically oriented therapists view a videotape of a young man in an interview. Half of each group of therapists were told that the young man was on a job interview, and the other half were told he was a patient. Therapists were then asked to make judgements about the man's mental health. The behaviorally oriented therapists were relatively unaffected by the label, while the dynamic therapists rated the "patient" as more disturbed than the "job interviewee." The point of the study is not, however, to say who was right and who was wrong in their judgements. Rather, it illustrates the importance of paradigmatic sets. Behavior therapists are trained to evaluate overt behavior and were less affected by the label. Dynamic therapists, in contrast, are trained to look beyond the obvious and were inclined to interpret the "patient's" behavior as symptomatic.

Another paradigm clash is illustrated in a box in which opposing views of hypnosis are examined. The basic controversy is whether hypnosis involves some special psychological processes such as unconscious experience, or whether it is a response to an expected social role. Empirical reports can be used to support each point of view, and the clash of paradigms is illustrated by the critical commentary and the new experiments each camp offers in response to new data from the opposing camp.

Chapter 1

STUDENTS SHOULD KNOW . . .

Key Points

1. The text takes a scientific rather than a phenomenological approach to understanding abnormal behavior. Because so little is known at this time, the kinds of questions asked rather than particular answers constitute the essence of the field.

2. The different types of professionals involved in the field of mental health. Students should realize that a particular therapist's approach to clinical work is more a reflection of the orientation of their school of training than of their academic degree.

3. While there have been differing views on the causes of abnormal behavior throughout the course of history, the roots of contemporary thought are embedded in the past. The somatogenic viewpoint was first postulated by Hippocrates more than 2,000 years ago, and the psychogenic point of view emerged in the late 18th century. These remain the major points of view regarding the causes of abnormal behavior.

4. Abnormal behavior has been treated differently and often inhumanely in the past. However, neither were past practices as inhumane nor are current practices as enlightened as they are sometimes portrayed.

5. Although it strives to be objective, there are elements of subjectivity that intrude upon the scientific enterprise. The assumptions scientists make about the types of questions to ask and the types of methods that should be used to collect data are more subtle indications of subjectivity (paradigms).

New terms
(key terms underlined)

phenomenological, clinical psychologist, psychiatrist, psychoanalyst, psychiatric social worker, psychopathologist, demonology, somatogenic, psychogenic, asylum, moral treatment, mesmerize, hypnosis, general paresis, symptoms, syndrome, germ theory, hysteria, cathartic method, paradigm, behavior therapy, psychoanalysis

New figures
(key figures underlined)

Hippocrates, Galen, Philippe Pinel, Benoni Buck, Thomas Sydenham, Wilhelm Griesinger, Emil Kraepelin, Franz Mesmer, Jean Charcot, Pierre Janet, Joseph Breuer, Thomas Kuhn

NOTES

LECTURE LAUNCHERS

Masturbatory Insanity

E.H. Hare (1962, <u>Journal of Mental Science</u>, <u>108</u>, 2-25--now <u>British Journal of Psychiatry</u>) presents a scholarly review of a seemingly outlandish hypothesis: masturbation causes insanity. The historical documentation of the rise and fall of this hypothesis affords the opportunity to illustrate an interesting bit of history, while demonstrating how many errors and biases can enter into the pursuit of "objective" information.

The notion that masturbation causes insanity arose among the 18th century political and religious beliefs that masturbation was wrong, as the purpose of sex was procreation. A popular book was written about the evils of masturbation--<u>Onania or the Heinous Sin of Self-Polution</u>. Not surprisingly, the book, which went into many editions, also offered a "cure" for an additional price. For reasons that are unclear, some leading medical authorities adopted and elaborated upon the masturbatory insanity hypothesis. One explanation offered as a link between masturbation and insanity was that blood flow was drawn away from the brain. The writings of the authorities of the time served to spread the belief further among medical professionals that masturbation did indeed cause insanity, thus reinforcing the popular view. Once widely held, like any theory, the hypothesis was difficult to disprove. Furthermore, "scientific" data were brought to bear to support the notion. In the crowded and inhumane asylums of the era, it was not unusual to observe an insane individual masturbating openly. This was a rare event for individuals to witness elsewhere, however, and there was little information on or consideration of the prevalence of masturbation, in private, among sane individuals. Case studies provided further data in support of the masturbatory insanity hypothesis. Physicians, believing the hypothesis, found patients who would confess to the practice, thus confirming the suspected etiology. Those patients with mental problems who did not admit to masturbating could well be lying (denying?), of course. Finally, since few rival hypotheses were available, there were few challenges to the masturbatory insanity notion. Indeed, to challenge the theory was to challenge morality.

With the rise of more plausible hypotheses, the gathering of some data, and the gradual change in attitudes about sex, the masturbatory insanity hypothesis faded. Still, from the 18th through the early 20th century the hypothesis had managed to survive in one form or another.

Such leading figures in the history of psychopathology as Freud, Rush, and Maudsley each, at least temporarily, adopted the hypothesis. In fact, Hare suggests that Freud's ideas about castration anxiety may have partially stemmed from childhood recollections about his father's warnings against masturbation. (Castration and clitorectomy were among the treatments employed for masturbatory insanity; prevention was more common in that parents were educated about its potential dangers and warned to be vigilant about their children's sexual play.)

The history of the masturbatory insanity hypothesis can be used to illustrate several important points about the scientific enterprise. It demonstrates the intrusion of popular beliefs into "objective" science. (How does our assumption that "all men are created equal" influence contemporary psychology?) The influence of authorities on our beliefs about what is true is also conveyed in this history. Finally, some points about the scientific method are illustrated: the fact that correlation does not mean causation (insane masturbating openly); the need for comparison groups (the base rate of private masturbation); limitations on case history data; and the value of considering rival hypotheses (a counterpoint to paradigm clash).

After illustrating how silly the masturbatory insanity hypothesis was, another useful lesson can be learned -- humility and skepticism. Who could believe the masturbatory insanity hypothesis now? In a **New York Times** article on life in China (**N. Y. Times Magazine**, Jan. 13, 1980), an excerpt is contained about a young man who wrote to a Peking newspaper concerned about the consequences of masturbation. A professor from Peking Medical College replies:

> Masturbation itself is not a sickness but an impulsive act . . . If done regularly, it will stimulate sex nerves which will produce fatigue, dizziness, listlessness, bad memory, and other phenomena which will hamper work and study. In more severe cases, it will lead to nervous breakdown.

The masturbatory insanity hypothesis and the potential for bias in science live!

Law and Lunacy in the Middle Ages

Neugebauer (1979, Medieval and early modern theories of mental illness. Archives of General Psychiatry, 36, 477-483) reviewed English legal documents dating back to the 13th century. He argues that around that time, the Crown assumed the right and responsibility for caring for the property and person of the mentally disabled. When a person was thought to be mentally incompetent, a petition requesting the Crown's guardianship would be filed, usually by friends or relatives of the person in question. The local sheriff then formed a jury and a hearing was held to establish if, and if so why, the person was incompetent and the extent of his estate. Two groups of incompetents were distinguished: idiots or natural fools and lunatics. These terms seem to roughly correspond to our terms "retarded" and "insane." For instance, a 16th century source defined idiot as:

> he that is a fool natural from his birth and knows not how to account or number 20 pence, nor cannot name his father or mother, nor of what age himself is, or such like easy and common matters; so that it appears he has no manner of understanding or reason, nor government of himself, what is for his profit or disprofit.

Commonsensical explanations were offered for the person's disturbed state. Consider the following cases: In July, 1490, John Fitzwilliam was said to be mentally disabled starting when he was "gravely ill." In 1502, John Norwick "lost his reason owing to a long and incurable infirmity" and on September 18, 1291, a jury declared Bartholomew de Sadewill mentally deranged and attributed that condition to "a blow received on the head." Robert Barry's insanity was, in 1366, thought to have been "induced by fear of his father." Similarly, a 1568 hearing found James Benok to have been "afflicted by reason of a fright on 20 Oct. 1556 and has so continued from that time to the present."

In reviewing at least 5 centuries of hearing records, Neugebauer found only one demonological explanation. The facts that those requesting and those subjected to competency hearings came from all walks of life and that the juries that heard them were made up of townsmen suggest that these views were not those of a minority or a particular social group. The commonsense definitions and explanations documented here stand in marked contrast to the conventional view that the insane were held to be possessed and tested by the terrible tortures of religious inquisition.

Hysteria or Malingering?

To lay the groundwork for discussion in Chapter 3 of the problems of diagnosis and classification, the historical roots of the concept of mental illness, traced by Thomas Szasz in The Myth of Mental Illness (1961, New York: Harper and Bros.), might be presented at this point in the course. Szasz reviews Charcot's influence on psychiatry and on the public's view of mental disorders. Before Charcot's time, hysteria was considered to be a form of malingering (faking real physical illness), and such counterfeiters were treated with anger and hostility by physicians who resented the deception. After Charcot had lent his expertise and authority to the problem of hysteria, it was elevated to the status of "illness;" Szasz asserts that this shift has led to the present-day classification of all human conduct as falling within the purview of mental illness.

How did this shift take place? Szasz suggests that Charcot's goal was to get hypnosis and hysteria accepted by the medical profession as respectable phenomena, worthy of study; further, he asserts that rather than use logical analysis or scientific investigation to understand hysteria, Charcot simply changed the rules of classification such that "malingering" became "illness." Given that the new illness could nevertheless be considered counterfeit in the sense that it mimics a physiological dysfunction, medicine acquired the responsibility of distinguishing, not only real from imitated physical illness, but conscious from unconscious faking. If the sufferer counterfeits unknowingly, he is not a malingerer, but a hysteric. While this change in label may have been humane in the sense that such sufferers were no longer shunned by physicians, Szasz argues that it has obscured our understanding both of true organic neurological disorders and of problems in living that may only look like physical disorders. Further confusion arises when, as is the case today, conscious malingering itself is seen as a form of mental illness; Szasz quotes Bleurer: "Those who simulate insanity with some cleverness are nearly all psychopaths and some are actually insane. Demonstration of simulation, therefore, does not at all prove that the patient is mentally sound and responsible for his actions" (p. 48).

Discussion might focus on the following questions: What are the consequences of labeling a phenomenon an "illness?" How does such a label obscure or clarify that which it describes? Should psychiatry be considered a branch of medicine? What is the value of distinguishing "conscious" from "unconscious" malingering? How can such a distinction be made? The story of hysteria may also be discussed in the context of a shift from somatogenic to psychogenic viewpoints in psychiatry. If hysteria had continued to be seen as simple malingering, would the psychogenic hypothesis of psychopathology have been advanced?

NOTES

Asylums in Modern Times

A discussion of the conditions in contemporary institutions for the mentally disturbed can supplement the material on the historical development of asylums. A variety of interesting and impressive exposes of institutions are available:

Burton Blatt's work exposing the condition of institutions for the mentally retarded as recently as the late 1970s may prove especially enlightening for students, who are often shocked by the conditions of asylums in the Middle Ages. Excellent sources include <u>Christmas in Purgatory: A Photographic Essay on Mental Retardation</u> (1966, Blatt, B. & Kaplan, F., Boston: Allyn & Bacon) and its follow-up volume <u>The Family Papers: A Return to Purgatory</u> (1979, Blatt, B., Ozolins, A., & McNally, J., New York: Longman Inc.), as well as <u>Exodus From Pandemonium</u> (1970, Blatt, B., Boston: Allyn & Bacon), which details Blatt's work to document and reform institutional care of the mentally retarded. Discussion might be sparked by reading the following quotes from the latter volume and asking students to guess the year (or century!) which they describe:

> The children's dormitories depressed me the most. Here, cribs were placed - as in the other dormitories - side by side and head to head. Very young children, one and two years of age, were lying in cribs without any contact with any adult, without playthings, without apparent stimulation. In one dormitory that had over 100 infants and was connected to nine other dormitories that totalled 1,000 infants, I experienced my deepest sadness. As I entered, I heard a muffled sound emanating from the "blind" side of a doorway. A young child was calling, "Come, come play with me. Touch me." (p. 18).

> . . . I found two young women in one cell, lying nude in the corner, their feces smeared on the walls, ceiling, and floor - two bodies huddled in the darkness, on a bare terrazzo floor . . . On the next floor was a girl who has been in a solitary cell for five years, never leaving - not for food or toileting or sleep. This cell - this concrete and tile cubicle - without furniture or mattress or washstand, is one human being's total universe (pp. 72-73).

The words describe institutions visited by Blatt in the 1960s.

Asylums: Essays on the Social Situation of Mental Patients and Other Inmates (Goffman, E., 1961, Chicago: Aldine Publishing Company) offers a sociological perspective on life in institutions, researched during the 1950s. In the essay "On the Characteristics of Total Institutions," Goffman discusses institutional life (with a particular focus on mental institutions) from the point of view of both the "inmates" and the staff. Discussion might focus on the loss of identity, personal possessions, meaningful work, and control over personal needs (asking permission to go to the bathroom, use the telephone, spend money, mail letters), which characterizes institutional life, as well as the perspective of the staff who must reconcile patients' self-destructive behavior and the resulting need for measures which curtail their rights, incompatible standards for different patients (e.g., if the gates are left open for those patients who have "town privileges," patients who could otherwise have enjoyed the use of the grounds might have to be kept in locked wards), and the conflict between humane treatment and institutional efficiency (e.g., collective clothing is depersonalizing, yet much more efficient to clean and keep track of than personally owned clothing). Students might be encouraged to think about ways that institutional life could be improved, as well as the question of whether it is possible to truly effect reform without abandoning the institutional system altogether (foreshadowing the discussion of de-institutionalization discussed in Chapter 20).

For those students who believe that our current enlightened recognition of the problem of institutionalization is sufficient to alleviate the conditions in institutions, it can be pointed out that the following quote first appeared in the _Journal of Mental Science_ in 1856:

> Asylums . . . might justly be called manufactories of chronic insanity. If a case recovers, and few indeed are those that do recover within their walls, it is certainly the result of fortuitous circumstances, and not of any special treatment applied to it (Aldridge, p. 1979, _British Journal of Psychiatry_, 134, p. 333).

Awareness and outrage, while starting points, would seem to be insufficient motivators for change in institutional care when viewed from an historical perspective.

Chapter 1

Careers in Mental Health

Most students are extremely interested in the different mental health professions. Many may be considering careers in one of these fields, making more detailed review of the professions interesting and worthwhile. Each profession can be listed on the board and compared on various dimensions, such as years of training required, difficulty of acceptance into training programs, criteria for acceptance (courses, grades, national exams, outside activities), focus of academic training, and career possibilities. Students are also likely to be interested in comparisons such as opinions that each profession holds of each other, interprofessional conflicts, lines of authority and power structure, salaries (the $50 - $100 hour amazes most students), and similar "insider" information. Current topics of interest in the mental health field might be discussed, such as: (1) Should clinical psychologists be allowed "admitting privileges" at psychiatric hospitals? (2) Which professionals should be eligible to receive Medicare payments for their services? (3) Should professionals other than psychiatrists be allowed to prescribe psychotropic medications? (4) Should training of clinical psychologists focus on clinical or research training, or both?

A recent article in American Psychologist (Purdy, J. E., Reinehr, R. C., & Swarx, J. D., 1989, 44, 960-961) reported on results of a survey of 106 graduate programs in experimental, clinical, and counseling psychology regarding their admissions criteria. Students might be interested in hearing the conclusions:

> the ideal graduate school applicant has a high GRE combined score, strong letters of recommendation, some research experience, and a high overall GPA, with particularly high grades for the final two years. For applicants for a clinical or counseling program, previous clinical experience is desirable. Undergraduate course work would include statistics, experimental methods, and at least some laboratory experience (p. 961).

DISCUSSION STIMULATORS

Pre-Post Assessment of Students' Views of Abnormal Behavior

Students have many reasons for taking a course in Abnormal Psychology. They may need to fulfill major subject requirements, have a free hour when the course is given, possess a copy of the textbook handed down from someone, want to learn "how to help people," or want to learn to understand themselves better.

The latter motivation is probably the most prevalent, and may be responsible for the immense popularity of courses in Abnormal Psychology. You may want to explain to students that they may gain insight into their own behavior through taking the course, but this is not the major purpose of the course. The goal of the course is to expose students to a wide range of human behaviors, conventional and bizarre, and to illustrate the scientific research being conducted on the causes and methods of changing abnormal behavior. Furthermore, it can be emphasized that process is being taught as much as content is. Students are not just learning information; they are learning a method of scientific inquiry.

The questionnaire presented here may be useful for helping students examine their biases and expectations at the beginning of the course. Students can be asked to write their answers to the questions and hand them in; at the end of the course, they can be given a blank copy of the questionnaire to fill out again, and the two sets of answers can be compared and discussed.

VIEWS ON ABNORMAL PSYCHOLOGY

Name _____

(circle one:)   pre   post

1) How would you define "abnormality"?

2) Where do you think "mental illness" comes from? Is the root of abnormal behavior primarily physical/organic, early childhood experiences, current environmental forces, or some other factor?

3) How do you think mentally disturbed people should be treated?
What treatment approach(es) do you think work best?

4) What do you hope to learn from this course? (Or, if post-course, what have you learned that is most valuable?)

The Case of Ernest H.

Students' interest will be sparked by discussing the case of Ernest H. presented in the first pages of the book. Questions to discuss: What more would you like to find out about Ernest in order to understand him better? Is there anything you feel was left out of the case presentation which would be important to know? What factors do you think may have led to Ernest's current difficulties? Which of his problems seem most important to focus on first in trying to help him? What approach do you think would be helpful in treating him?

Again, it may be helpful to have students record their ideas and refer to them as the course progresses, to observe changes in their views about the case of Ernest as they learn more about abnormal behavior.

"Medical Student's Syndrome"

Just as medical students often "diagnose" themselves as having many of the diseases they read about in such detail, Abnormal Psychology students frequently see themselves in the symptoms of mental illness described in this course. It is important to be sensitive in lecturing about various topics, as some students will be wondering if they are in need of therapy, or they may have a friend or relative who has emotional problems and want to do something to help. It is good practice to give the class information about a student counseling center or other psychological services early on in the course. Still, be prepared during office hours to answer questions that are more personal than academic in nature, and have referral sources available for such times.

Paradigms: Brain Teasers

One of Kuhn's important arguments is that scientists' investigations are directed by the assumptions that they begin with. Sometimes the assumptions facilitate the discovery of interesting phenomena; other times the assumptions stand in the way. The following demonstrations and "brain teasers" help to illustrate the influence of one's mental set. (In fact, Kuhn links most of scientific activity to puzzle solving.)

1. Using a slide projector, show several slides of any scene (a natural landscape, a cityscape, your pet dog), beginning with the slide blurry and unrecognizable. (Be sure to set the projector out of focus in advance, so the students cannot identify the picture.) Ask a volunteer from the class to describe what he/she sees on the screen, and write the comments on the board. Have an assistant or another student gradually bring the slide into focus as the volunteer continues to describe the picture and you continue to write the description on the board. Several points can be brought out through this demonstration:

- The blurry picture can be likened to the state of science in the early gropings for understanding, and the later recognition of the picture to the experience of scientists discovering a new phenomenon more clearly. This experience can be compared to Kuhn's view about how "normal science" progresses: rather than developing in a continuous, smooth manner, our recognition of scientific phenomena often occurs by fits and starts. Similarly, students will find themselves fumbling to understand the picture during the "pre-recognition" phase, followed by what is usually an "aha!" experience of recognition.

- In order to grasp the "true" meaning of the picture, we must start out with numerous hypotheses but remain flexible about changing our perspective as new data becomes available. Students who take a longer time to recognize the subject of the picture may be wedded to cognitive "sets" established early in the exercise and not abandoned.

Chapter 1

2. Brian Teasers:

a) To what does the following enigma, written by Lord Byron, refer?

I'm not in earth, nor the sun, nor the moon.
You may search all the sky -- I'm not there.
In the morning and evening -- though not at noon,
You may plainly perceive me, for like a balloon
I am suspended in air.

Though disease may possess me, and sickness and pain,
I am never in sorrow nor gloom;
Though in wit and wisdom I equally reign,
I am the heart of all sin and have long lived in vain;
Yet I ne'er shall be found in the tomb.

Odds are it will take the class a long time to recognize that the answer is the letter "i". (But ask students not to shout out answers right away; some one may have heard this before or be bright enough to figure it out, and puzzling over the brainteaser increases the impact of the point being made.) Once given the answer (and a new "set"), the following puzzle should be easily solved:

The beginning of eternity
    the end of time and space,

The beginning of every end,
    the end of every place.

The answer is "e", of course.

b) "A boy is riding down the highway with his father and gets into a terrible accident. His father is killed immediately and the boy is in critical condition. He is rushed to the hospital in an ambulance, where the emergency room doctor exclaims, `That's my son!' How can this be?"
About half the class will get the answer fairly quickly, so warn people to keep their solutions to themselves. The solution to this puzzle not only illustrates the concept of set once again, but can lead to a discussion of sex roles if you choose. The answer, naturally, is that the doctor is the boy's mother.

c) Hold a box of tacks and a candle in front of the class. Ask how these materials can be used to fasten the candle to a wall. Students are likely to provide many ingenious answers, but most are unlikely to be able to break their "paradigmatic set." The key is to think of using the box as a candleholder. The box can be fastened to the wall, and the candle can be set in the box.

These brainteaser demonstrations can serve as a lead in to a discussion of paradigms and their role in science. What is a paradigm? It is a set of beliefs or a model which explains something about the world. Most importantly, it is universally accepted as being the best way to look at and understand a specific problem. There are many characteristics of mature, paradigmatic science. Among them is that there are no competing schools, each with a claim to the "only true paradigm." Another characteristic is that knowledge is accumulated and studied for its present worth, while the historical predecessors and false starts that led to the knowledge are generally ignored. By-products of these two characteristics of a mature science are the progressive obscurity of specific knowledge to the layman and the increasing proliferation of scholarly reports and papers at the expense of longer books which try to cover a topic from every angle. A useful question for students to think about (or write about on an exam) is whether or not psychology is a pre-paradigmatic or a paradigmatic science. The discussion of abnormal psychology in the text would tend to indicate that the former is the case. The clash of paradigms is very evident both in the conception and in the treatment of mental disorders.

Paradigms and Bias Today

To illustrate the potential for bias and error in the presentation of historical information, bring in reports of a significant current news event from two popular media sources differing widely in their political views. Each report is likely to differ greatly when providing a "factual account" of the same event; this demonstration serves as an example of a paradigmatic set. One culture's "freedom fighters" are another culture's terrorists. One's paradigm--in this case a political perspective--influences one's perceptions of "objective" data.

INSTRUCTIONAL FILMS

(A list of film distributors can be found at the end of this manual.)

1. <u>Abnormal Behavior</u>. (CRM, 26 min., color, 1971) A general film on abnormal behavior, this deals with the influence of childhood experience on later psychopathology, neurosis and anxiety, and psychosis. Included are views of schizophrenics in a mental hospital and even a scene showing a clinical application of ECT.

2. <u>Abnormal Behavior: A Mental Hospital</u>. (McG, 28 min., 1971) A documentary about life in a modern psychiatric hospital. Includes a tour of the hospital, diagnostic sessions, and therapy sessions.

3. <u>Hurry Tommorrow</u>. (TFC, b & w, 1976) A documentary film in a Los Angeles psychiatric hospital, depicting the attitudes of staff and patients and the treatment of patients.

4. <u>King of Hearts</u>. (UA, color, 1967) This classic film stars Alan Bates as an English soldier sent to scout out a German-occupied French villiage, abandoned by all but members of the local insane assylum. The film focuses on what happens when these residents occupy the town. An excellent and humorous portrayal of normal and abnormal behavior.

5. <u>Mental Health: New Frontiers of Sanity</u>. (EMC, 22 min., color, 1971) Documents the extent of mental health problems in North America, and traces the history of therapy.

6. <u>Hypnosis: Can Your Mind Control Pain</u>. (FI, 53 min., color, 1982) Several case histories are presented in which hypnosis is used as anesthesia. One of a series of four films on hypnosis produced by the BBC.

CHAPTER 2

Current Paradigms in Psychopathology and Therapy

CHAPTER SYNOPSIS

This chapter is concerned with the principal paradigms that have been used to conceptualize abnormal behavior--the physiological, psychoanalytic, learning, cognitive, and humanistic paradigms. The goal of the chapter is to convey the general assumptions made by each paradigm to lay the groundwork for the examination of diagnostic categories in later chapters.

The Physiological Paradigm

The historical link between medicine and abnormal behavior has led to a medical or disease model which likens abnormal behavior to a physical disease. However, the multitude of theories to explain physical illness suggest that there exists no single paradigm for explaining "disease," whether mental or physical. Therefore, the term physiological paradigm (rather than "medical model") has been chosen to describe the theory that behavioral abnormality may be attributed, at least in part, to a disruption in one or more physiological processes.

A box discusses some criticisms of the application of the "medical model" to abnormal behavior, such as the difficulty of independently verifying the existence of a mental disease, the subjectivity of symptoms of mental illness (Szasz), and the lack of a known etiology for many mental illnesses.

Physiological Approaches to Treatment

An important implication of the physiological paradigm is that somatic treatments will be effective. Knowledge that PKU is caused by an enzyme deficiency, for example, has led to testing for evidence of the deficiency and to dietary treatments that reduce exposure to the amino acid that causes brain damage. However, other physiological interventions, such as ECT, do not follow from knowledge about etiology. In addition, nonphysiological treatments can have beneficial effects on the soma.

The Psychoanalytic Paradigm

Sigmund Freud's psychoanalytic or psychodynamic view is probably the most widespread paradigm of psychopathology. Freud divided the mind into three principal parts, the _id, ego, and superego_. The id, the primary instinctual core, operates on the _pleasure principle_, seeking immediate gratification via reflex activity and _primary process_ (the satisfaction of needs in fantasy). The id is fueled primarily by life-integrating psychic energy or _libido_. The ego mediates between the instinctual demands of the id and the demands of reality, using _secondary process_, or logical planning. The superego is the carrier of society's moral values as interpreted by one's parents. The interplay between these three competing psychic structures is referred to as the _psychodynamics_ of the personality. According to Freud, most of this interplay is _unconscious_.

According to Freud, the personality develops through four psychosexual stages: the _oral_, _anal_, _phallic_, and _genital_. Between the phallic and genital stages is the _latency period_ during which the child behaves asexually. Life-long personality traits are determined by the child's resolution of conflicts at each stage of development. Too much or too little gratification can cause _fixation_ of the personality at an immature point. Perhaps the most important developmental crises are the _Oedipal_ (for boys) or _Electra_ (for girls) conflicts. Identification with the same-sex parent resolves these crises and leads to the development of the superego.

Freud proposed two different theories of anxiety. In his first formulation (1895), anxiety was hypothesized to stem from the repression or blockage of id impulses, leading to _neurotic anxiety_. In his second formulation (1926), the conditions which caused an individual to repress id impulses were made more explicit, and anxiety was seen as functional, serving as a warning to the ego of impending overstimulation. Freud differentiated two other forms of anxiety: _objective anxiety_ or realistic fear, and _moral anxiety_ or guilt.

Initially, Freud maintained that traumatic childhood sexual experiences were the central cause of neurotic anxiety. Because this would mean that sexual acts with children were more prevalent than he assumed, Freud altered his theorizing and suggested that his clients were reporting fantasy rather than fact. Ironically, recent evidence on the prevalence of childhood sexual abuse suggests that Freud's initial speculation may be more nearly correct.

According to Freud, objective anxiety could be reduced by removing or avoiding the external danger in a rational way. In contrast, neurotic anxieties are reduced through an unconscious distortion of reality by the _defense mechanisms_, which protect the ego from anxiety. Some defense mechanisms are: 1) _repression_, whereby impulses unacceptable to the ego are pushed out of consciousness; 2) _projection_, attributing unacceptable impulses to external agents; 3) _displacement_, redirecting emotional responses from a dangerous object to a safer substitute; 4) _reaction formation_, converting one feeling, such as hate, into its opposite, love; 5) _regression_, retreating into the behavioral patterns of an earlier age; and 6) _rationalization_, inventing a reason for an action or attitude.

Post-Freudian Psychodynamic Perspectives

A number of theorists adapted Freud's ideas in forging their own approaches. _Carl Gustav Jung_ broke with Freud in 1914; he de-emphasized the sexual nature of libido, seeing it as a general biological life energy, introduced the idea of a _"collective unconscious"_ containing information from the history of humankind, and asserted that each of us has both masculine and feminine traits as well as basic spiritual and religious needs. Jung also catalogued various personality types (e.g., extraversion vs. introversion) and developed the concept of _self-actualization_ which was later emphasized by the humanists. Finally, Jung focused on _teleology_ (purposiveness, decision-making, and goal-setting) rather than on the determinism of Freudian thinking.

Alfred Adler's "individual psychology" focused on the individual's _phenomenology_ as the key to understanding the person. He anticipated contemporary cognitive therapy in his efforts to help patients change their illogical beliefs. His interest in the prevention of problems influenced the development of child guidance centers and parent education.

As an _"ego psychologist,"_ _Erik Erikson_ emphasized the formation of ego identity and psychosocial development. His major contribution is in _lifespan developmental psychology_, as he proposed eight stages of psychosocial development which detail the growth and change of individuals throughout the lifespan. For example, the _identity crisis_ reflects the transition from childhood to adulthood, a time when we struggle to define ourselves.

Psychoanalytic Therapy

Psychoanalytic therapy attempts to lift repression so that the patient can resolve childhood conflicts in the light of adult reality. Two techniques for lifting repression are <u>free association</u>, in which the patient is asked to speak without self-censoring, and <u>dream analysis</u>, based on the assumption that repressed material is present in symbolic form in dreams. Ego analysts emphasize the <u>analysis of defenses</u>: the analyst <u>interprets</u> the patient's behavior by pointing out its defensive nature. While psychoanalytic treatment in the past extended over several years of as many as five sessions per week, contemporary "psychoanalytically oriented psychotherapy" tends to be briefer and more present-oriented than traditional analysis, while continuing to focus on examining the true sources of tension and unhappiness by a lifting of repression.

In a box, the authors review methodological and conceptual problems in Freud's work, including the limited reliability of case study data, his highly referential theorizing, the small and select nature of his sample of patients, and the reification of many Freud's theoretical concepts.

Learning Paradigms

The roots of <u>behaviorism</u> lie in the dissatisfaction of <u>John Watson</u> and others with <u>introspection</u> as a means of experimental investigation, and the suggestion that a focus on observable responses would be more profitable. Watson borrowed from psychologists who were investigating learning in animals; thus learning rather than thinking became the dominant focus in psychology.

<u>Classical conditioning</u> is a form of learning discovered by Pavlov: he paired the presentation of food (<u>unconditioned stimulus</u>) with ringing a bell (<u>conditioned stimulus</u>) and found that the ringing of the bell alone came to evoke salivation. Salivation in response to food is a natural event (<u>unconditioned response</u>), but in response to the bell it is a conditioned event (<u>conditioned response</u>). Watson and Rayner induced Little Peter to fear a white rat through the use of classical conditioning, suggesting a possible etiology of certain disorders.

<u>Operant conditioning</u> is based on Thorndike's <u>law of effect</u>, which suggested that behavior followed by satisfying consequences would be repeated, while behavior followed by unpleasant consequences would decrease. Skinner renamed this the principle of <u>reinforcement</u>, and argued that all behavior is determined by the positive and negative reinforcers provided by the social environment.

Modeling is a third type of learning in which observing someone perform certain behaviors can increase or decrease the likelihood that the observer will perform that behavior. Albert Bandura distinguishes four types of modeling: 1) observational learning, 2) inhibitory and disinhibitory effects, 3) response facilitation effect, and 4) environmental enhancement.

Finally, the mediational theory of learning holds that an environmental stimulus does not initiate an overt response directly; rather some internal response plays a mediating role. According to this theory, fear may be both a learned internal response and a drive which can mediate avoidance behavior.

Applying the learning paradigm to deviant behavior, both normal and abnormal behaviors are seen as learned responses which may be precisely observed. While effective treatments have developed from the learning theory approach, abnormal behavior has not yet been convincingly traced to particular learning experiences.

Behavior Therapy

The terms behavior therapy and behavior modification have been applied to therapeutic techniques that are outgrowths of the learning paradigm. The principle that a response to a given stimulus can be eliminated by eliciting a new response in the presence of that stimulus is called counterconditioning. Wolpe's systematic desensitization is one example of counterconditioning, as people are taught to replace fear with relaxation in a step by step learning process. In assertion training, people are encouraged to express both positive and negative feelings. In aversive conditioning, an attractive stimulus is paired with an unpleasant event in hopes of endowing it with negative properties. A token economy is a procedure based on operant conditioning in which explicit rules of behavior and rewards are established. Modeling is also used to teach new behaviors, with role playing and behavior rehearsal being two variations of modeling techniques.

The Cognitive Paradigm

The focus of cognitive psychology is on how people structure their experiences, transforming environmental stimuli into information that is usable. According to the cognitive view, the learner plays an active role, fitting new information into an organized network of accumulated knowledge or schema. Researchers in the cognitive paradigm suggest that cognitive sets may lead to psychopathology; a pre-existing set toward helplessness, for example, may cause depression. At this point, however, cognitive explanations of psychopathology tend to focus on current determinants, and have shed little light on the etiology of mental disorders.

Cognitive Behavior Therapy

Cognitive restructuring is an attempt to change patients' thinking processes. Albert Ellis, for example, holds that maladaptive feelings are caused by irrational beliefs, and he challenges the patient's irrational assumptions in the process of rational-emotive therapy. Aaron Beck proposed that depressed individuals distort experience by, for example, selectively abstracting from a complex event those features which maintain their gloomy perspective on life.

Learning and Cognitive Paradigms

There is great controversy as to whether the learning and cognitive paradigms should be combined or treated separately. Some of the assumptions of each viewpoint seem quite different, but many cognitive behavior therapists use both cognitive and learning techniques. Moreover, the two approaches share the rigorous standards of proof of experimental psychology.

Chapter 2

The Humanistic Paradigm

Reacting against the dominance of the psychoanalytic and behavioristic views, Maslow offered the humanistic paradigm as a more positive perspective on human behavior. He and Rogers suggested that humans are innately good, with a natural drive toward self-actualization, and that suffering comes from the denial of that goodness. The phenomenological world is of utmost importance to the humanists, as a person's actions are said to be decided by the way he or she experiences the world. Finally, the humanistic view reflects an abiding belief in free will or freedom of choice.

Humanistic Therapy

Carl Roger's client-centered therapy focuses on helping the client become aware of and express feelings from the inner self. Rogers assumes that an individual's innate capacity for growth and self-direction will assert itself in a warm, attentive, and receptive therapeutic atmosphere. Thus, their basic tool is unconditional positive regard--complete and unqualified acceptance and respect for the client. Empathy, or the reflection of feeling, is also used to help clients to clarify their thoughts and to listen to their inner feelings. Since the humanist's goal is self-actualization, therapists do not give direct advice and therapeutic techniques are de-emphasized.

Consequences of Adopting a Paradigm

Abnormal behavior is too diverse to be adequately explained by any one of the current paradigms, and in fact, most practicing clinicians describe their approach as eclectic, borrowing techniques from other schools. The authors favor the diathesis-stress paradigm, which considers abnormal behavior to be a consequence of the interactions between a physiological or psychological predisposition toward pathology and life stress.

As discussed in a box, none of the paradigms provides an explicit definition of abnormal behavior. The statistical definition (deviation from average), the personal discomfort definition (self-defined abnormality), the disability definition (impairment in social or occupational functioning), and the norm violation definition (transgressions against social rules) are all reviewed, but each is found to be less than fully satisfactory.

STUDENTS SHOULD KNOW . . .

Key Points

1. What a paradigm is.

2. That the physiological paradigm assumes that the roots of psychopathology are somatic in nature, how the authors distinguish the physiological paradigm from the medical model, and the criticisms of the disease analogy in explaining "mental illness."

3. That the psychoanalytic paradigm traces psychopathology to unconscious conflicts. Students should be aware of Freud's ideas about the structure of the mind, the stages of psychosexual development, anxiety, and the defenses. Students should also be able to distinguish the views of the major post-Freudian psychodynamic theorists.

4. That the learning paradigm asserts that abnormal behavior is learned much the way normal behavior is learned. Classical conditioning, operant conditioning, and modeling are the major learning processes proposed.

5. That the cognitive paradigm shares much in common with the learning view, while putting much more emphasis on the role played by unobservable (but testable) cognitive processes and the active role of the learner.

6. That the humanistic paradigm was developed in reaction to the dominance of the psychoanalytic and learning views, asserting that humans are innately good and that human behavior is a product of free will.

7. Students should be aware of the different therapeutic approaches that emanate from each of the five paradigms.

8. That paradigms are both an aid and a limitation to scientific research and that no one paradigm adequately accounts for human behavior.

9. That the diathesis-stress paradigm is an attempt to integrate some of the seemingly contradictory views of different paradigms.

10. That most psychologists do not align themselves with one school of thought, but instead see themselves as eclectic.

Chapter 2

New Terms
(Key terms underlined)

- physiological paradigm, medical model, etiology

- psychoanalytic paradigm, id, ego, superego, libido, pleasure principle, primary process, secondary process, reality principle, psychodynamics, defense mechanisms, unconscious, oral stage, anal stage, phallic stage, latency period, genital stage, fixation, Oedipus complex, Electra complex, neurotic anxiety, objective anxiety, moral anxiety, repression, projection, displacement, reaction formation, regression, rationalization, collective unconscious, teleology, ego psychologist, lifespan developmental psychology, psychosocial stages, identity crisis, free association, dream analysis, analysis of defenses

- learning paradigm, introspection, classical conditioning, unconditioned stimulus, unconditioned response, conditioned stimulus, conditioned response, learning curve, extinction curve, operant conditioning, law of effect, reinforcement, mediators, shaping, modeling, observational learning, inhibitory and disinhibitory effects, response facilitation effect, environmental enhancement, arousal-induction, avoidance conditioning, counterconditioning, systematic desensitization, assertion training, aversive conditioning, token economy, role playing, behavior rehearsal

- cognitive paradigm, schema, cognitive set, cognitive restructuring, irrational beliefs, rational-emotive therapy

- humanistic paradigm, self-actualization, existential approach, phenomenological world, client-centered therapy, unconditional positive regard, empathy

- diathesis-stress paradigm, predisposition, eclectic, normal curve

New Names
(Key figures underlined)

Thomas Szasz, Sigmund Freud, Carl Jung, Alfred Adler, Erik Erikson, Karen Horney, Harry Stack Sullivan, John B. Watson, Ivan Pavlov, Edward Thorndike, B. F. Skinner, Albert Bandura, O. Hobart Mowrer, Neal Miller, Albert Ellis, Aaron Beck, Abraham Maslow, Carl Rogers

LECTURE LAUNCHERS

The Misuse of "Behavior Modification"

The label which is used to describe a paradigm of abnormal behavior can create various positive and negative connotations that can be important to the evaluation of that paradigm. Many students in an abnormal psychology class are naive about the implications of the various paradigms and may react to their presentation in this chapter based on public misconceptions rather than more detailed evaluation. Students, for example, may find themselves attracted to the humanistic paradigm as opposed to the learning view because the words sound more attractive rather than because they find one set of ideas more sensible. The instructor may wish to alert students to this issue when discussing various paradigms.

The popular misuse of the term "behavior modification" serves as an example of public misconceptions. Turkat and Feuerstein, for example, (1978, _American Psychologist_, _33_, 194) documented the misuse of this term. While, in psychology, behavior modification is a label used to describe certain learning paradigm approaches to treating abnormal behavior, these authors found that a very reliable public medium, the _New York Times_, equated behavior modification with "Chinese torture, revolutionaries, convicts, and Nazi Germany." The popular but confusing term "behavior modifying drug" is an ironic misnomer, since it brings together two conflicting paradigms whose respective proponents might agree on just one thing: the term misrepresents both perspectives. Overall, Turkat and Feurstein found that 48% of the _Times_ articles written between 1973 and 1977 misused the term behavior modification. Thus, it is likely that students will have to be disabused on popular misconceptions about this and other terms before they can begin to objectively evaluate the various paradigms of abnormal behavior.

Maslow's Hierarchy of Needs

As the text notes, the humanistic paradigm differs radically from the other views on abnormality in its focus on health, growth, and self-fulfillment. There is perhaps no better example of this unique orientation than Maslow's hierarchy of needs (Maslow, A., 1968, Toward a psychology of being. New York: Van Nostrand Reinhold). If they haven't already encountered the concept in an introductory psychology class, it may be worth briefly outlining the hierarchy for students.

Typically presented as ascending steps in a psychological triangle, Maslow outlines five basic classes of human needs. At the bottom come physiological needs such as thirst, hunger, and sexual drives. Next are the safety needs of being secure and out of danger posed by a threatening environment. Safety needs are followed by belongingness and love needs--an innate human desire to be accepted and valued by others. The need to be held in esteem, to achieve, to be competent is the fourth step discussed by Maslow. Finally, the need for self-actualization comes at the top of the triangle.

Two points should be made clear about Maslow's hierarchy. First, he views the desire to satisfy these needs as innate--our goal of achieving self-actualization is every bit as much a part of our human make-up as is our goal to survive. The second point sets some limits on the first, however. According to Maslow, we can only satisfy higher needs on the triangle when the lower ones are fulfilled. Physiological needs are more basic than safety needs, and we will risk our safety in order to fulfill them. (A starving man will take considerable risks in order to find food.) Similarly, self-actualization needs must be subordinated to esteem needs and only can be pursued when the lower desires are fulfilled.

Carl Rogers (1902-1987)

Carl Rogers died suddenly in 1987 at the age of 85, following surgery for a broken hip. Obituaries from the Los Angeles Times (February 6, 1987) and the American Psychologist (1988, 43, 127-128) offer a glimpse into the life of this influential champion of the humanistic paradigm. Rogers was born Jan. 8, 1902, in Oak Park, Illinois. He received his doctorate from Columbia University Teachers College in 1931. Rogers founded the Center for the Study of the Person in La Jolla, California in the 1960's, where he remained active until his death. Those who knew Rogers describe him as a quiet but intent listener, who was able to convey his real interest in and empathy for the phenomenological world of the individual. While caring deeply about individual persons, he doubted authority, institutions, credentials, and diagnosis. Accused in the 1940s of "destroying the unity of psychoanalysis," Rogers successfully pioneered the new method of nondirective, client-centered therapy, turning the tables on the authority of analysts. One of Rogers' most important contributions was his concern with conducting research in psychotherapy. He was one of the first to assert that therapists should demonstrate that their methods work; he even went so far as to tape therapy sessions at a time when the analytic relationship was considered almost sacred. Friends report that on his 80th birthday, Rogers announced that he would devote the rest of his life to working toward world peace, and to that end traveled to the Soviet Union in 1986 and led workshops in Hungary, Brazil, and South Africa.

The Family Systems Paradigm

While the family systems approach is presented as a type of therapy in Chapter 20 of the text, students may be interested in contrasting the view which family systems theorists take of abnormal behavior with the viewpoints presented in this chapter. Of particular interest is the idea that a person's behavior and emotions need to be examined within their social context, rather than as isolated phenomena. The following basic tenets of the family systems view of "abnormal behavior," originally developed during the 1950's and modified in the ensuing years, might be contrasted with the views espoused in other paradigms. Sources for these views include two books by Jay Haley: Problem-solving therapy (2nd Ed.), San Francisco: Jossey-Bass, 1987, and Reflections on therapy and other essays, Chevy Chase, MD: The Family Therapy Institute of Washington D.C., 1981, (Chapter 4: Behavior modification and a family view of children).

1) Rather than studying and classifying abnormal behaviors within individual persons, family systems theorists view behavior (both normal and abnormal) as an interaction between two or more persons.

2) When viewed within their social context, symptoms may be discovered to be appropriate and adaptive behavior, rather than pathological. For example, the dog phobia of an 8-year-old boy described in "Case Report: A Modern `Little Hans'" (Haley, 1987) would be explained not by internal conflict or classical conditioning, but as an

adaptive response within the family. The boy's symptoms were helpful to his mother; she was a lonely woman with no activities outside the home and little contact with her hard-working husband, and the boy's phobia kept him from leaving the house and leaving her alone. For the boy, his phobia was an effective means of maintaining closeness with his father, with whom he only spent time when he needed a protective escort. Finally, the symptom was helpful to the marriage; it gave the parents a common concern, demanding much of their energy and enabling them to avoid facing their marital problems.

3) Many family systems theorists take an anti-diagnostic stance, in part because they may see a given symptom as adaptive, but also because they are mindful of their own role in the system; the label of an expert may make change more difficult by crystallizing the problem and making it chronic.

Students might be asked to consider the similarities and differences between the family systems approach and the other paradigms described in the text. While family systems theory is perhaps most similar to the learning paradigm (both focus on the impact of the environment in creating and maintaining behavior), Haley (1981) presents a case for important differences between them, particularly in their approaches to therapy. While the behavior therapist who treats a child's disruptive behavior by teaching new discipline techniques to a parent is working within the social context, he differs from the family therapist in several ways.

First, the family therapist is likely to consider a wider social context, exploring the role of a grandparent or father in addition to the concerned mother who brings the child to the clinic. Second, the family systems thinker is acutely aware of possible disagreement between the parents about the plan of discipline the behavior therapist proposes. If, for example, the child's symptoms have an adaptive role in the family, one or both parents may unwittingly sabotage the new discipline plan. Finally, the family systems theorist considers the complex interplay of several types of learning contexts occurring simultaneously. Consider the following example: a father tells his son not to smoke, but that if he must smoke, he should do so openly and not "sneak around." The boy is then punished for smoking at home in the presence of his father. In addition, the mother defends the boy's right to smoke. The operant conditioning context (smoking is followed by punishment, which should decrease the behavior) malfunctions because of another learning context (the punishment is dependent not only on the boy's behavior, but also on the mother's behavior; she may forbid her husband to punish the boy). In addition, the boy finds himself in a learning context in which no voluntary action will influence reinforcement (his parents use him in their struggle with each other, thus ensuring that the reinforcements will be determined, not by his behavior, but by their feelings toward one another).

At this point, students might be asked to consider whether family systems theory offers a new paradigm for explaining abnormal behavior, or if its uniqueness lies only in its methods of therapy.

The Biopsychosocial Paradigm

"Mental illness is a myth. Psychiatrists are not concerned with mental illnesses and their treatments. In actual practice they deal with personal, social, and ethical problems in living." (Szasz, T., 1961, The Myth of Mental Illness, New York: Harper and Bros., p. 296)

Szasz' attack on psychiatry, and particularly on psychoanalysis, was notorious at the time his book was first published. He proposed that the attempt to explain "psychiatric symptoms" as significantly similar to diseases of the body was not only incorrect but an affront to personal responsibility. Instead, Szasz presented what was then a new view of the role of the psychiatrist. Students could be asked to compare his viewpoint to those of the non-psychoanalytic paradigms which have developed in greater depth since his book was written. For example, how does Szasz' view of the therapist as teacher, who helps people learn to adapt to new environments, fit with the views of behavior therapists? How is his portrayal of psychotherapy as a theory of human relationships and social arrangements reflected in family systems theory? How would more recent findings within the physiological paradigm, such as those regarding the etiology of schizophrenia and manic-depression, challenge Szasz' premise that psychiatry should be divorced from medicine? This discussion could be coordinated with the film, "Is Mental Illness a Myth" (reference below).

Engels (1977, Science, 196), providing another view of the relationship between psychiatry and medicine, asserts that the medical model is an outmoded approach to understanding both mental and physical illness. He proposes that rather than divorcing psychiatry from medicine (as Szasz proposes), both disciplines should adopt a "biopsychosocial model," in which physicians take into account "the patient, the social context in which he lives, and the complementary system designed by society to deal with the disruptive effects of illness, that is, the physician role and the health care system" (p. 132). Students might enjoy debating the similarities and differences between medicine and psychiatry, in conjunction with the box in the text on criticisms of the medical model.

NOTES

Chapter 2

DISCUSSION STIMULATORS:

Mastering New Material

A large number of new terms are introduced to students
in this chapter. This may be a bit overwhelming to students
so early in the class, yet many of the terms and concepts in
this chapter form the backbone of the text. Providing
students with a list of terms and their definitions may
help. Use the above list and get definitions from the
glossary in the text. Terms can be discussed in class, or
this may be a good time to give a short quiz on the
definitions of some of the key concepts in the chapter.

Applying Paradigms to People

Students often enjoy and learn from applying the
material in this course to actual cases. Divide the
students into five sections, and have each group adopt one
of the paradigms described in the chapter. Using the case of
Ernest H. or a case from your own practice (explaining how
you have protected the confidentiality of your client), have
the groups discuss how their paradigm might be used to
understand the client. Questions for the groups to consider
in the case of Ernest H.:

- What (if any) are the important aspects of Ernest's
childhood history to consider in understanding his
current difficulty?

- What aspects of the case history would be down-played
or considered less important in this paradigm?

- What factors have led Ernest to drink heavily?

- What is the cause of Ernest's mood swings?

- Why is Ernest experiencing problems with impotence?

- What treatment approach would be recommended? What
specific techniques would be used?

After preparing answers to these questions, the groups could
be asked to debate each other on the various points. The
competition between paradigms should become clear as
students become wedded to particular views and attempt to
persuade their peers of their ideas.

Chapter 2

Free Will vs. Determinism

The issue of free will and determinism runs throughout
the book, and students often bring to the course strong
opinions on the subject. At this point in the course, the
strongly deterministic views of Freud and Skinner may be
pointed out as contrasting greatly with the emphasis on free
will by Rogers and Maslow. The following questions might be
discussed in class:
- What are the psychological implications of not
believing in free will? Determinism implies a loss of
control; belief in free will may be adaptive if it increases
our self-efficacy. This issue could be related to the
concept of internal vs. external locus of control, which
students may have encountered in an introductory psychology
course. Is it **healthier** to believe in free will, or to live
as if we have free will, whether or not it exists?
- Is the scientific study of human behavior compatible
with a belief in free will? Is free will something that can
be studied empirically? If so, how?
- What view of human behavior does our society hold, as
evidenced by various religious and legal beliefs? Can a
psychopathologist who believes in free will support an
exception for being not guilty by reason of insanity?

Personal Consequences of Paradigms

The view of behavior that a student adopts has an
effect not just on the student's view of psychology, but
also on the student's view of him or herself. Do I want to
think of my own behavior as being caused by unconscious
processes, by my biological make-up, by past learning
experiences, or by the way I construe the world? How can I
change myself, if I can change myself at all? Can I learn
new ways of behaving, must I have my biological make-up
altered if I want to change, will change only occur after
many years of analysis, or do I really need some
understanding and caring? While scientists (and students)
are striving to be objective, personal values can effect the
answers we seek and those we accept; at times our values may
persuade us more than the data we find.

Peak Experiences

Maslow's description of self-actualization includes the concept of "peak experiences," which students are often attracted by (1968, Toward a psychology of being. New York: Van Nostrand Reinhold). Reading the following passage might encourage students to consider their own experiences in the humanistic context:

> I would like you to think of the most wonderful experience or experiences of your life; happiest moments, ecstatic moments, moments of rapture, perhaps from being in love, or from listening to music or suddenly "being hit" by a book or a painting, or from some great creative moment. First list these. And then try to tell me how you feel in such acute moments, how you feel differently from the way you feel at other times, how you are at the moment a different person in some ways. (p. 71)

Focusing on these types of growth experiences is one element that distinguishes the humanist paradigm from those which focus on studying pathological behavior and emotions.

Somatogenic vs. Psychogenic Hypotheses in Modern Psychology

The relationship between the somatogenic and psychogenic hypotheses described in Chapter 1 and the major paradigms presented in this chapter could be made explicit by asking the class to categorize the paradigms as either somatogenic or psychogenic. The physiological paradigm is a clear example of the modern version of the somatogenic viewpoint, and psychoanalysis clearly grew out of the psychogenic hypotheses of Charcot and Breuer. More dissent might arise in classifying the learning and cognitive paradigms; they may represent a new view of abnormal behavior (environmentogenic?) which is not neatly defined as somatogenic or psychogenic.

In addition to recognizing their own biases regarding which paradigm is most appealing or "makes sense," students could be encouraged to think about what type of evidence would convince them of the value of one paradigm over another.

INSTRUCTIONAL FILMS:

1. **The Otto Series**. (IU, 25-27 min., color, 1975) A series of five films that begins with an open-ended dramatization of abnormality in a middle-aged man, then offers four perspectives for understanding and treatment: behavioral, phenomenological, psychoanalytic, and social.

2. **Sigmund Freud: His Office and Home, Vienna, 1938**. (Filmaker's Library, 17 min., color) "The film would be of real use in a history of psychology class or any class dealing with Freud and his ideas."

3. **Young Dr. Freud**. (FOTH, 97 min., b & w, 1977) Dramatic portrayal of Freud's youth, medical training, and discovery of the unconscious.

4. **Carl Gustav Jung**. (Time-Life Film, 38 min.) "In the warmth and privacy of his home on the shores of Lake Zurich, Dr. Jung talks about his friendship and later differences with Freud. (He humorously declines to reveal any details of the interpretations each made of the other's dreams.) He also reminisces about his childhood and the influences that led him to become a psychiatrist. The total span of his life and work are covered--right up to his view of death and his idea of the ongoing of the psyche."

5. **Everybody Rides the Carousel**. (PFP, 73 min., color, 1975) Real-life episodes are used to illustrate the stages of life that figure in Erikson's theory of personality.

6. **Professor Erik Erikson**. (AIM, 50 min.) A summary of Erikson's stages of personality development by Erikson himself.

7. **Pavlov: The Conditioned Reflex**. (Films for the Humanities, 25 min., b & w, 1974) "This absorbing film biography of Pavlov has been beautifully constructed . . . (his) devotion to science--and his contributions to psychology--are very well conveyed" (Mental Health Materials Center Review).

8. **Classical and Instrumental Conditioning**. (HAR, 20 min., color, 1978) Defines, compares and demonstrates these two basic learning principles.

9. **B.F. Skinner and Behavior Change**. (Research Press, 45 min., color) Skinner is joined by various eminent behavior therapists in a discussion of behavioral psychology and behavior therapy. Examples of on-site interventions are provided.

10. **Being Abraham Maslow**. (FLMLIB, 30 min., b & w, 1972) Excerpts from an interview in which Maslow discusses factors that influences his life and theory. Includes reasons for rejecting Freudian views and the behaviorist approach.

11. **Dialogues, Dr. Carl Rogers, Parts I and II**. (UCEMC, 100 min., 1971) Wide-ranging interview with Carl Rogers, covering basic client-centered theory and some contemporary issues.

12. **Is Mental Illness a Myth?** (NMAC-T 2031, 29 min., 1969) "Debates whether mental illness is a physical disease or a collection of socially learned actions." Panelists: Thomas Szasz; Nathan Kline; and F.C. Redlich.

NOTES

CHAPTER 3

Classification and Diagnosis

CHAPTER SYNOPSIS

There was great inconsistency in the way abnormal behavior was classified in the nineteenth century, and many of these problems extend into the twentieth century as well. Currently, the World Health Organization's <u>International Statistical Classification of Diseases, Injuries, and Causes of Death</u> and particularly the American Psychiatric Association's <u>Diagnostic and Statistical Manual - III Revised</u> have gained widespread use.

DSM-IIIR

A number of major innovations distinguish the DSM-III and its revised version, in particular its <u>multiaxial</u> system in which each individual is rated on five separate dimensions. Axis I includes all diagnostic categories except for the personality and developmental disorders, which make up Axis II. This distinction was made so that long-term disturbances would not be overlooked. Axis III is used to indicate any current physical disorders believed to be relevant to the mental disorder. Axis IV is a 1 to 7 rating of the level of psychosocial stress experienced by the patient, and Axis V is used to indicate both the current level of adaptive functioning and the highest level achieved in the past year.

Fifteen major diagnostic categories make up Axes I and II:

<u>Disorders usually first evident in infancy, childhood, or adolescence</u>. This broad-ranging category includes the intellectual, emotional, physical, and developmental disorders that usually begin between birth and 18 years of age.

<u>Organic mental disorders</u>, in which the functioning of the brain is known to be impaired. The primary symptoms are <u>delirium</u>--clouding of consciousness--and <u>dementia</u>--intellectual deterioration.

<u>Psychoactive substance use disorders</u>. In these disorders the use of various substances have led to an impairment of functioning.

<u>Schizophrenia</u>. These serious mental disorders involve a deterioration in functioning, communication disturbances, <u>delusions</u> and <u>hallucinations</u>.

Delusional disorders. Here, the individual experiences delusions of being persecuted or extreme and unjustified jealousy.

Mood disorders include major depression and bipolar disorder, which involves episodes of mania or both mania and depression.

Anxiety disorders include phobias, panic disorder with agoraphobia, generalized anxiety disorder, obsessive-compulsive disorder, and posttraumatic stress disorder.

Somatoform disorders. These disorders are characterized by the presence of physical symptoms that have no known physiological cause but seem to have a psychological purpose.

Dissociative disorders. A sudden alteration in consciousness affecting memory and identity is the major symptom of these problems which include amnesia, fugue, multiple personality, and depersonalization disorder.

Sexual disorders. These disorders include people who choose unconventional objects for sexual expression (paraphilias) and those who experience problems in their sexual response.

Psychological factors affecting physical condition. This diagnosis is given when psychological factors seem to cause or exacerbate a physical illness.

Sleep disorders include disturbances in the amount, quality, or timing of sleep (dyssomnias) and the parasomnias, in which an unusual event occurs during sleep.

Personality disorders. These disorders, listed on Axis II, are inflexible and maladaptive patterns of behavior.

Developmental disorders include mental retardation, pervasive developmental disorder, and specific developmental disorders in the areas of reading, arithmetic, and writing skills.

Code V. This all encompassing category is for "conditions not attributable to a mental disorder that are a focus of treatment," such as marital problems, occupational problems, or uncomplicated bereavement.

The Relevance of Classification

One group of critics assert that classification per se is irrelevant to the field of abnormal behavior, because it leads to a loss of information and hence overlooks the uniqueness of the person being studied. While such simplification may be useful depending on the purpose of the classification system, the classified individual may be stigmatized. Assuming that various types of abnormal behavior do differ from one another, however, it is essential to classify them; the differences may constitute keys to discovering causes and inventing treatments.

Criticisms of Diagnostic Practice

A second group of critics finds specific deficiencies in the way diagnoses are made, particularly focusing on the reliability and validity of diagnostic practice. Reliability indicates whether or not different diagnosticians will agree on the application of a given diagnostic label. The reliability of earlier classification systems has been demonstrated to be disappointingly low.

Whether or not accurate statements and predictions can be made from a classification is the test of its validity. Three kinds of validity are considered: etiological validity is present if the classification provides information on the cause of the disorder; concurrent validity is established if the classification conveys information about current functioning that is not used in making the diagnosis; and finally, predictive validity refers to the ability of the diagnosis to predict future behavior, particularly the course of the disorder or the likely response to treatment.

DSM-IIIR and Criticisms of Diagnosis

DSM-III and DSM-IIIR were designed to be more reliable and valid than their predecessors. Extensive descriptions of the various disorders are provided, and specific diagnostic criteria are spelled out. Results of field trials indicate that this effort has led to improved reliability.

Problems remain with DSM-IIIR, however. It is unclear whether the rules for making diagnostic decisions are the best, and subjective factors still play a role in making diagnoses. Furthermore, the system's reliability in day to day practice may be considerably lower than what was achieved in the field trials. Even if reliability is higher, there is no guarantee of improved validity. Finally, some of the diagnostic categories seem overly broad. The most promising aspect of the new classification systems is their attempt to be explicit about the rules for diagnosis, making problems in the system easier to detect.

STUDENTS SHOULD KNOW . .

Key Points

1. DSM-III and DSM-III Revised are quite different from earlier classification systems, and that their multiaxial structure is perhaps the most distinctive innovation. The five axes call for ratings of: current mental disorders (Axes I and II), related physical disorders (Axis III), level of psychosocial stress (Axis IV), and both the current and highest levels of adaptive functioning (Axis V).

2. Some critics object to the concept of classifying abnormal behavior, raising issues of losing information, overlooking individual uniqueness, and creating social stigmatization.

3. Other critics see value in classifying abnormal behavior, but question the reliability and validity of past and current classification systems.

4. Diagnostic reliability refers to whether or not different diagnosticians will agree on a given diagnosis.

5. The validity of a classification is measured by whether or not accurate statements and predictions can be made from knowledge of class membership. A diagnosis can have etiological, concurrent, or predictive validity.

6. DSM-III and DSM-IIIR are more reliable than their predecessors because they contain specific diagnostic criteria, but the manual is still far from perfect.

New Terms
(Key terms underlined)

WHO International Statistical Classification of Diseases, Injuries, and Causes of Death, Diagnostic and Statistical Manual III and IIIR, multiaxial, diagnostic category, reliability, validity, etiological validity, concurrent validity, predictive validity, diagnostic criteria

New Names

American Psychiatric Association

LECTURE LAUNCHERS

On Being Sane in Insane Places

D. L. Rosenhan (1973, Science, 179, 250-258) conducted one of the best known and most controversial studies about the ability of mental health professionals to define abnormality. Rosenhan had several individuals who showed no signs of any emotional problems try to get themselves admitted to mental hospitals. These normal "pseudo-patients" acted like themselves during their screening interviews and simply reported on the events that had occurred in their lives. There were two ways in which they acted_atypically, however. First, they contacted and asked to be admitted to a psychiatric ward, something that most people who consider themselves to be well-adjusted do quite rarely. Second, when asked by the admitting psychiatrist to describe their problems, the pseudo-patients claimed that they were hearing voices that said "empty," "hollow," or "thud." Such a complaint is not a symptom of any known mental disorder.

In every instance in which they tried, the pseudo-patients got themselves admitted to the mental hospital, and in eleven out of twelve cases they were diagnosed as suffering from schizophrenia. Even more surprising, although they immediately stopped complaining of their "symptom" following admission, none of the pseudo-patients was suspected of being a fake by the hospital staff. (Several fellow patients harbored these suspicions, however.) In fact, the behavior of the pseudo-patients while they were "patients" on the psychiatric ward, as well as their accounts of their life experience, were often interpreted by the ward staff as being consistent with their "mental disorder." Consider the following excerpt from a case summary of a pseudo-patient's report on his "normal" upbringing:

> This white 39-year-old male . . . manifests a long history of considerable ambivalence in close relationships, which begins in early childhood. A warm relationship with his mother cools during adolescence. A distant relationship with his father is described as becoming very intense. Affective stability is absent. His attempts to control emotionality with his wife and children are punctuated by angry outbursts and, in the case of the children, spankings. And while he says that he has several good friends, one senses considerable ambivalence embedded in these relationships also . . .

Is it abnormal for a young man to get closer to his father and more distant from his mother as a teenager? Is it unusual to sometimes be angry with your spouse and children? Is it a symptom of mental disorder to spank your children? If you start with the premise that someone is "insane," apparently so.

Rosenhan has argued that the results of his study indicate that sanity and insanity cannot be distinguished, and he suggests that when mental health professionals make such distinctions, they do so on the basis of pre-existing expectations. He asserts that the label that is given to a person is very sticky and sets up a self-fulfilling prophecy.

Rosenhan's criticisms suggest that we should not attempt to classify mental disorder, but whether or not his study suggests this conclusion is a matter of considerable debate. (See replies to the study, 1973, Science, 180, 1116-1122.) If I prove that it is possible to fool a physician into falsely believing that I am suffering from a physical disease, does that mean that physical illness does not exist? Did the pseudo-patients really behave normally? Wouldn't the normal thing to do be to never try to get admitted to a mental hospital or to try to get out immediately upon admission?

While flawed in many respects, this interesting study illustrates many important points: the question of whether we should attempt to classify mental disorder, issues about the reliability and validity of the diagnoses used at the time of the study, concern about the ill-effects of labeling, and evidence regarding the treatment of patients on a psychiatric ward. Not only are these broad and important issues, but also the study can be used to illustrate limitations in research design and interpretation of findings.

False Positives and False Negatives

Whenever decision rules are other than completely accurate, as is the case in clinical psychology and psychiatry, of necessity errors must be made. Given that errors will be made, the question arises as to what sort of bias in decision-making will be adopted. That is, will decisions be made in such a way as to minimize false positives--concluding that something is not present when in fact it is not, or will there be a bias toward minimizing false negatives--concluding that something is not present when in fact it is. One of the many analyses of this important issue was conducted by Thomas Scheff (Decision rules, types of error, and their consequences in medical diagnosis. In R. Price & B. Denner [1973], The making of a mental patient, New York: Holt, Reinhart, and Winston).

Consider the bias that exists in criminal law. The assumption is that a man is innocent until he is proven guilty. Furthermore, the maxim, "Better a thousand guilty men go free, than one innocent man be convicted," makes clear that the Western law wishes to minimize false positives at the expense of risking an increase in false negatives.

Other areas where error exists in decision-making are not so clear about the biases that are adopted. What is the bias in medicine? A moment's reflection suggests that, in most cases, it is the opposite of that adopted by law. Physicians would seem to be more willing to tolerate false positives, offering treatment to a patient who in reality is healthy, than to risk false negatives, denying treatment to someone who in reality is ill. Such a posture seems prudent when the treatment carries a low risk (e.g. the prescription of antibiotics), but becomes more questionable as the risk involved in the treatment increases (e.g. major surgery).

What about the risk ratios in the specialties of psychiatry or clinical psychology? Scheff argues that a bias similar to medicine exists, but he suggests that the risk associated with the treatment for mental disorder may be higher than it first appears. Among his concerns are the potentially stigmatizing effects of labeling, the anxiety a diagnosis of mental disorder causes, and so on. While what the consequences are of various decision rules in psychiatry and psychology is a matter that is open to debate (and should provoke a healthy discussion in class), a bias toward making false positives certainly fits with Rosenhan's findings, as discussed above. In any regard, students will benefit from being introduced to the concepts of false positives and false negatives, and from considering these in relation to such topics as: (1) what is best from the patient's perspective? (2) how does the clinician's financial reward influence decision-making? and (3) specific topics such as the prediction of dangerousness, fitness as a parent, and suicidal risk.

The Diagnoses of Autism and Schizophrenia: Examples of the False Positives/False Negatives Problem

Comparing the diagnostic criteria for autism in DSM-III and DSM-IIIR, Volkmar, Bregman, Cohen, and Cicchetti (1988, American Journal of Psychiatry, 145, 1404-1408) found that the new system is substantially broader, leading to a larger number of false positives and fewer false negatives. The implications of this change are discussed, and provide interesting material regarding the differing standards for diagnosis depending on the purpose the system will be used for. For example, the broader criteria may increase the number of people eligible for social services. In genetic research, including a broader range of individuals within the diagnosis of autism may cloud findings of genetic links. Finally, having differing systems in use makes it difficult to compare studies using differing criteria for diagnosis.

In the area of schizophrenia, in contrast, changes made in the DSM have led to a narrower definition of the disorder (Fenton, McGlashan, & Heinssen, 1988, American Journal of Psychiatry, 145, 1446-1449). The impetus for such narrowing has been the hope that a specific biological cause will be found if a less heterogeneous group of patients is studied. However, as the authors note, a single etiology might result in multiple symptom patterns, and conversely, multiple etiologies may lead to the same set of symptoms.

The use of the DSM for both clinical diagnosis and research means that different users of the manual may have different purposes for making diagnoses and, thus, different priorities concerning false positives and negatives.

Symptom, Syndrome, Disorder, Disease

In medical taxonomies, the terms symptom, syndrome, disorder, and disease are carefully defined concepts that imply knowledge at increasingly higher order levels of analysis. Understanding the definitions and implications of these terms is important to students in its own right, and this should aid in their understanding of the DSM-IIIR and the implications of the manual. Numerous discussions of these terms can be found. A particularly clear and useful exposition of these levels of classification and their implications for child behavior therapy has been written by Alan Kazdin (1983, Behavior Therapy, 14, 73-99).

A symptom refers to an observable behavior or state. When the term is used, there is no implication that an underlying problem necessarily exists or that there is a physical etiology. Rather, a symptom is the simplest level of analyzing a presenting problem. Depressed affect is a symptom; a sore throat is a symptom too.

A _syndrome_ is the next higher level of analysis, and this term is applied to a constellation of symptoms that occur together or covary over time. Again the term carries no direct implications in terms of underlying pathology. Whether, in fact, certain sets of symptoms covary with one another is an empirical questions.

A _disorder_, like a syndrome, refers to a cluster of symptoms, but the concept includes the idea that the set of symptoms is not accounted for by a more pervasive condition. For example, a depressed mood, vegetative symptoms, and a sense of helplessness may be a syndrome that could be subsumed under some specific disorder. Bipolar illness, on the other hand, appears to be independent of other problems and is not readily accounted for by another problem. It is therefore appropriately thought of as a disorder. So is the common cold, whereas a sore throat, running nose, and a headache is a syndrome. As with symptom and syndrome, there is no implication of etiology associated with the term disorder.

A _disease_ is a disorder where the underlying etiology is known. It is the highest level of conceptual understanding. A cold is not a disease as its etiology is unknown. Bipolar illness is not a disease either. Strep throat is a disease, as are some of the organic mental disorders. For the most part, however, the categories of emotional problems listed in DSM-IIIR are appropriately thought of as being syndromes and disorders.

The Reliability of Medical Tests

The modest reliability obtained in classifying mental disorders is dismaying to many psychologists and may be viewed critically by students. An interesting perspective on this issue can be gained by examining the reliability of medical tests. Medicine is often held up as the standard for psychology to aspire to as a precise science of healing. Thus, it may be surprising to learn just how unreliable many medical tests are. In a wide-ranging review in the New England Journal of Medicine, Lorrin Koran (1975, _293_, 642-646; 695-701) concluded:

> physicians studied almost always disagreed at least once in ten cases, and often disagreed more than one in five cases, whether they were eliciting physical signs, interpreting roentgenog rams, electrocardiograms, or electroencephalo- grams, making a diagnosis (from incomplete information), recommending treatment or evaluating the quality of care.

Some specific examples:

Two groups of physicians classifying 561 electrocardiograms as either normal or as showing signs of any of six abnormalities agreed on 60% of the cases. In another EEG study, agreement among pairs of physicians on the normality of the tracings occurred 84% of the time.

Three M.D.'s interviewing patients referred for chest pains in an attempt to diagnose angina agreed 75% of the time.

Two groups of experienced physicians reading a very large series of x-rays agreed on the presence or absence of black lung in 78% of the cases.

Eight pairs of M.D.'s reviewed over 250 case records of patients treated for urinary tract infections, hypertension, or ulcer. Agreement between physician pairs on whether the patient received good care ranged from 56% to 84% (median=72%).

These figures do not correct for chance agreements and thus are inflated estimates of reliability. Furthermore, the more physicians who were asked to make a judgement, the less chance there was of complete agreement. Finally, Koran notes that the "reliability of many signs, procedures, and diagnostic and therapeutic judgements has never been studied."

Revising the DSM

The text introduces DSM-IIIR as a scientific tool and discusses the manual in terms of coverage, reliability, and validity. While concerns can be raised about the manual in its scientific context, most professionals agree that DSM-III and IIIR are a dramatic improvement over their predecessors. It may be worthwhile to spend some time discussing the political implications of the manual, as well as its scientific merit, however. Since the list of "mental disorders" in the manual becomes the operational definition of mental illness for insurance companies and other institutions, the manual does indeed have political implications.

A report on the process of revising the DSM-III criteria for the melancholic subtype of depression was recently published by Zimmerman and Spitzer (1989, American Journal of Psychiatry, 146, 20-28). (Spitzer headed the committees to create both DSM-III and IIIR.) This article provides a fascinating look at the inner circle of professionals who decide the fate of the diagnoses of mental disorders. The steps taken to decide how to change the DSM-III version of the melancholia diagnosis included reviewing the remarkably limited number of research studies addressing questions of reliability and validity, and then suggesting and discussing specific changes that might be made and voting on which should be adopted. (The qualifications of the committee members for the job are unfortunately not described; interesting questions for students to discuss would be who should be included on such committees, and who should choose them?) Some excerpts from the article reveal the nature of the decision-making process:

> In the vote on the alternatives, one individual
> voted for retaining the DSM-III criteria, no one
> voted to adopt a symptom-based polythetic
> approach, six members voted to define melancholia
> on the basis of both symptom and non-symptom
> features, and four persons supported the proposal
> to eliminate melancholic subtyping and replace it
> with a severity distinction. (One of the
> committee members left the meeting early, thus
> leaving 11 votes.) (p. 24)

While students might object to the process of voting on diagnostic criteria, they should be encouraged to consider what alternative means of decision-making might be more appropriate and still feasible. They might also consider that while inadequate data may exist to make scientific decisions, a classification system is necessary in order to define groups to use in the research that will improve later systems (e.g., "The absence of stress was rejected [as a criteria for melancholia] because the group believed that it lacked empirical support as a treatment outcome predictor. [After the meeting, one of us reviewed this literature and found that the lack of precipitating stress has been a consistent predictor of favorable outcome.]" [p. 25]).

See suggestions below for ways to encourage students to tackle the problem of devising classification systems themselves.

Chapter 3

DISCUSSION STIMULATORS

On Being Sane in Insane Places

Rosenhan's article, "On being sane in insane places," is engaging for students to read and can be counted on to provide material for classroom discussion (1973, _Science_, _179_, 250-258). Replies to the article are also particularly valuable to assign, as they present a wide variety of viewpoints on the study (1973, _Science_, _180_, 1116-1122). A few questions such as: Was Rosenhan setting up the psychiatrists? Is insanity in the eye of the beholder? What are the effects of the label "insane?" Can medicine detect liars? should be sufficient to sustain discussion on this controversial piece of research.

Classification

The notion that different classification systems can have different functions can be demonstrated to the class by bringing in several items from your desk. Several different classifications could be created from this set of items depending upon the purpose of the system. They could all be classified together as items from a desk. They could be classified according to function so that pens, pencils, and magic markers formed one group, while paper clips, staples, and rubber bands formed another. Material could define the classification purpose so that metal pens now join paper clips and staples. The point is that classification is an arbitrary function of our purpose: we impose a classification, we do not discover it. While information is lost in the process of classification, the simplification may be of value for other purposes. What are our purposes in attempting to classify abnormal behavior?

Controversial Diagnoses

Discussing several of the tentative diagnoses included in an appendix of DSM-IIIR is likely to generate lively controversy, as it did when the committee to revise the DSM-III considered including them in the body of the manual. Such categories include premenstrual syndrome (which critics see as a gynecological disorder, not a mental illness, and has prompted threats of a law suit against the American Medical Association, author of DSM-IIIR), self-defeating personality disorder, and sadistic personality disorder. The latter two proposed disorders have been criticized as blaming abused women for their suffering (they are mentally ill for staying in the relationship) and then giving a legally acceptable mental defense--sadistic personality disorder--to their abusers. Other controversial diagnoses to discuss might include homosexuality (included as ego-dystonic homosexuality in DSM-III and then dropped altogether in DSM-IIIR), and learning disabilities in children (are these mental disorders?).

Case Vignettes

The DSM-III Training Guide (1981, Webb, L. J., DiClemente, C. C., Johnstone, E. E., Sanders, J. L., & Perley, R. A., New York: Brunner/Mazel, Chapter 24) provides brief case vignettes for practice in making DSM diagnoses. Brief discussions of the diagnoses suggested are included with each case. For practice in using the multiaxial system, students might be given the cases first without the discussion, and asked to suggest diagnoses and ratings for each axis, using the Table included in the chapter. (This will of course be more practical for Axes III through V, given the students' lack of familiarity with the specific Axis I and II diagnoses.)

Reliability and Chance Agreement

The concept of accounting for chance agreement in evaluating reliability is an important idea to get across to students. Ask them this: Two psychiatrists are engaged in a study of the reliability of the diagnosis of schizophrenia. They are only making the diagnosis of schizophrenic or not schizophrenic, and each psychiatrist assigns the diagnosis of schizophrenic to 10% of the cases she sees. After seeing 1000 cases the psychiatrists discover that they agreed on the diagnosis in 82% of the cases. Is this reasonable reliability? On the surface it doesn't sound too bad, but in reality the two diagnosticians would be agreeing at a purely chance level. (Given the base rates, this is exactly chance--draw a Chi-square contingency table on the board for the students.) You can go on to discuss different statistical measures of reliability (e.g. Kappa coefficient) or simply make the point that students should have a general idea of random joint probabilities when evaluating reliability statistics.

Improving Clinical Judgement

A useful and well-written article, "Representative Thinking in Clinical Judgement" (Dawes, R. M., 1986, Clinical Psychology Review, 6, 425-441), demonstrates to the reader the common fallacy of basing clinical judgements (particularly probability estimates) on the degree to which characteristics are representative of our cognitive schemas while ignoring the rules of probability theory. For example, ask students to answer the following question:

Linda is 31 years old, single, outspoken, and very bright. She majored in philosophy. As a student, she was deeply concerned about issues of discrimination and social justice, and also participated in anti-nuclear demonstrations. Which is a more likely description of Linda's current life?

1) Linda is a bank teller.
2) Linda is a bank teller and active in the feminist movement.

(from Tversky, A. and Kahneman, D., 1983, Psychological Bulletin, 90, 293-315.)

Most students will answer (2), because their "schema" of Linda is compatible with "feminist" but incompatible with "bank teller." Point out to them that it is never more likely for two possibilities to be true than for one of them to be true. While we might expect that experts making judgements in their field would be unlikely to make these kinds of logical errors, Tversky and Kahneman found that 91% of medical experts thought it would be more likely that a woman with a blood clot in the lung would have both shortness of breath (an associated symptom) **and** partial paralysis (an unassociated one) than partial paralysis alone.

Both the Dawes article and another by Arkes (1981, Journal of Consulting and Clinical Psychology, 49, 323-330) conclude with suggestions for minimizing errors in clinical judgements. Students might discuss and practice such ideas as considering alternatives to one's hypothesis, considering base rate information, and decreasing reliance on memory, using more examples selected from the articles.

NOTES

INSTRUCTIONAL FILMS:

1.   <u>Simulated psychiatric patient interview</u>, videorecording by John Snibbe et al.   (Los Angeles, University of Southern California, School of Medicine, 6 cassettes, 90 min., color, 3/4 inch, 1976)   This program provides an excellent method of teaching trainees in the mental health field about the common psychiatric disturbances, including schizophrenia, organic brain syndrome, phobia, and phenomena characteristic of each diagnosis, and shows methods used by skilled interviewers to elicit the necessary facts.

2.   <u>Assessment and Diagnosis of Childhood Psychopathology</u>. (PSUPCR, 26 min., color, videocassette, 1980)   An overview of standardized child psychiatric assessment based on DSM-II and DSM-III.

CHAPTER 4

Clinical Assessment Procedures

CHAPTER SYNOPSIS:

All clinical <u>assessment procedures</u> are more or less formal ways of finding out what is wrong with a person, what may have caused a problem, what steps may be taken to improve the individual's condition, and, in some cases, to evaluate the effects of therapeutic interventions.

Assessment of Psychopathology

Clinical Interviews

Clinical interviews differ from other interpersonal encounters in that the clinician pays close attention to <u>how</u> the person answers questions, rather than only to content. Establishing <u>rapport</u> with the client through the use of empathic statements is essential for gaining the person's trust and thus encouraging disclosure of personal material.

While it is clear that vast amounts of information can be obtained by means of the interview, the dependability of the information gleaned has been questioned. <u>Situational factors</u> may exert strong influences over what is said, and many interviews are unstructured, leading clinicians to rely on intuition and general experience.

Structured interviews, such as the Structured Clinical Interview for DSM-IIIR (SCID), have been developed to facilitate the collection of standardized information for making diagnostic judgments based on operational criteria.

Psychological Tests

Psychological tests structure the assessment process further. Statistical norms are established for tests by analyzing the responses of many people; this process is called <u>standardization</u>. Three types of psychological tests are discussed: projectives, objective personality tests, and intelligence tests.

The Rorschach inkblot test and the Thematic Apperception Test are examples of <u>projective techniques</u>. These tests assume that the unstructured stimulus materials will reveal unconscious material about the client's attitudes, motivations, and modes of behavior (the projective hypothesis). The reliability and validity of projective tests is often quite low. Mindful of the problems with traditional projective test interpretation, current use of the Rorschach concentrates more on the form of the person's responses than on their content. The test is then viewed as a perceptual-cognitive task, rather than a stimulus to fantasy.

In personality inventories, examinees are asked to give their self-report as to whether or not a large number of statements apply to them. The Minnesota Multiphasic Personality Inventory (MMPI) is a well-known test designed to simplify the differential diagnosis of mental patients; computerized scoring and interpretation services have more recently been developed. In designing the test, items that empirically distinguished between different diagnostic groups were selected from a large number of items suggested by clinicians. The scales have been found to relate well to psychiatric diagnosis, and several scales are designed to detect deliberately faked responses. Still, problems with social desirability need to be considered.

Intelligence tests are widely used to predict how well a person will do in school, to diagnose learning disabilities, to identify areas of strength and weakness for academic planning, to identify gifted children, and as part of neuropsychological evaluations. It must be remembered that "intelligence" as measured by the tests is an invention of psychologists; while the tests are good predictors of school performance, if the demands of the educational system changed, so would our definitions and measures of intelligence.

Effects of Considering Minority Cultural Differences in Diagnosis

In a box, the authors consider the question of whether diagnosticians consider cultural factors that may influence the significance of particular symptoms. Lopez and Hernandez (1986) found that surveyed mental health practitioners sometimes err on the side of minimizing the seriousness of a patient's problems by attributing them to a subcultural norm. On the other hand, Lopez and Nunez (1987) found that cultural variables were hardly mentioned in the standard diagnostic classification systems and interview schedules, revealing an insensitivity to cultural differences in psychopathology. In the end, it remains unclear whether it is best for clinicians to be sensitive to cultural factors, or to downplay such factors to avoid the risk of missing significant psychopathology by attributing it to cultural norms.

Assessment of Brain Abnormalities

"Seeing" the Brain

Recent technology has led to advances in assessing brain abnormalities. Computerized axial tomography, the CAT scan, gives a two-dimensional view of the brain that can show the location of tumors and blood clots. Positron emission tomography, the PET scan, involves injecting a radioactive isotope into the bloodstream to produce moving visual images of the working brain. Newer techniques include nuclear magnetic response imaging (NMR), superior to CAT scans because of the higher quality pictures produced without radiation; magnetic force is used to move hydrogen atoms in the body. The "pictures" of living tissue are used to discover previously undetectable organic problems and study the neural bases of thought, emotion, and behavior.

Neurologists are distinguished from neuropsychologists: neurologists are physicians who specialize in medical diseases affecting the nervous system; neuropsychologists are psychologists who study how dysfunctions of the brain affect the way we think, feel, and behave. Both kinds of specialists work to understand the nervous system and how to ameliorate problems caused by disease or injury to the brain.

Neuropsychological Assessment

Since organic brain dysfunctions affect behavior, it is possible to infer the location of brain damage by using neuropsychological tests. By analyzing a pattern of performance, psychologists can use tests like the Halstead-Reitan and the Luria-Nebraska batteries to locate the affected area of the brain. Increasingly sophisticated measures have been developed for detecting negative effects of even minor head injuries.

Behavioral Assessment

While traditional assessment concentrates on measuring underlying traits, behavioral assessment is more concerned with the situational determinants of behavior. Behavioral clinicians are concerned with four sets of variables, referred to by the acronym SORC. S stands for the stimuli that precede the problem, O stands for organismic factors (both physiological and psychological), R stands for the overt response, and C stands for the consequent variables.

Direct Observation of Behavior

In their observations, behavior therapists try to fit physical events into a learning framework, consistent with their point of view. Behavior therapists are particularly concerned with linking assessment to intervention.

Artificial situations are sometimes contrived to control the conditions under which behavior is observed. For example, Barkley (1981) sets up a "living room" within a laboratory in order to observe the interactions of mothers with their hyperactive children. "Significant others" in the environment may also be used to collect behavioral observations; teachers and parents can be given a rating scale to report on a child's behavior, for example, or spouses can rate each other. Behavioral therapists also use observations of overt behavior to infer internal states like anxiety. Finally, self-monitoring, in which an individual monitors her own behavior, can be used. While self-monitoring is often unreliable, this can be used to therapeutic advantage; people often experience reactivity and increase desirable behavior while decreasing undesirable behavior.

In a box, the authors discuss the new trend toward behavior therapists scrutinizing their own work with the zeal once reserved for evaluating competing paradigms. For example, subjective evaluations which people make of their own behavior are now considered, rather than confining assessment to the direct observation of overt behavior.

Interviews and Self-Report Measures

For all their interest in direct observation of behavior, behavioral clinicians still rely very heavily on the interview to assess the needs of their clients. Self-report inventories are also used, although these are typically much more detailed and specific than those used by other clinicians.

Cognitive Assessment

The thoughts of patients may be probed in both interviews and by self-report inventories; however, replies in these circumstances may differ from what is experienced in the actual situation. The Articulated Thoughts in Simulated Situations (ATSS) method is one attempt to avoid this problem, as patients are asked to give their thoughts while listening to a hypothetical situation. Different types of cognitive assessment methods are useful for different purposes.

The interest in cognitive assessment has brought cognitive-behavioral clinicians into contact with the literature in experimental cognitive psychology. For example, the concept of a schema (a basic, underlying assumption that influences the way a person experiences the world) has been used to study memory phenomena. Clinical researchers have applied that work to studies of a hypothesized "failure schema" among depressives.

Physiological Measurement

The discipline of psychophysiology is concerned with the bodily changes that accompany psychological states; experimenters have studied such changes using physiological measures of such phenomena as blood pressure or skin conductivity.

Measurement of autonomic nervous system activity is discussed in a box. The mammalian nervous system can be divided into the somatic or voluntary and the autonomic or involuntary systems. The autonomic system, which innervates many bodily organs, can be further divided into the sympathetic system, which prepares the organism for stress, and the parasympathetic system, responsible for maintenance functions. Electronic and chemical measurements of the autonomic nervous system, such as heart rate and electrodermal responding (also known as galvanic skin response), are used to study emotion.

Behavioral Marital Assessment

Marital assessment serves to advance understanding of relationships, to identify problems to be addressed in marital therapy, and to measure changes in the relationship brought about by intervention (Margolin, Michelli, & Jacobson, 1988). Areas of focus include the traditional arenas of overt behavior and contingencies of rewards and punishment between spouses as well as a growing interest in the cognitive and affective aspects of relationships and systems variables such as dominance and flexibility.

Measures used in marital assessment include Spanier's Dyadic Adjustment Scale, a self-report scale used to distinguish distressed from satisfied marriages, and direct observations of overt behavior, such as the Spouse Observation Checklist (SOCL). The SOCL asks spouses to track each other's behavior, providing important information on the nature of marital distress and marital satisfaction. Behavioral observation techniques have been extended to marital interaction or communication between partners, and cognitive assessment examines how distressed and satisfied couples differ with respect to such variables as irrational beliefs, attributions, and expectations. Gottman has developed methods for measuring affective variables, combining physiological measures with observed interactions during a conflictual discussion. Finally, behavioral researchers have become interested in studying systems concepts, making the relationship, rather than the individual, the unit of study.

One area yet to be systematically studied is the issue of sex roles. In this area in particular, the biases of the observer will inevitably affect both the research conducted and the direction an intervention takes.

Assessment of Anxiety

Different attempts to measure anxiety are discussed in a box, including self-report, observation, and physiological assessments. Several issues are raised including: (1) the importance of knowing about the environmental situation when interpreting physiological evidence; (2) the lack of intercorrelation often found between somatic, behavioral, and cognitive measures of anxiety; and (3) the value of anxiety as an elusive but helpful construct.

Reliability and Validity of Behavioral Assessment

Is behavioral assessment more reliable and valid than traditional, less direct, assessment methods? Maybe. Reliability between observers is affected both by the complexity and difficulty of the assessment task and by how closely observers are monitored. The more inference is necessary in the task, the more difficult it is to establish reliability.

In addition to the problem of reactivity discussed earlier, external or ecological validity is an issue in behavioral assessment. That is, does the observation apply to the actual situation of interest? Another concern is the Rosenthal effect (expectancy effect) in behavioral observation. Finally, we must consider whether the indicators we choose measure the constructs of interest to us.

Chapter 4

The Consistency and Variability of Behavior

Trait theorists argue that people will behave consistently in a variety of situations and over time, while Walter Mischel (1968) has argued that behavior is much more situation specific. Considerable controversy has been generated by Mischel's arguments. Wachtel asserts that people with clinical problems may, in fact, be less flexible than the normal people Mischel studied, that disturbed people may perceive different situations as similar (and thus respond in similar ways to them), and that personality dispositions affect the kinds of situations an individual selects or construes. Block argued that Mischel's original position was too extreme and cites research supporting trait theory. Epstein has suggested that observational studies employ too small bits of behavior, missing the consistency that is found when one averages observations of behavior across situations. Bandura, on the other hand, suggests that the reliance of trait theorists on self-report questionnaires colors their conclusions, since people describe themselves as more consistent than they really are.

The emerging picture is a growing appreciation for the way personality factors **interact** with different environments, a paradigmatic perspective that overlaps with the diathesis-stress viewpoint.

NOTES

STUDENTS SHOULD KNOW . . .

Key Points

1. That the clinical interview is a widely used assessment method, but may be strongly influenced by situational factors. Structured interviews reduce subjectivity in interpreting interview data.

2. Projective tests are deliberately made to be ambiguous so that the testee may project onto the stimulus material. While these tests traditionally present problems with reliability and validity, recent use of the Rorschach as a perceptual-cognitive task has reduced these problems.

3. Personality inventories like the MMPI are highly structured, empirically developed tests used to simplify differential diagnosis of mental patients.

4. Intelligence tests are used mainly to predict progress in school, aid in academic placement and planning, and in neuropsychological assessments.

5. While clinicians are often encouraged to take minority cultural differences into account in their assessments, research suggests that clinicians may be oversensitive to cultural differences, leading them to downplay significant psychopathology.

6. Neurological techniques may reveal brain abnormalities through living pictures of the brain; neuropsychologists' assessments are based on the relationships between brain structures and behavior.

7. Behavioral assessment focuses on situational specificity, rather than looking for stable traits. While observational assessment is the hallmark of the behavioral approach, self-report, cognitive, and psychophysiological measures are also used.

8. Behavioral marital assessment focuses on traditional areas such as overt behavior and contingencies of reinforcement between spouses, while also considering cognitive and affective aspects of relationships, and systems variables.

9. Debate continues as to whether people are consistent in their behavior across situations or whether behavior is situation specific.

New Terms
(Key terms underlined)

assessment procedures, clinical interview, rapport, psychological tests, standardization, projective techniques, Rorschach inkblot test, projective hypothesis, personality inventory, self-report, MMPI, social desirability, intelligence testing, CAT scan, PET scan, NMR, neuropsychological tests, neurologist, neuropsychologist, Halstead-Reitan battery, Luria-Nebraska battery, behavioral assessment, situational determinants, traits, SORC, direct observation, self-monitoring, reactivity, cognitive assessment, schema, psychophysiology, somatic nervous system, autonomic nervous system, sympathetic nervous system, parasympathetic nervous system, electrodermal responding, galvanic skin response, affective, content analysis, hypothetical construct, external or ecological validity, Rosenthal effect

New Names
(Key figures underlined)

Hermann Rorschach, Walter Mischel

NOTES

LECTURE LAUNCHERS

The History of the Inkblot:
An Illustration of Changing Paradigms

The history of the Rorschach Inkblot Test provides an excellent illustration of the influence of paradigms on assessment approaches and the changes occurring in paradigms in the United States over the last 50 years. Exner (1986, The Rorschach: A Comprehensive System, Volume I, New York: John Wiley & Sons) reviews changes in the scoring and interpretation of the test since its early development, revealing influences of the psychoanalytic, behavioral, and cognitive paradigms:

Original Rorschach: When Hermann Rorschach began studying the inkblot test in the 1920s, he used empirical methods to develop the test as a diagnostic tool. He was particularly interested in determining how the responses of schizophrenics differed from those of non-schizophrenics.

Psychoanalytic Paradigm Influences: After Rorschach's untimely death at the age of 37, numerous clinicians became interested in the inkblot test. In the United States, the strong influence of psychoanalytic theory in the 1930s and 40s led to the practice of interpreting Rorschach responses for their symbolic content, and the "projective hypothesis" was born, suggesting that the examinee projects unconscious material onto the ambiguous stimulus of the inkblot. The psychoanalytic interpretations were based on analysis of content alone, and often involved inferential leaps (e.g., a person who sees a bird in a Rorschach card is described as "immature and inept sexually and [failing] to establish enduring heterosexual relationships" (1953, Phillips, L. & Smith, J. G., Rorschach interpretation: Advanced technique, New York: Grune & Stratton). By the 1950s, over 3000 books and articles on the Rorschach had been published, and numerous systems of scoring and interpretation were in use.

Behavioral Paradigm Influences: In the 1950s, as behaviorism became influential in the United States, strong criticism was made of the weak psychometric properties of the Rorschach and its inability to predict behavior. The Rorschach Test fell into disfavor in academic circles, although many clinicians continued to use it in their work.

Cognitive Paradigm Influences: Most recently, the cognitive paradigm, gaining prominence in the 1970s and 80s, has led to a new view of the Rorschach as a cognitive-perceptual problem-solving task, rather than a stimulus to fantasy. Exner developed the "Comprehensive System," widely taught in training programs today, which bases its scoring and interpretation on empirical data about the responses of different clinical groups (coming full circle, in fact, to Rorschach's original work). The current system includes standardized administration and scoring methods and extensive normative data for use in interpretation.

Integrated Assessment in Clinical Practice

Students will likely be interested in learning about how the several assessment approaches described in the text are integrated in clinical practice. The following steps may be outlined in class to give an overview of the clinical use of assessment.

(1) Referral Question(s). A good assessment begins with a carefully formulated referral question. Possible goals might be to diagnose a client, to recommend appropriate placement, to aid in treatment planning, or to provide baseline data at the beginning of a planned intervention.

(2) Data Collection. The collection of information often begins with meeting with the referral source and examining the client's file (if available) for relevant historical information, cultural background, and results of previous testing. In addition to an interview with the client, "significant others" such as teachers, parents, or individual therapists are often contacted to obtain additional information. Finally, test materials are used to collect standardized data for comparison with normative groups. This step may include personality testing, intelligence testing, neuropsychological evaluation, behavioral assessment, or, most often, some combination of approaches.

(3) Interpretation and Integration of Data. Keeping the referral question in mind, the hypothetico-deductive method may be used to generate hypotheses about the client and use the test data collected to look for evidence for and against the hypotheses. More information may need to be gathered to clarify conflicting information.

(4) <u>Recommendations</u>. The assessment culminates in practical suggestions related to the referral question. Usually, a summary of the test results and recommendation is offered to the referral source, the client, and, if indicated, significant others such as teachers and parents.

Integrating Psychiatric Diagnosis and Behavioral Assessment

While behaviorists have traditionally been skeptical of the value of psychiatric diagnosis, a recent chapter by Hersen and Last (1989, in C. G. Last and M. Hersen [Eds.], <u>Handbook of Child Psychiatric Diagnosis</u>, New York: Wiley, pp. 517-528) outlines grounds for rapprochement. While clarifying the value of classification as contributing to organization of data, communication with professionals, identification of treatment strategies, etc., the authors point out some problems in current diagnostic schemes. Particularly relevant to the issue of integrating diagnosis with behavioral assessment, DSM-IIIR includes many terms such as "increase," "excessive," "slowed down," etc. Unfortunately, these terms are not described in behavioral terms, leaving the diagnostic process open to considerable subjective judgement in determining whether a client's symptoms are out of normal limits in these areas. For example, one of the symptoms of attention-deficit hyperactivity disorder is "excessive jumping about." But what is excessive? For what age group? In what setting? Here the behavioral assessor has much to contribute, by developing norms for patient and normal populations to assist the diagnostician in making judgements about behavioral symptoms. Students might be encouraged to think of other ways in which behavioral assessment could contribute to improved diagnostic classification systems in the future.

The Barnum Effect

P. T. Barnum created circuses that had "a little something for everybody." He also declared that "there is a sucker born every minute." Both of these quotes likely played a role in Paul Meehl's honoring Barnum in naming a psychological phenomenon for him. The "Barnum effect" refers to the tendency for people to accept vague and generally applicable personality descriptions as being characteristic of them personally, thus the popularity of horoscopes, handwriting analysis, and the like. Rather than recognizing that interpretations or predictions such as those found in the horoscope column could apply to most anyone, people tend to view these brief paragraphs as characterizing them in particular.

What are the characteristics of those people who are so gullible as to accept these general personality interpretations? Snyder, Shenkel, and Lowery (1977, <u>Journal of Consulting and Clinical Psychology</u>, <u>45</u>, 104-114) reviewed the research on this topic and concluded that few such factors have been identified. However, characteristics of the testing situation which enhance acceptance of Barnum interpretations have been identified: (1) general, high base-rate interpretations; (2) presenting the information as being specifically derived for the individual; (3) giving favorable feedback; and (4) using short, psychologically ambiguous procedures.

The identification of these enhancing variables helps to explain why and how palm readers and other "seers" remain in business. But what about psychological testing? Many of the above factors characterize the psychological test situation as well. A psychologist cannot, therefore, use a client's feedback about her terrific testing insight as evidence of that insight, any more than a mystic can legitimately use a client's belief in her powers as evidence for those powers. Once again, we see the difficulty in using self-report data as a measure of "truth."

A demonstration to the class can vividly illustrate the Barnum effect. (See Discussion Stimulators for this chapter.) It is also likely, through embarrassment, to create some healthy skeptics among the class members.

The Unreliability of Eye Witness Testimony

Students may feel that behavioral psychologists' elaborate examination of the reliability and validity of direct observation is little more than an esoteric academic exercise. After all, how wrong can you be about what you actually see?

Elizabeth Loftus examines that question in detail in her book <u>Eyewitness Testimony</u> (1979, Boston: Harvard Press) and concludes that we are often mistaken in our recollection of what we see. She presents evidence that a variety of factors, including the length of the observation, the frequency with which something is seen, the salience of the details asked for, and the stress under which the scene is observed all can significantly affect how well subjects recall what they see. Some of her most interesting work involves the influence that information received after an event has on memories of that event. In one experiment two groups of subjects watched the same film of a minor car accident. Afterwards they each filled out questionnaires asking about what they saw. One group was asked the question: "About how fast were the cars going when they smashed into each other?" The other group was asked: "About how fast were the cars going when they hit each other?" Subjects in the first group guessed that the car was going much faster than did subjects in the second group. And, when asked one week later whether they had seen any broken glass in the film, members of the first group said "yes" significantly more often than did members of the second. Apparently, the information introduced by the words "smashed" and "hit" had a lasting effect on the subjects' memory of the event. Loftus presents an impressive array of evidence suggesting that verbal memories are quite vulnerable to unconscious, after-the-fact distortion.

Presentation of this material could be enhanced by preceding it with the demonstration of eyewitness testimony described in the Discussion Stimulators section.

Why I Do Not Attend Case Conferences

Paul Meehl, one of the most brilliant clinical psychologists and a champion of statistical prediction, takes the case conference to task in an insightful, engaging, and caustic essay entitled "Why I Do Not Attend Case Conferences" (1973, Meehl, P. E., Psychodiagnosis. New York: Norton). A practicing therapist as well as a researcher, Meehl deplores the "muddleheadedness" that too frequently characterizes case conferences. (By implication, many of these problems pertain to the clinical interview in general; see above material on the Barnum effect.) Among Meehl's complaints are:

Buddy buddy syndrome. "Somehow the group situation brings out the worst in many people, and results in an intellectual functioning that is at the lowest common denominator, which in clinical psychology and psychiatry is likely to be pretty low" (p. 232).

Shift in evidential standard, depending upon whose ox is being gored. "When you are putting your own diagnostic case, you permit indirect inferences, . . . then when the other fellow is making his case for a different diagnosis, you become superscientific and behavioristic . . . " (p. 232).

Sick-sick fallacy. "There is a widespread tendency for people in the mental health field to identify their personal ideology of adjustment, health, and the social role, and even to some extent their religious and political beliefs and values, with freedom from disease or aberration" (p. 237).

<u>"Me too" fallacy</u>.   "This is the opposite of the overpathologizing "sick-sick" fallacy . . . If you find yourself minimizing a recognized sign or symptom of pathology by thinking, "Anybody would do this," think again. Would just anybody do it?" (pp. 237-239).

<u>Uncle George's pancakes fallacy</u>.   "A mitigating clinician says, "Why, there is nothing so terrible about that--I remember good ole Uncle George from my childhood, he used to store uneaten pancakes in the attic" (p. 239).

<u>Crummy criterion fallacy</u>.   "We do not ordinarily say, `The social worker thought Johnny was dumb, but he has a WISC IQ of 160; isn't it a shame that the test missed again!' But if an MMPI profile indicates strongly that a patient is profoundly depressed . . . this psychometric finding is supposed to agree with the global impression of a first-year psychiatric resident, and if it doesn't the psychologist typically adopts a posture of psychometric apology" (p. 241).

<u>"Doing it the hard way"</u>.   "By this I mean employing some clinical instrument or procedure, such as a time-consuming projective test, to ascertain something that documents in the patient's social record or an informant could tell one in a few minutes" (p. 262).

And a good one to close on:

<u>Identifying the softhearted with the softheaded</u>. "While there is surely no logical connection between having a sincere concern for the suffering of the individual patient . . . and a tendency to commit logical or empirical mistakes in diagnosis . . . one observes clinicians who betray a tendency to conflate the two" (p. 255).

Meehl's essay details a number of additional logical errors and social pressure which conspire to stand in the way of clear thinking regarding diagnosis and causal inference. This very readable essay serves as a reminder that doing what "feels good" is not the same as doing what is best.

DISCUSSION STIMULATORS:

Rorschach Demonstration

Most students are interested in seeing the Rorschach cards and trying their hand at answering and interpreting them. A demonstration might accompany a lecture on the influence of paradigms on Rorschach interpretation (see lecture material, above): Show several cards to the class, ask them, "What might this be?", and have them write down their associations. (Brave students might volunteer to have their responses written on the board, but have them wait until others have had a chance to respond in writing.) This exercise alone exposes students to the discomfort of responding to an ambiguous stimulus, as many will ask for more structure (Can I look at the card upside down? Can I give more than one answer? Am I supposed to use the whole thing? How did they make these?).

As in standard Rorschach administration, follow with an inquiry: "What makes it look like that to you?" and again have students write down their explanations.

In conjunction with the lecture above, students' answers could be used to illustrate the psychodynamic, stimulus to fantasy approach (try offering wild symbolic interpretations) as compared to Exner's perceptual-cognitive approach. You might explain how some of the structural elements are scored, such as Human Movement, Form Quality, use of Color, and Location of the response, and what they mean about a person's structuring of experience.

Practice in Integrating Assessment Approaches

To expose students to the use of assessment procedures in clinical practice, you might present a case from your own practice, or refer to the case of Ernest H. described in Chapter 1 of the text. Students could be asked to formulate a referral question for the case and choose appropriate measures for collecting data relevant to the referral question. This might best be done in small groups, with the class reconvening to discuss their suggestions.

Demonstrating the "Barnum Effect"

To familiarize students with the "Barnum Effect" and illustrate the form of personality inventories, give students a "personality test" (you could invent an MMPI-like test, or lift one from Cosmopolitan Magazine, introducing them as real tests). In the next class meeting, tell them you have scored their tests and have feedback for them. Hand out two forms of feedback (one form to each student) such that half the class receives negative feedback, and half receives positive feedback. Ask the students whether or not they agree with the feedback. By keeping track of which type of feedback they received, you should be able to demonstrate that people accept positive feedback as accurate (along with other "Barnum effect" findings). Be sure to fully debrief students after the demonstration.

Vocational Interest Test

For an alternative way to expose students to personality inventories, you could try giving them a vocational interest test. Like the MMPI, most of these inventories have been validated using a contrasted groups criterion. Students who find that the inventory tells them they want to be a psychologist, for example, have answered questions in a manner similar to the way psychologists answer. The student counseling center at many colleges and universities will give these tests for free, or perhaps you could arrange for a group administration in class.

"Seeing" the Brain

The January, 1987 issue of National Geographic (Sochurek, H., 171, 2-41) contains fascinating color pictures of various brain imaging techniques which students may enjoy seeing. Included are such innovative technologies as magnetic resonance imaging (MRI), digital subtraction angiography (DSA), radioisotope imaging (PET and SPECT), computed tomography (CT scans), and sonography.

Self-Monitoring Exercise

Self-monitoring is an interesting and easily used assessment technique, which students can try themselves. You could mimeograph the attached materials and pass them out in the class before the session on assessment.

In class, after the students have tried self-monitoring for a week, discuss their experiences. What was it like to monitor themselves? How faithfully did they keep records? Did they experience reactance? What are some advantages and disadvantages of self-monitoring as an assessment tool? How might students use the data they collected to change their behavior? More complicated records, such as (for someone trying to eat less) where food is eaten, with whom, and at what time, might help in developing a behavior-change plan.

Self-Monitoring Exercise

INSTRUCTIONS:

1. Select one of your own behaviors that you find troublesome or undesirable (Examples: biting your fingernails, smoking, eating between meals, swearing in front of your grandmother, etc.).

    A. Choose a behavior that occurs relatively frequently.
    B. Choose a behavior that you have tried to change in the past or would like to change.

2. Starting tomorrow, record the frequency of your target behavior every day for one week on the form provided.

3. Before class, graph the frequency of your target behavior on the grid provided.

4. Bring your self-monitoring records to class for discussion.

SELF-MONITORING RECORD

TARGET BEHAVIOR: _____

ESTIMATED FREQUENCY OF BEHAVIOR **BEFORE** MONITORING:

_____

UNIT OF MEASUREMENT (e.g. number of cigarettes, hours of T.V., etc.):

_____

FREQUENCY OF TARGET BEHAVIOR (Mark each time behavior occurs):

Day 1	Day 2	Day 3	Day 4	Day 5	Day 6	Day 7

GRAPH (plot a graph of the frequency of behavior for each
      day of the week, using your own units on the frequency
      axis):

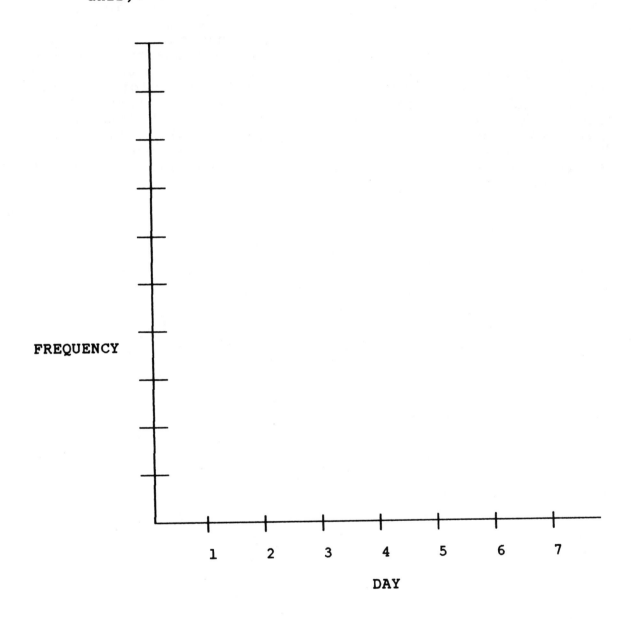

Eyewitness Testimony Demonstration

A dramatic demonstration of the unreliability of eyewitness testimony can be made through the following exercise: Arrange for a confederate to burst into your classroom while you are lecturing, steal a wallet from your desk at the front of the room, and run out. After the startled students have calmed down and been assured that the robbery was a fake, have them write down as much as they can remember about the "perpetrator:" his dress, color of hair, height and weight, age, and other identifying information. Comparing students' answers should provide interesting material for discussing the problems with eyewitness testimony outlined above in the section on lecture material. An alternative to this demonstration is the film, "Fidelity of Report," described below.

NOTES

INSTRUCTIONAL FILMS:

1. <u>Intelligence: A Complex Concept</u>. (MGHF, 28 min., color, 1978) Examines a variety of intelligence tests and discusses the problems that confront the effort to provide measures of intelligence.

2. <u>Personality</u>. (CRM, 30 min., color, 1974) Explores the complexity of personality development through an in-depth analysis of a college senior, including interviews with the subject, his parents, girlfriend, and roommate, and the use of personality assessment techniques such as the Draw-a-Person Test and the Thematic Apperception Test.

3. <u>Unconscious Motives</u>. (IU, 40 min.) Shows how psychological tests and interview techniques are able to uncover a situation implanted in the "unconscious" of two subjects through hypnosis.

4. <u>Eye of the Beholder</u>. (LUCEMC-2759, 25 min., 1955). A series of events during 12 hours in the life of an artist are seen through the eyes of people who have observed them: his mother, a cab driver, a headwaiter, his landlord, a model, and himself.

5. <u>Fidelity of Report</u>. (PCR-95, 6 min., silent, 1964). "Audience participation demonstration of accuracy of observation and report. Dramatic action sequence concerns woman robbed while waiting for bus. Action takes 60 seconds, after which projection is stopped. Standard set of questions given to audience for answer. Dramatic action repeated by continuing projection and each observer asked to check accuracy of own observation." Standard set of questions appears in Ray, W. S., 1967, <u>Journal of Psychology</u>, <u>24</u>, 297-312 or may be ordered with film.

CHAPTER 5

Research Methods in the Study of Abnormal Behavior

CHAPTER SYNOPSIS

Science and Scientific Methods

Science, as currently practiced, is the pursuit of systematized knowledge through observation. Scientific propositions must be amenable to systematic testing that could show them to be wrong. In addition, scientific observations must be <u>reliable</u>--they must occur repeatedly under prescribed conditions. A <u>theory</u> is a set of propositions meant to explain a class of phenomena; a primary goal of science is to test the adequacy of theories. Theories themselves guide research by suggesting which data be collected. Inferred from observational data, theories go beyond what can actually be seen or measured. In this way they may bridge spatiotemporal relations, or formulate lawlike generalizations to account for observed relationships.

The Research Methods of Abnormal Psychology

Empidemiological Research

<u>Epidemiology</u> is the study of the frequency and distribution of illness in a population; data are gathered about the rates of illness and possible correlates of illness in a large sample or population. <u>Prevalence</u> refers to the proportion of the population that has the disorder at a given point in time; <u>incidence</u> is the number of new cases of a disorder that occur in some period; and a <u>risk factor</u> is a condition that, if present, increases the likelihood of developing the disorder. Epidemiology research is important for documenting the rates of various disorders and contributes to understanding the causes of illness.

The Case Study

In developing a case study, the clinician collects historical and biographical information from the individual and other sources. While they lack control and objectivity, case studies have played some important roles in the study of abnormal behavior. They have been used (1) to describe rare or important phenomena; (2) to disconfirm allegedly universal aspects of theories; and (3) to generate hypotheses. The case history fares less well in providing evidence in favor of a theory, as the validity of the information gathered is sometimes questionable and the means for confirming one hypothesis and ruling out alternative hypotheses are usually absent. The case study is an ideal idiographic method, but it is less useful in the nomothetic or group context, and in illuminating cause-effect relationships.

The Correlational Method

The correlational method establishes whether there is a relationship between or among two or more variables. The Pearson product-moment correlation coefficient (r) has values from -1.00 to +1.00 and reflects both the magnitude and direction of a relationship. The statistical significance of correlation coefficients must be evaluated to determine the likelihood that the obtained relationship happened by chance. However, statistical significance does not ensure social or real-life significance.

While correlational studies are often performed in laboratories, they are not experiments; classificatory variables like diagnosis are naturally occurring and cannot be manipulated by the researcher. The correlational method does not allow us to determine cause-effect relationships because of two major problems of interpretation: directionality and third variables. The directionality problem refers to the fact that we do not know which of two correlated variables caused the other. Longitudinal designs in which the hypothesized "cause" is measured before the "effect" help avoid this problem. The high-risk method of longitudinal research selects for study only those individuals who have a greater than average risk of developing the disorder. While correlation does not imply causation, causation does imply correlation. As for the third variable problem, it may be that neither of the two variables studied in the correlation produces the other; rather, some unspecified variable may be responsible for the correlation.

The Experiment

The experiment is considered the most powerful tool for determining causal relationships between events. The experimenter typically begins with an <u>experimental hypothesis</u> and chooses an <u>independent variable</u> that can be manipulated by the experimenter. The <u>dependent variable</u> is expected to vary with manipulations of the independent variable. When variations in the independent variable lead to differences between groups, an <u>experimental effect</u> has been produced.

At least one <u>control group</u> is included in an experiment to secure <u>internal validity</u>. The control serves as a <u>baseline</u> to compare against the treatment group and rules out <u>confounds</u>--variables other than the independent variable that can influence the dependent variable. <u>Random assignment</u> of subjects to groups is used to minimize pre-treatment differences between groups.

Even with both a control group and random assignment, the results of the experiment may still be invalid. The <u>Rosenthal effect</u> refers to the potential biasing influence of the experimenter. To avoid bias, many studies use <u>double-blind</u> procedures in which both the subject and the person administering the treatment are unaware of what the treatment is. To decide whether an experimental effect is important, experimenters determine its statistical significance. Finally, the extent to which the results of a particular piece of research can be generalized beyond the immediate experiment is a measure of their <u>external validity</u>.

Practical and ethical issues prohibit the use of the experiment as a means of addressing many questions related to abnormal behavior. The <u>analogue experiment</u> is commonly used by studying a related phenomenon, an analogue. While internally valid results may thus be obtained, the external validity of such experiments is more difficult to ensure.

Single-Subject Experimental Research

While relying on a single subject prohibits the use of a control group and limits generalizability, it can be effective for certain purposes. <u>Reversal</u> or <u>ABAB designs</u> obtain a baseline, introduce treatment, reinstate the baseline conditions, and finally reintroduce the treatment. This design allows one to attribute experimental effects to the independent variables, but cannot be employed when the baseline state is not recoverable or when ethical considerations prohibit reversing a treatment. In multiple baseline procedures, two or more behaviors are monitored and one at a time is treated; an experimental effect is demonstrated if only the targeted behavior is affected by the treatment.

Mixed Designs

The mixed design combines experimental and correlational techniques: subjects who can be divided into two or more discrete populations are assigned as groups to each experimental condition, thereby identifying which particular treatment applies best to which group of subjects. Mixed designs may also be used to identify differential deficits in performance between two groups.

NOTES

STUDENTS SHOULD KNOW . . .

Key Points

1. Science, as currently practiced, is the pursuit of systematized knowledge through observation.

2. In order to be considered scientific, theories must be testable, or falsifiable, and reliable. Theoretical concepts must be subject to operationalization.

3. Epidemiological research studies the frequency and distribution of illness in a population.

4. The case study lacks control and objectivity, but is useful for (1) describing unusual phenomena; (2) disconfirming supposedly universal aspects of a theory; and (3) generating hypotheses.

5. The correlational method is a valuable means of systematically studying the association between two or more variables, but third variable and reverse causality interpretations prohibit causal inferences.

6. Diagnosis is a classificatory variable, and all comparison made between groups of patients with different diagnoses are correlation studies.

7. Statistical significance refers to a convention adopted by scientists wherein a finding is not considered to be reliable unless the chances are less than 5 in 100 that it occurred by chance. Statistical significance is no guarantee of social significance.

8. The experiment is a powerful means for determining causality, although ethical and practical problems often prohibit its use for studying abnormal behavior.

9. The basic features of the experiment include the experimental hypothesis, independent variables, dependent variables, experimental effects, control groups, and random assignment.

84

10. Internal validity refers to whether the results obtained can be confidently attributed to the independent variable. External validity concerns whether the results of a particular study are generalizable.

11. Analogue experiments are frequently used to study psychopathology.

12. Single-subject experimental designs lack control groups and are less generalizable, but can be used for certain purposes. Reversal or ABAB designs and the multiple-baseline procedure enable demonstration of experimental effects using single-subjects.

13. Mixed designs combine experimental and correlational techniques, usually dividing subjects into two discrete populations and assigning them as groups to each experimental condition.

New Terms
(Key terms underlined)

testability, falsifiability, theory, operationalize, epidemiology, prevalence, incidence, risk factor, case study, idiographic, nomothetic, correlational method, correlation coefficient, statistical significance, classificatory variables, directionality problem, third-variable problem, high-risk method, experiment, experimental hypothesis, independent variable, dependent variable, experimental effect, control group, confounds, internal validity, baseline, random assignment, Rosenthal effect, double-blind, external validity, analogue experiment, single-subject experiment, reversal design, ABAB design, multiple-baseline procedure, mixed design, differential deficit

New Name
(key figures underlined)

Baruch Spinoza

LECTURE LAUNCHERS

Threats to Internal Validity

Campbell and Stanley's _Experimental and Quasi-experimental Designs for Research_ (1966, Chicago: Rand McNally) is an invaluable source for understanding the factors which limit internal validity. Their list of plausible alternative hypotheses to the conclusion that the independent variable caused the change observed makes the concept of internal validity clear. Before providing the examples here (or your own), students might be encouraged to think of examples on their own.

1) _History_. All things that may have happened to the subjects between Time 1 and Time 2 in addition to the independent variable may affect the dependent variable. For example, in addition to the psychotherapy treatment she received (the independent variable), a manic-depressive subject may view a television program on bipolar illness which influences her behavior.

2) _Maturation_. Subjects may change from Time 1 to Time 2 because of autonomous growth or development. For example, a subject who is rated as hyperactive at Time 1 (age 3) may grow out of his overactivity by Time 2 (age 4). The problems of history and maturation increase the longer the time period between Time 1 and Time 2.

3) _Testing_. Taking the pre-test itself may affect the dependent variable. For example, taking a practice test for the SAT before an educational intervention (the independent variable) not only assesses the subjects' pre-treatment skills, but also teaches them something about test-taking and would improve their post-treatment performance even without the treatment.

4) _Instrumentation Change_. The measuring instruments may change between Time 1 and Time 2. For example, during a longitudinal study, it is likely that the DSM diagnostic criteria will have been revised, resulting in changes in diagnosis that are not due to the independent variable.

5) <u>Statistical Regression</u>. Extreme scores will regress toward the mean from Time 1 to Time 2, apart from independent variable effects. For example, people who do extremely poorly on an IQ test at the first testing are likely to do somewhat better on the second test (and vice versa) because of imperfect test-retest reliability and the random component to the abilities tested.

6) <u>Selection</u>. Non-random selection may influence the independent variable. For example, if subjects are self-selected for an SAT course, those who take the course are likely to vary from the no-treatment group on some factor (like achievement motivation) in addition to the independent variable (SAT course).

7) <u>Experimental Mortality</u>. Non-random loss of subjects influences the independent variable: schizophrenic subjects who drop out of a medication treatment study may have been responding less well to the treatment (causing them to quit); the resulting post-treatment group will not include those subjects who responded least well.

Analogues and External Validity

Students studying research methods in psychology often raise questions about the external validity of laboratory research: is the setting or the sample so artificial that it cannot apply to "real life." In his essay, "In Defense of External Invalidity" (<u>American Psychologist</u>, April, 1983, 379-387), Mook points out that such questions are relevant only for certain types of experiments with certain purposes; it would be worthwhile discussing this issue with students. To summarize his point, many experimental studies seek to test theories; in such cases, predictions are made, based on the theory, about what ought to happen <u>in the laboratory</u>. For example, the tension-reduction theory asserts that alcoholics drink in order to relieve tension. A prediction derived from that theory is that subjects made anxious in the laboratory should drink more to release the tension. In a test of this prediction, subjects who were made anxious did <u>not</u> drink more (Cappell, H. & Herman, C. P., 1972, <u>Quarterly Journal of Studies on Alcohol</u>, <u>33</u>, 33-64). This finding suggests that the theory needs to be qualified, <u>even though</u> the experimental conditions were not similar to real life. Indeed, more recent studies (e.g. Steele, C. M., Southwick, L. & Pagano, R., 1986, <u>Journal of Abnormal Psychology</u>, <u>95</u>, 173-180) have begun to specify conditions under which alcohol might be used to reduce stress, thus advancing the theory through analogue research.

In contrast, when researchers wish to <u>describe</u> what actually occurs in real life, external validity becomes a more potent issue; the following threats to external validity often arise in research designed to make generalizations about abnormal behavior: (1) Use of subject analogues, such as volunteer college students who score in the clinical range on questionnaires, to draw conclusions about how disordered individuals behave. Such subjects differ in important ways from diagnosed patients; for example, they have not sought professional help for their problems, despite scoring in the clinical range. (2) Use of therapist analogues, such as inexperienced graduate student therapists, to reach conclusions about the effectiveness of different types of therapy in the clinical setting. If no differences are found between types of therapies, this may relate to the lack of experience of the therapists; experienced therapists might, in fact, differ in their effectiveness depending on their theoretical orientation.

Skinner on the Scientific Method

Students may enjoy reading Skinner's entertaining account of the scientific process in action (1955, <u>American Psychologist</u>, 221-233). In his conversational tone ("imagine that you are all clinical psychologists--a task which becomes easier and easier as the years go by--while I sit across the desk from you or stretch out upon this comfortable leather couch" [p. 222]), Skinner elucidates the following "unformalized principles" of scientific practice as he describes his early conditioning research:

1) "When you run into something interesting, drop everything else and study it" (p. 223).

2) "Some ways of doing research are easier than others" (p. 224). Tiring of carrying rats around and delivering reinforcement, Skinner developed apparatuses to take care of these tasks. Later, tiring of preparing food for reinforcement, Skinner discovered the powers of periodic reinforcement.

3) "Some people are lucky" (p. 225). Skinner reveals how his mistakes led him to new ideas and ways of measuring phenomena.

4) "Apparatuses sometimes break down" (p. 225). The jamming of Skinner's food magazine led him to study the extinction curve.

5) "Serendipity--the art of finding one thing while looking for something else" (p. 227): trying to find a way to keep rats at a constant level of food deprivation, Skinner discovered instead the phenomenon of fixed-ratio reinforcement.

Skinner's irreverence for traditional scientific method ("I never attacked a problem by constructing a Hypothesis. I never deduced Theorems or submitted them to Experimental Check." [p. 227]) provides a thought-provoking counterpoint and compliment to the text.

Rogers on the Scientific Method

In his article, "Toward a More Human Science of the Person," (1985, Journal of Humanistic Psychology, 25, 7-24), Carl Rogers addresses the need for more research within the humanistic paradigm, and presents examples of studies employing a more phenomenological model of scientific inquiry. He notes common elements among several recent books and articles calling for a new model of science, including (1) the "Newtonian, mechanistic, reductionistic, linear cause-effect, behaviorist view of science is not thrown out but it is seen as simply one aspect of science . . . decidedly inappropriate for [investigating certain questions]" (p. 12); (2) recognition that our knowledge will always be uncertain; (3) the assertion that no one methodology is best, and approaches should be chosen to fit the question asked; (4) the importance of a methodology that includes an "indwelling" in the experience of the participants; and (5) the use of "participants" or "co-researchers" rather than "subjects" in studies.

Students might enjoy contrasting the perspective of Rogers with that presented by Skinner (above), as well as discussing how some of the humanistic concepts presented in Chapter 2 might be subjected to research (e.g., self-actualization and the phenomenological experience of the world).

DISCUSSION STIMULATORS

The Coke-Pepsi Experiment

An engaging method of teaching the concepts of the experiment is to conduct a taste-test in class. Get a few cans of Coke or Pepsi (or new Coke and Coke Classic) and pour them into cups which you have marked to identify the soda (but which students can't identify, of course). Select 20 or so student volunteers and pass out the cups at random. Next have students provide some ratings on the drinks, such as whether they drank Coke or Pepsi, how much they liked the soda on a scale of 1 to 10, etc. While students will get caught up in which soda wins the challenge, conclude by asking questions like: What was the independent variable? What were the dependent variables? What was the experimental hypothesis (if you have one)? Is the study internally valid? Externally valid? Was this a double-blind study? If you compared results for men and women, would this be a mixed design?

Critiquing Research

A useful way to get students to utilize their knowledge about research design is to have them critique research. You could:

(1) Assign a couple of research reports (Science is a good source for brief reports) and discuss them in class or have students write a one page evaluation, including the following points: (a) identify the type of research design, (b) note what theoretical constructs were discussed and how they were operationalized, (c) critique the report in terms of external and internal validity and the causal inferences made.

(2) Have students locate their own "research reports" from sources such as Cosmopolitan, the National Enquirer, or the local newspaper. Having students critique media reports of psychological research will teach them to apply some of their newly-learned concepts, make them a bit more skeptical about what they read, and introduce you to hundreds of new facts about diets, childhood experiences, and the effects of stress!

Reliability and ESP

The concept of reliability of an experimental finding and the importance of this criterion can be easily demonstrated to the class by having them take part in an "ESP" experiment with you. You think of a number between 1 and 10 and ask the entire class to use ESP to divine the number. About 10% of the class will guess correctly, but after being amazed at the number of psychics in your class, you might begin to wonder if the finding is reliable. Replications of the experiment will eventually eliminate all of the numbers of the first group of psychics and demonstrate why a finding must be reliable before it is accepted by the community of scientists.

Falsifiability

Present the class with your "theory" of human behavior. Your theory goes like this: we each have an invisible little Martian sitting on our shoulder and whispering into our ears telling us what to do. Can the class disprove your theory? No--nor could you prove it. The students' attempts to disprove your theory can be used to point out why theories, in order to be scientific, must be testable. This demonstration also illustrates why, in scientific research, the null hypothesis is that no effect is accepted until it is demonstrated. If I assert that schizophrenia can be cured by hemodialysis, that florescent lights cause hyperactivity, or that masturbation causes insanity, it is my obligation to prove the assertion to be true, not your obligation to prove me wrong. Ask the class to apply some of their newly-learned rules of science to some of the theories discussed in Chapter 2.

Ethics in Research

The ethics of doing research on human subjects is discussed in the last chapter of the text, but discussion of the issues might begin now. Many students have probably served as subjects in psychology experiments to earn extra credit for courses. How do they feel about their experience? Were they deceived as a part of an experimental manipulation? Past experiments such as Milgram's obedience to authority studies can be discussed from an ethical perspective. While certain studies are obviously unethical, there is a conflict between the benefit of advancing knowledge and the protection of research participants. When discussing this topic, be prepared to answer questions about the ethics of animal experimentation as well.

NOTES

INSTRUCTIONAL FILMS

1. Search for Solutions: Investigation.   (PHPE, 22 min.,
color, 1979)   An exciting portrayal of the progress of
science.   One point made in this film is that "to solve a
problem, one must ask the right question." This is one film
in a series focusing on problem solving. Other "Search for
Solutions" topics include evidence, adaptations, context,
modeling, theory, patterns, prediction, and trial and error.

2. Methodology: The Psychologist and the Experiment.   (CRM,
30 min., color, with discussion guide, 1975) Highlights
Schachter's "fear and affiliation" research and Riesen's
visual deprivation research to teach the concepts of
independent and dependent variables, control groups, random
assignment to conditions, and the use of statistics.

CHAPTER 6

Anxiety Disorders

CHAPTER SYNOPSIS:

Anxiety occurs in many psychopathologies, is a principal aspect of the disorders considered in this chapter, and plays an important role in the lives of normal people. While the disorders considered in this chapter were called neuroses in the past, this term, associated strongly with psychoanalytic theory and encompassing a broad array of behaviors, has been dropped from the DSM.

Phobias

A phobia is a disrupting, fear-mediated avoidance, out of proportion to the danger posed by the object or situation, and recognized by the sufferer as groundless. In classifying types of phobias, behaviorists rely on a functional explanation of the behavior, rather than a topographical framework. Simple phobias, which are more common in women and usually begin in early childhood, are relatively unusual. Agoraphobia, now considered a form of panic disorder, is a cluster of fears centering on being unable to escape or find help when in public places. This serious problem accounts for about 60% of the phobias seen in treatment, and occurs more often in women. Social phobias are persistent, irrational fears related to the presence of other people.

Psychoanalytic Theory of Phobias

According to Freud, phobias are a defense against the anxiety that is produced by repressed id impulses. The anxiety is displaced onto the feared object and avoidance of the object enables the person to avoid dealing with repressed conflicts. The classic case of Little Hans, discussed in a box, illustrates the psychoanalytic view and the inferential leaps it requires. More recently, Arieti has proposed that an interpersonal problem is repressed, not an id impulse.

Behavioral Theories of Phobias

The avoidance conditioning model of learning theorists asserts that phobias result first from learning to fear a situation through classical conditioning, and second, learning to avoid the situation as a result of operant conditioning. While some clinically reported phobias seem to fit this model, research has not supported the model as explaining all phobias. As is explained in a box, the concept of preparedness suggests that organisms may only associate certain CSs with certain UCSs.

Vicarious learning or modeling is supported by experimental evidence as an explanation for phobias. Again, however, the model is not sufficient to explain all phobias. Problems also plague a purely operant model of phobias.

Social anxiety has been explained in several ways: as a result of classical conditioning, as a consequence of having inadequate social skills, and as a product of cognitions such as a vulnerability schema.

Physiological Factors in the Development of Phobias

Autonomic lability, the tendency to be readily aroused by a wide range of stimuli, seems to be partially determined by genetics and may play a role in phobias.

Therapies for Phobias

Psychoanalytic approaches view phobias as symptomatic and attempt to identify the underlying conflicts that are held to cause them. Contemporary ego analysts focus less on historical insights and encourage their patients to confront the phobia. The principle behavioral treatment of phobias is systematic desensitization. Flooding forces exposure to the source of the phobia at full intensity, while operant techniques reward approach behavior. Cognitive approaches focus on changing irrational beliefs. Research indicates that spouses should play a role in treating agoraphobia. Evidence suggests that all of these treatments must include real-life exposure to be effective. Medications that reduce anxiety (anxiolytics) have been found to be effective in treating phobias, but they may be difficult to discontinue without relapse.

Chapter 6

Behavior Genetics

Behavior genetics, the study of individual differences
in behavior that are attributable in part to genetic makeup,
is discussed in a box. The genotype is the genetic makeup,
while the phenotype is the total observed characteristics.
The two major methods of study in behavior genetics are to
compare members of a family and pairs of twins. After
obtaining index cases or probands with a certain diagnosis,
relatives are studied to determine the frequency of the same
diagnosis. In the twin method monozygotic and dyzygotic
twin pairs are compared; when twins are diagnosed similarly,
they are said to be concordant. In order to control for the
effect of environment on family similarities, children
raised by adoptive parents or twins reared separately are
often studied.

Panic Disorder

In panic disorder the person experiences frequent panic
attacks, including depersonalization, derealization, and
fears of losing control, going crazy, or even dying.
Explanations of the disorder's etiology include a genetic
link and physiological causes, such as cardiac problems
leading to panic attacks, overactivity in the B-adrenergic
nervous system, and hyperventilation leading to lactate
sensitivity and panic attacks. Psychological explanations
include the hypothesis that panic may result from
overconcern with slight physical symptoms. Treatment
efforts for panic disorder include medication and training
patients in slow breathing.

Generalized Anxiety Disorder

Individuals with generalized anxiety disorder are
chronically and persistently anxious, often with
accompanying somatic complaints, apprehensiveness, and
muscle tension. Psychoanalytic theory attributes this
problem to unconscious conflicts similar to those
experienced by the phobic, but since the anxiety is not
displaced on a specific source, there is no way to avoid it.
Learning theorists examine the environmental elicitors of
the anxiety, and cognitive-behavioral models focus on the
role of control and helplessness. Humanistic theories
suggest that people become anxious when their basic natures
are not expressed. Data on a genetic component to
generalized anxiety disorder are equivocal. Neurobiological
models suggest that panic disorders result from
overactivation of the noradrenergic system, while the GABA

neurotransmitters are implicated in generalized anxiety disorder.

Behavioral clinicians treat generalized anxiety using systematic desensitization (if they can locate specific sources for the anxiety) or more generalized treatments such as relaxation training. Helplessness might be reduced through training in skills which lead to "self-efficacy." One humanistic treatment, Gestalt therapy, helps the client confront basic wants and fears using methods such as the empty-chair technique. Tranquilizers are probably the most widely used treatment, but have negative side effects. Finally, community psychologists view anxiety as a normal reaction to untenable living conditions and seek to change those conditions rather than the individual.

Communication in the Nervous System

A box in this chapter explains the action of neurons and the neurotransmitters.

Obsessive-Compulsive Disorder

Obsessions are intrusive and recurring thoughts which appear irrational and uncontrollable. A compulsion is an irresistible impulse to repeat some ritualistic act over and over. The disorder often has a negative impact on the individual's relationships with other people.

In psychoanalytic theory, obsessions and compulsions are viewed as resulting from instinctual forces which are not under control because of excessively harsh toilet training. Adler suggested instead that compulsive acts are attempts to gain a sense of mastery which is missing because of excessively doting or dominating parents. Behavior theorists view compulsions as learned behaviors reinforced by anxiety reduction. However, not all compulsions reduce anxiety, and obsessions actually increase anxiety. A cognitive view suggests that obsessive-compulsives overestimate the likelihood of harm. Finally, biological factors including brain damage and genetic transmission have been associated with the disorder.

While focusing on insight, some analytic writers use more active approaches to treating obsessive-compulsives to encourage them to tolerate anxiety and confront reality. Behavioral approaches focus on active interruption of symptoms, including the promising technique of response prevention. Medication and even a surgical technique called a modified leucotomy have been found to be effective.

Posttraumatic Stress Disorder

In posttraumatic stress disorder, a catastrophe brings an aftermath of difficulties with thinking, relaxation, and psychic numbing, frequently accompanied by "flashbacks" and recurring nightmares. New to DSM-III, this disorder highlights the fact that extreme stress can cause psychological difficulties. PTSD has received particular attention following the Vietnam War; a box discusses the hypothesis that PTSD was delayed in Vietnam veterans because the stressors eliciting the symptoms occurred upon the return home. Treatment of PTSD has included temporary removal of the soldier from the battlefield, hypnotism, and currently, "rap groups" and other group therapy for Vietnam veterans.

NOTES

STUDENTS SHOULD KNOW . . .

Key Points

1. The term _neurosis_ is based on the psychoanalytic idea that anxiety is caused by unconscious conflict, and has been replaced by more descriptive terms in the DSM.

2. Phobias, panic disorder, generalized anxiety disorder, obsessive-compulsive disorder, and posttraumatic stress disorder are the major categories of anxiety disorders listed in DSM-IIIR.

3. A phobia is a disrupting, fear-mediated avoidance, out of proportion to the danger of a particular object or situation that is feared. Agoraphobia accounts for most of the phobias seen for treatment.

4. Psychoanalytic theory views phobias as a defense against the anxiety produced by repressed id impulses. Behavioral theories of phobias include avoidance conditioning, vicarious learning, and operant models. Physiological factors such as autonomic lability have also been implicated.

5. Research indicates that successful treatment of phobias includes exposure to the feared stimulus.

6. Behavior genetics is the study of individual differences in behavior that are attributable in part to differences in genetic makeup.

7. Panic disorder has been explained by both physiological and psychological causes.

8. Cognitive theories of the cause of generalized anxiety disorder focus on the role of helplessness and loss of control.

9. Obsessive-compulsive disorder includes intrusive and recurring thoughts and the irresistible impulse to repeat acts over and over. Response prevention is a promising behavioral treatment for the disorder.

10. Posttraumatic stress disorder refers to the after-effects of a trauma. PTSD has received particular attention in Vietnam veterans.

Chapter 6

New Terms
(key terms underlined)

neurosis, psychosis, phobia, agoraphobia, social phobia,
simple phobia, preparedness, vicarious conditioning,
vulnerability schema, autonomic lability, behavior genetics,
genotype, phenotype, index cases, probands, monozygotic and
dizygotic twins, concordant, family studies, twin studies,
flooding, anxiolytics, depersonalization, derealization,
panic disorder, panic attack, generalized anxiety disorder,
Gestalt therapy, empty-chair technique, community
psychology, neuron, neurotransmitter, obsessive-compulsive
disorder, obsessions, compulsions, response prevention,
modified leucotomy, posttraumatic stress disorder, group
therapy

New Names
(key figures underlined)

Little Hans, Little Albert

NOTES

LECTURE LAUNCHERS

Whatever Happened to Little Albert

An interesting aside to Watson and Rayner's famous experiment with Little Albert is the misinterpretations and distortions that have been found in subsequent accounts of the study (Harris, B., 1979, American Psychologist, 84, 151-160). Textbook reports of the study have made such simple errors as misspelling Rayner, getting Albert's age wrong, and substituting a rabbit for a rat. More serious errors include falsely reporting that Albert's fear of the white rat generalized to a fur pelt, a man's beard, a cat, a teddy bear, all white furry things, his aunt who wore fur, and his mother's fur coat. Some accounts managed to combine Watson and Rayner's study with Mary Cover Jones' report of deconditioning a child's fear of a rabbit, giving Little Albert's story a happy ending.

In fact, the experiment with Little Albert was not nearly as successful as it has been portrayed. It has been difficult to replicate, it did not contain proper controls, and the extent to which the fear generalized to other objects is not clear. This does not mean, however, that Watson and Rayner were wrong; it does suggest that they were not necessarily right. Given the historical significance that the case of Little Albert has taken on, the elements of persuasion that are a part of the pursuit of science are evident once again.

Treating Social Phobia

Social phobia involves both behavioral problems (avoiding contact with other people) and cognitive distortions (fear of being evaluated negatively, for example), making it particularly suited to cognitive-behavioral approaches to treatment. In a special issue of Clinical Psychology Review devoted to social phobia, Butler (1989, 9, 91-106) describes the application of cognitive-behavioral therapy to social phobia. The wealth of clinical examples and practical guidance included in the article make it clear how cognitive and behavioral principles can be combined in clinical practice.

As presented by Butler, the first steps of treatment include specifying the situations in which anxiety occurs, identifying available resources in the client's life, and agreeing on goals of treatment. As with other types of phobias, exposure to the feared stimulus is the primary behavioral intervention used. In the case of social phobia, this approach takes on added complexity because of the difficulty of predicting how a dynamic stimulus like social interaction will unfold. Unlike the case of a simple dog or snake phobia, it may be difficult to decide what exposure tasks are appropriate: "In order to meet someone of the opposite sex at a `disco' should you offer them a drink, ask them to dance or first go and buy some new clothes?" (p. 97). Role-playing may be an especially effective behavioral technique for social phobia, allowing the client to try out new behavior in the safety of the office first.

While exposing the client to the feared situations is an essential part of treatment, Butler points out that the cognitive aspects of social phobia, such as the fear of being evaluated negatively, often do not subside with exposure alone. Thus, cognitive techniques are often combined with behavioral tasks to dispute maladaptive beliefs. For example, a person who remembers only the negative social events that have occurred might be asked to monitor and write down instances of positive social exchange at the end of each day. A particularly valuable technique is encouraging people to test out their pessimistic or self-conscious expectations. A client who was afraid everyone would notice and critically evaluate him when he entered a room (making him afraid to enter a lecture hall) was given the assignment of purposely dropping his books on entry to class, and then taking note of people's reactions. When he found that most people took little notice of his behavior, he became less self-conscious.

A review of research on cognitive and behavioral treatments in the same issue of <u>Clinical Psychology Review</u> (Heimberg, R. G., pp. 107-128) documents the effectiveness of these techniques in relieving social phobia.

<u>Wolpe on the Etiology of Panic Disorder</u>

In a clear and compelling presentation of their theory of the etiology of panic disorder, Wolpe and Rowan (1988, <u>Behavior Research and Therapy</u>, <u>26</u>, 441-450) argue that, while first panic attacks have a variety of causes, recurring attacks are the result of classical conditioning. First panic attack may be caused by organic or psychological factors: Organic causes may be direct (as in the case of panic induced by amphetamines, cocaine, or other drugs) or indirect (as when a person experiencing non-pathological heart palpatations--intermittent tachycardia--perceives the symptoms as dangerous). The psychological pathway to a first panic attack involves the following steps: (1) the person is habitually anxious and oversensitive, and is also going through a stressful period, (2) this person finds herself in a particularly stressful circumstance, (3) the anxiety and stress precipitates hyperventilation (a common consequence of anxiety), (4) the hyperventilation is accompanied by physical symptoms such as dizziness, shortness of breath, and tingling in the extremities, and (5) the physical symptoms escalate into a panic attack. The person _may_ interpret the attack as impending death or insanity, leading to a misattribution; however, such misattributions do not _cause_ panic attacks, according to Wolpe and Rowan, but rather _follow_ them. In a pilot study involving interviews with panic disordered patients, they found that in the first panic attack, the physical symptoms always _preceded_ the panic, and if misattributions occurred, they followed the attack.

While numerous experiences may cause a person to have their first panic attack, Wolpe and Rowan assert that _recurrent_ attacks, or panic disorder, have a single cause: classical conditioning. According to their model, the first panic attack is an _unconditioned response_ to the physical symptoms caused by hyperventilation. Contiguous stimuli, both endogenous (bodily sensations) and exogenous (sunlight, driving in a car, being away from home) become _conditioned stimuli_ for panic, as they are associated with the first attack. These stimuli thus become triggers for recurring attacks.

The classical conditioning model leads directly to an effective treatment technique which Wolpe describes: (1) The person is taught to prevent hyperventilation through breathing retraining (holding the mouth shut and breathing through the nose is remarkably effective). (2) The next step is to extinguish the anxiety response to the physiological effects of hyperventilation. This is done by exposing the person to these physical symptoms by inducing hyperventilation (through breathing CO_2) in the office. Repeated exposure to the symptoms extinguishes the anxiety response: hyperventilation no longer leads to panic. (3) Finally, it is necessary to eliminate the maladaptive anxiety response habits which the person has developed, through systematic desensitization or cognitive restructuring.

Chapter 6

PTSD in the War Zone

Feinstein, acting as psychiatric medical officer for a counterinsurgency unit on active patrol, writes an interesting account of symptoms of Posttraumatic Stress Disorder on the battlefield (1989, _American Journal of Psychiatry_, _146_, 665-666). Following an ambush involving intense and prolonged crossfire and casualties on both sides, Feinstein decided to monitor the soldiers for symptoms of PTSD. He found that all of the DSM-III criteria were frequently reported one week after the ambush, including, for example, hyperalertness, recurrent and intrusive recollections of the event, sleep disturbance, and guilt about surviving. The men would have fit a DSM-III diagnosis of PTSD, although they continued to function efficiently in their duties (all but one soldier, who had to be evacuated because of the severity of his symptoms), and most symptoms subsided within a few weeks.

The author concludes that periods of distress are normal following traumatic life events, and supports the changes made in the DSM-IIIR PTSD criteria, which introduced a minimum duration of 1 month as a criterion for labeling such distress a disorder.

Survivor's Syndrome: Long-term Consequences of the Holocaust

The term "survivor's syndrome" was coined following World War II to describe the problems afflicting survivors of the Holocaust. Recent reports by Nadler and Ben-Shushan (1989, _Journal of Consulting and Clinical Psychology_, _57_, 287-293) and Solomon, Kotler, and Mikulincer (1988, _American Journal of Psychiatry_, _145_, 865-868) confirm the long-lasting and far-reaching consequences of such massive traumatization.

Nadler and Ben-Shushan present results from a forty-year follow-up study comparing Holocaust survivors (now in their 60s) and a control group of similar age and cultural background who had not been victims of the Holocaust. None of the subjects had received psychiatric treatment. Structured personality inventories revealed that survivors had significantly lower psychological well-being, poorer interpersonal functioning, and more psychopathological symptoms than controls. Interviews with the survivors revealed considerable problems with anxiety: almost all reported frequent nightmares, insomnia, and frequent anxieties and fears, even forty years after the trauma.

Not only do Holocaust survivors show lasting effects of the traumatization, but their children, who were not directly exposed, have been found to react with severe anxiety when under stress, as well as experiencing survival guilt and conflict about the expression of aggression. Solomon and colleagues compared Israeli combat stress casualties from the 1982 Lebanon War whose parents were Holocaust survivors with a control group of casualties without such family history. None of the subjects had evidenced psychiatric problems before serving in the Lebanon War. The authors found that soldiers whose parents had been Holocaust survivors had significantly higher rates of Posttraumatic Stress Disorder than the controls. Several alternative explanations are offered for the results: (1) survivors' children may be particularly vulnerable to stress reactions; (2) failure to continue in combat may be seen as particularly shameful to survivors' children, who see themselves as guardians and protectors of their parents, or (3) the survivor parents may be more protective and reluctant to have their children return to war, leading to secondary gains for PTSD symptoms. Regardless of the interpretation, these studies reveal the far-reaching psychological consequences of massive traumatization.

NOTES

DISCUSSION STIMULATORS

Superstitious Behavior and Compulsions

Skinner drew an analogy between what he described as "superstitious behavior" resulting from chance reinforcement and compulsions. We all engage in a certain amount of superstitious behavior; students might be encouraged to consider ritualistic superstitions they may hold-- professional athletes are prime examples of this. What similarities or differences are there between these behaviors and compulsions?

Developmental Changes in Fears

Specific fears and phobias are common during the childhood years (see graph in Chapter 15), however, they seem to increase or decrease in prevalence over time. Have the class discuss some of the implications of the developmental changes in fears such as fear of falling, separation anxiety, fear of the dark, anxiety over death, accident or injury, and so on. Issues about biological predispositions, preparedness, outgrowing fears, common cultural myths and experiences, and overcoming fear should come out of this discussion.

Trying Out Behavioral Techniques

If time allows, you might do an exercise teaching the class the basics of systematic desensitization. Have students pair up, pass out the following instructions, and have them take turns acting as behavior therapist and client. To make the exercise briefer, tell students to assume they have been taught how to relax in previous sessions, and are ready for the desensitization procedure. Following the exercise, bring the group back together to discuss their experiences: How did it feel, both from the client perspective and the therapist perspective? What problems arose in constructing the hierarchy or visualizing the scenes? Do students feel this technique would be helpful? Be sure to highlight the differences between this exercise and use of technique in a real-life therapy situation (in which you would spend more time, build a relationship, proceed more slowly through the hierarchy, build in in vivo exposure, etc.). The instructions which follow are adapted from Goldfried and Davison's Clinical Behavior Therapy (1976, New York: Holt, Rinehart, & Winston, pp. 112-135).

SYSTEMATIC DESENSITIZATION EXERCISE
INSTRUCTIONS

Instructions for "Client":

Choose a situation that actually makes you anxious, or make up a situation. Examples might include fear of driving on the freeway, fear of speaking in class, test-taking anxiety, fear of being in closed spaces, fear of talking to strangers, or fear of dogs.

Work with your "behavior therapist" to construct a hierarchy from the least anxiety-provoking situation to the most feared situation. Think of your anxiety as a large balloon filled with stimuli, each of which is associated with a given amount of anxiety. In constructing your hierarchy, you will choose examples from this balloon which represent all its elements, sampling items of varying degrees of aversiveness. Make your examples as concrete as possible, so your "therapist" can help you imagine them vividly. You will be asked to sit comfortably in your chair, imagine that you are very relaxed, and visualize the scenes which your "therapist" will describe for you, signalling him or her when you feel any anxiety.

Instructions for "Behavior Therapist":

(1) _Interview_. Begin with a brief interview with your "client" to determine what is making him or her anxious. (We are assuming that anxiety is the presenting problem.) As well as making the person feel comfortable during the interview, find out as much detail as you can about the specific situations which make him/her anxious: time of day, other people present, where it occurs, how long it lasts, and (briefly) how they have tried to overcome it in the past. These details are essential for use in the next step, constructing a hierarchy of anxiety-producing situations. Take notes to help you remember the details.

(2) _Construct hierarchy_. Together with your "client," come up with a list of anxiety-producing situations (related to the particular problem they described in the interview), and order them from least to most anxiety-producing. You should help your "client" come up with 10-12 situations, and collect enough information about them so that you will be able to help your "client" visualize them as if they are actually occurring.

(3) **Systematic desensitization procedure.** Instruct your client to relax (you might ask them to rate on a scale from 1 to 100 how relaxed they feel, with 1 being extremely relaxed, and 100 being extremely tense). Tell them to signal you by raising a finger whenever they feel at all anxious. When the client appears relaxed or reports feeling relaxed, begin describing the <u>least</u> anxiety-producing situation from the hierarchy. Describe it briefly, then pause to let the person imagine it. After about 10 seconds, ask them to stop visualizing the situation and simply relax again. If the person has not signalled any anxiety, proceed to the next scene, in the same manner. Continue up the hierarchy, describing each scene in turn, giving the client time to visualize them, and pausing to relax in between.

At any point that the person signals anxiety, instruct them to stop visualizing the scene and relax. They might choose a relaxing scene to imagine, such as lying on the beach, instead of the anxiety-producing one. When the person reports feeling relaxed again, try having them visualize a scene lower on the hierarchy, that is, one that will be less anxiety-producing. If it is difficult to find a scene that does not provoke anxiety, you have made the hierarchy too difficult; you need to come up with smaller steps.

NOTES

Case Studies in Abnormal Psychology

Neale, Oltmanns, and Davison have written a book of illustrative cases that provides interesting examples of the various disorders, as well as offering supplementary material on most of the psychological problems presented in the text. Students really appreciate the way a case can bring material alive, and Case Studies in Abnormal Psychology is something to seriously consider as a supplement to the text.

Disorders on T.V.

At the risk of letting your students know that you occasionally do something as mundane as watching T.V., you can help to illustrate some of the disorders (and what does not constitute a disorder) discussed in this and subsequent chapters by "diagnosing" various characters from T.V., movies, and novels. Some possibilities based on my own mundane experience include: Felix Unger, Radar and Frank Burns from M*A*S*H, Dennis the Menace or Calvin (from Calvin and Hobbes comic) . . . As an alternative, have the class go to see virtually any of Woody Allen's earlier movies. Play It Again Sam and Manhattan are particularly good examples of his creative neurosis, as well of a series of irrational beliefs.

NOTES

INSTRUCTIONAL FILMS

1. <u>Anxiety: The Endless Crisis</u>. (IU, 59 min., 1975) Examines a wide range of anxiety-producing situations, from fleeting anxiety to anxiety that ultimately leads to death. Discusses state and trait views of anxiety.

2. <u>Descriptions and Interventions</u>. (CM, 17-25 min., filmstrips) The films deal with the origins of abnormal behavior, anxiety disorders (in two parts), personality disorders, and schizophrenia.

3. <u>Pathological Anxiety</u>. (PCR-2122, 30 min., 1961) Case study of an office worker who experiences panic and terror that prevents him from leading a normal life.

4. <u>Image in a Mirror</u>. (N.Y.U. Film Library, 9 min., color) "Carol goes through visible agony during tests and is always convinced that she is going to fail, despite excellent report cards. Even her teacher's constant encouragement has not helped. What can the teacher do to help Carol gain self-confidence? Solution left to viewer."

5. <u>Anxiety: Decision at the Synapse</u>. (Abbott Laboratories, 27 min., color, 1975) Summarizes information on the etiology and physiology of anxiety, including its clinical symptoms and management.

6. <u>What Happens in Emotions?</u> (IU, 30 min., b & w) Discusses bodily functions that operate during emotional states, including charts and diagrams to explain the sympathetic and parasympathetic nervous systems. Stresses the way in which facial expressions provide clues in determining different emotions.

7. <u>Experimental Neuroses by Control of Emotion</u>. (The Film Center, 30 min.) Demonstration of the use of hypnosis and conditioning to produce emotions.

8. <u>Rational Emotive Therapy</u>. (Research Press, 30 min., color) Albert Ellis describes his therapeutic techniques and his model for understanding emotions.

CHAPTER 7

Somatoform and Dissociative Disorders

Somatoform Disorders

Somatoform disorders involve physical symptoms which have no known physiological explanation, are not under voluntary control, and appear to be linked to psychological factors. The chapter focuses on two forms of somatoform disorders, conversion disorder and somatization disorder, or Briquet's syndrome. Both occur most often in women, and usually begin in adolescence or early adulthood. The two disorders share many of the same symptoms and may be applicable to the same patient. DSM-IIIR identifies several additional somatoform disorders about which little is known: somatoform pain disorder refers to pain which cannot be accounted for by organic pathology; body dysmorphic disorder describes those who are preoccupied with defects in appearance; and hypochondriasis refers to people who are preoccupied with fears of having a serious disease.

Conversion Disorder

In conversion disorders, some bodily function is impaired although the organ itself is sound. Conversion symptoms usually appear suddenly in stressful situations, allow patients to avoid some activity, or secure them attention. The term "conversion" is derived from Freud's thinking, reflecting the belief that anxiety and psychological conflict are converted into physical symptoms. Hysteria is an earlier term for the disorder, dating back to Hippocrates' view that it was caused by the uterus traveling through the body.

True neurological problems may be misdiagnosed as conversion disorders, and patients diagnosed with the disorder have high rates of subsequent physical disorders. Malingering presents a problem in diagnosis as some people may intentionally fake incapacity to avoid responsibility. La belle indifference may help make this distinction--some patients with conversion disorders act unconcerned about their symptoms and talk about them at length, while a malingerer is likely to be more guarded.

Somatization Disorder (Briquet's Syndrome)

This syndrome, first described by Pierre Briquet, is characterized by recurrent, multiple somatic complaints which have no known physical cause. These patients may have frequent medical treatments, menstrual difficulties, and sexual indifference. DSM-IIIR's distinction of somatization disorder (characterized by complaints about symptoms) and hypochondriasis (fear of disease) is of dubious value.

Theories of Somatoform Disorders

Conversion disorders are central to psychoanalytic theory; Breuer and Freud proposed that they are caused by a traumatic emotional experience which remains unexpressed. Freud later proposed that sexual impulses stemming from the Electra complex were primary. The primary gain of conversion disorder was avoidance of sexual impulses, while secondary gain or real-life benefits from the symptoms were also considered. Evidence from experimental research on hysterical blindness and other phenomena indicates that many mental processes are unconscious, as Freud suggested. The difference is that Freud used "unconscious" as a noun, whereas experimental psychologists use it as an adjective.

Sociocultural theories are based on the supposed decrease in conversion disorders over the last century; the repression of sexual attitudes in Freud's day are implicated in the disorders, while modern relaxation of sexual mores is seen as decreasing their incidence. A behavioral account of somatoform disorder suggests that the problem is a role enactment of how a person with such a problem should behave. Such a view would not seem to distinguish the disorders from malingering, however. Researchers have found no evidence for a genetic role in conversion disorders. More conversion symptoms are found on the left side of the body, leading to speculation that the left hemisphere (where verbal capacities are centralized) somehow blocks impulses carrying painful emotional content from the right hemisphere.

Therapy for Somatoform Disorders

Most people with somatoform disorders contact physicians for help, presenting a dilemma to medical personnel as to whether to treat them or refer to an (unwanted) mental health professional. There is no evidence on the relative efficacy of different treatments for this disorder. Psychoanalytic therapy uses catharsis, while behavioral clinicians are likely to focus on changing situations that create anxiety and attempting to eliminate the reinforcement the patient receives for being "sick."

Dissociative Disorders

In all three dissociative disorders there is a sudden, temporary alteration in the normal functions of consciousness, identity, and motor behavior. Depersonalization disorder, also classified as a dissociative disorder, is controversial because there is no disturbance in memory.

In psychogenic amnesia, the person becomes unable to recall important personal information following a stressful episode. In psychogenic fugue, not only is total amnesia present, but the person moves away and assumes a new identity. Multiple personality is characterized by the existence of two or more independent ego states; each personality is fully integrated and complex and determines actions when in command. As with conversion disorders, it is possible for the symptoms of dissociative disorders to be faked.

Theories of Dissociative Disorders

According to psychoanalytic theory, dissociative disorders are instances of massive repression relating back to unacceptable sexual wishes of the Oedipal stage. One theory suggests that multiple personality is established in childhood by self-hypnosis in order to cope with extreme trauma; this view is supported by evidence that many cases of multiple personality report childhood traumas, usually abuse, and such patients are high in hypnotizability.

Learning theorists view the disorder as a set of avoidance responses that serve to protect the individual from stressful events. Evidence suggests that subjects can adopt the role of a multiple personality to escape punishment. Finally, experimental research on state-dependent memory indicates that it may play a role in dissociative disorders.

Therapies for Dissociative Disorders

Little systematic research is available on the treatment of dissociative disorders. Psychoanalytic treatment pursues the goal of lifting repression. Multiple personalities are usually treated by attempting to "fuse" the different personalities. Free association, a review of life history, hypnosis, sodium amytal ("truth serum") and skills training have all been used in attempts to achieve this goal.

STUDENTS SHOULD KNOW . . .

1. Conversion disorder and somatization disorder (Briquet's Syndrome) are the two major categories of somatoform disorder.

2. The operation of the musculature or sensory functions are impaired in conversion disorder, although there is no apparent organic problem.

3. It is difficult to distinguish conversion disorders from true physical illnesses and from malingering.

4. Somatization disorder is characterized by recurrent, multiple somatic complaints for which medical attention is sought but which have no apparent physical basis.

5. Conversion disorders occupy a central place in psychoanalytic thinking, as some of Freud's major ideas, particularly regarding the unconscious, were based on his work with patients with this problem.

6. Freud suggested that the primary gain of a conversion disorder was avoidance of repressed id impulses, but he also allowed for secondary gain or direct reinforcement for the symptoms.

7. Evidence from experimental psychology supports the notion that many mental processes are unconscious; this is distinguished from Freud's notion of an entity called "the unconscious."

8. The dissociative disorders include psychogenic amnesia (a sudden loss of memory), psychogenic fugue (memory loss plus the assumption of a new identity), and multiple personality (the existence of two or more complex egos in the same person).

9. The dissociative disorders suggest the plausibility of Freud's concept of repression.

10. Little is known about the relative efficacy of treatments for either somatoform or dissociative disorders.

New Terms
(key terms underlined)

somatoform disorders, conversion disorder, somatization disorder, Briquet's Syndrome, somatoform pain disorder, body dysmorphic disorder, hypochondriasis, hysteria, malingering, la belle indifference, social-skills training, dissociative disorders, psychogenic amnesia, psychogenic fugue, multiple personality disorder, depersonalization disorder, state-dependent memory

New Names
(key figures underlined)

Pierre Briquet

NOTES

LECTURE LAUNCHERS

Hypochondriasis and Functional Somatic Symptoms

While discussed only briefly in Chapter 7, hypochondriasis and various functional somatic symptoms are important public health phenomena. Various estimates suggest that somewhere between 20% and 84% of the patients who consult medical practitioners fit into one of these two categories, and the prevalence of hypochondriasis is between 3% and 13% of the population. A recent review of the topic provides some additional interesting information on the disorders (Kellner, R., 1985, Archives of General Psychiatry, 42, 821-829).

Anxiety and depression are two complaints commonly associated with hypochondriasis, to such an extent that some investigators suggest that hypochondriasis is not a separate entity. Most experts on the topic suggest, however, that there is a subgroup of patients for whom the physical symptoms constitute the major complaint. Fear of death commonly accompanies hypochondriasis, a fear which can intensify to the extent that it is properly considered a phobia. Particular hypochondriacal complaints tend to run in families, and the disorders are more common among lower class patients who complain less about psychological symptoms and more about physical ones. Life stressors-- particularly bereavement or witnessing illness or death-- often appear to precipitate hypochondriasis, and symptoms can mimic those of an illness that the patient recently read about. Finally, it has been noted in several investigations that hypochondriacal patients are generally more sensitive to their physiological functioning.

Little in the way of controlled research has been conducted on the treatment of functional somatic symptoms and hypochondriasis. Several investigators have suggested that the presence of hypochondriasis is an indication of poor prognosis in therapy, but treatment successes have also been reported using both psychotherapy and antidepressant and anti-anxiety medications. It has also been noted that simple reassurance is often sufficient. Perhaps what is most surprising is the relative neglect of a topic that presents an important challenge to both medical and mental health professionals.

Sexual Histories of Women with Somatization Disorder

Studying the sexual histories of women with somatization disorder is important for several reasons. First, such women typically report sexual dissatisfaction and unhappy marriages. In addition, historical inquiry into hysterical disorders, beginning with Freud, focused on experiences with sexual molestation in childhood, though later dismissed as fantasy by Freud. A recent study by Morrison (1989, American Journal of Psychiatry, 146, 239-241) involved in-depth interviews with 60 women diagnosed as having somatization disorder by DSM-III criteria, and a control group of 31 women with primary affective disorder. While the groups did not differ in their reports of the usual childhood sexual experiences, including, for example, age at which they first played "doctor," masturbated, kissed, or had voluntary intercourse, (indicating that the women with somatization disorder were not globally exaggerating their sexual experiences), women with somatization disorder were significantly more likely to have been sexually molested as children. Over half of the women with somatization disorder had been molested, as compared to 16% of the control group. These results suggest that sexual abuse is a common event in the childhood histories of women with somatization disorder.

Update on Multiple Personality Disorder

Kluft (1987, Hospital and Community Psychiatry, 38, 363-373) reviews a range of issues involved in multiple personality disorder, including controversy over its prevalence and phenomenology, etiology, diagnostic criteria and differential diagnosis, and treatment:

Prevalence. A recent exchange of letters in the American Journal of Psychiatry (Ludolph, 1985, 142, 1526-1527; Bliss, 1985, 142, 1527; Kluft, 1986, 143, 802-803; Chodoff, 1987, 144, 124; and Kluft, 1987, 144, 124-125) explores the controversy surrounding the prevalence of multiple personality. One group of clinicians assert that the disorder is rare or nonexistent; they suggest that the recent increase in reported cases is due to loose diagnostic criteria, the overenthusiasm of a few diagnosticians, or even the creation of the disorder through hypnosis treatments, and conceptualize the disorder as maintained and perhaps created by secondary gains. Those who believe that the prevalence of the disorder is much higher than previously believed conceptualize it as a child's attempt to cope with trauma through inward flight; a child who cannot physically escape extreme abuse, for example, may find that dissociation provides an inner escape.

Etiology.   Support for the view that multiple personality disorder is a kind of posttraumatic stress reaction to childhood trauma comes from findings that up to 97% of cases of multiple personality have experienced child abuse, usually sexual. A combination of the following factors is seen as leading to development of the disorder: (1) the child is dissociation-prone (for example, multiple personalities have been found have high hypnotizability), (2) she is harshly abused or molested, (3) she cannot escape the abuse, perhaps because it is perpetrated by a member of her family, (4) the child dissociates, thus escaping psychically from a physically inescapable, ongoing trauma. Once established, this mode of coping may be repeated to deal with less traumatic events in the future. The author suggests that the disorder may be treated with much greater success if it is discovered in childhood near its onset, before the pattern has become an ingrained mode of coping.

Treatment. As described in the text, most treatment methods involve attempting to integrate the split personalities. In addition, Kluft points out the importance of teaching the client new ways of coping with stress, to replace the previously ingrained dissociation pattern. Thus, after integration has been achieved, coping skills such as relaxation and assertion training and new interpersonal skills become an important aspect of treatment to prevent relapse. Interestingly, Braun (1984, Psychiatric Annals, 14, 34-40) reports that integration may result in physiological changes; patients report changes in allergies, color blindness, eyeglass prescription, and insulin requirements (in diabetics) following integration.

Internal Group Therapy for Multiple Personality Disorder

Students may be intrigued by the use of "internal group therapy" in treating multiple personality disorder: the therapist "invites" the alter personalities to attend a therapy session and communicate with one another directly (Caul, D., 1984, Psychiatric Annals, 14, 43-50). The goals of such an intervention include arriving at an agreement between the personalities as to the goals and directions of therapy (to prevent one personality from sabotaging treatment), reducing "sibling rivalry" between the personalities, and encouraging the alters to work out conflicts which may interfere with integration. In the procedure described by Caul, the patient is put in charge of the session, determining who will attend, the subject matter, and the length of the session. The therapist's presence helps to maintain structure and safety, though he or she does not intervene except in an emergency. The following excerpt from an internal group therapy session will likely fascinate students:

The patient was placed in a trance. She reiterated her willingness to proceed with the session. The ISH [Internal Self Helper, a personality who had been helpful in therapy before, and was chosen by the patient to lead the session] assumed control and emerged from the trance. . . . [She then greets the other personalities and outlines the areas that need to be discussed.]

Apparently, there had been an incident at work the night before [the patient is a nurse]. The host personality had become angry. In frustration, she had struck the closet door in a patient's room. The ISH, in a very controlled manner, and with a well-modulated voice devoid of any anger, told the host personality that her actions on the previous night had been inappropriate. She explained to the alter personalities that they had to learn to control their "nasty tempers." A spontaneous switch took place and the host personality emerged. She was an indecisive and insecure individual with a quavering voice. She said that she realized what she did was wrong, but she had been unable to control herself. Then another came out, a very hostile, resentful, and aggressive personality. She voiced her anger and introduced her own topic: strong concerns about rivalries among the personalities for the therapist's attention. She was especially upset about another alter personality, whom she felt was the primary therapist's "pet." She felt the primary therapist had exhibited a great deal of favoritism toward her, and tended to hold her up to the others as a model of good behavior. (p 47)

In this case, the session served to alert the therapist to the fact that he was, unwittingly, alienating some of the personalities.

Case Study of a Multiple Personality: Sally Beauchamp

Recent studies of the life history of "Sally Beauchamp," one of the most famous cases of multiple personality, reveal fascinating information about the idiodynamics of this intriguing disorder (Rosenzweig, S., 1988, _American Psychologist_, _43_, 45-48). Information gleaned from articles by Morton Prince, Sally Beauchamp's therapist, and newspaper accounts of the period reveal a co-incidence of death, dates, and weather patterns occurring at the time of her dissociations. The first alter personality emerged June 7, 1880; Sally's newborn brother had just died, and she had a sense of complicity in the death. The new personality was defiant of conventional rules of behavior. The second personality emerged June 7, 1893. At this time, the trial of Lizzie Borden for the axe murder of her parents was going on in the town where Sally lived; the author suggests that this event recalled for Sally the deaths of her two infant brothers, which she felt guilty about. The personality that emerged at this time was described as "saint-like." Finally, a third personality emerged on June 7, 1899; at this time, a prominent newspaper account of a death in Prince's family had startled Sally.

Rosenzweig explores an additional characteristic of all three dissociation crises: cloudy and rainy weather conditions in the evening or night hours. Reports from Prince's account of Sally's treatment reveal a connection between the weather patterns and her dissociation experiences. On one occasion,

> while she was in a restaurant, dark clouds came up; on going out, from the looks of the sky she got the idea that a thunderstorm was coming up, and at the thought she became stricken with terror. At once she became affected with palpitation, nausea, hot and cold feelings and a sinking sensation . . .

Under hypnosis, the patient recalls the first occasion when she was frightened by lightening, coinciding with her second dissociation experience at the time of the Lizzie Borden murder trial. Finding that thunder storms were prominent on all three occasions of Sally's dissociations, the author suggests that the combination of death which she feels complicity in and an ambience of rainy weather, triggered the dissociations. It may be interesting to compare this analysis to Wolpe's theory of classically conditioned panic disorder (see Instructor's Manual, Chapter 6); perhaps the gloomy weather conditions had been associated with death and altered consciousness through classical conditioning.

This article could also be used to discuss the advantages and disadvantages of the case study method. While it may generate hypotheses about the circumstances eliciting dissociation experiences, it is difficult to test such hypotheses using this method (one wonders, for example, how often stormy weather was <u>unaccompanied</u> by dissociation in Sally's life).

<u>NOTES</u>

Chapter 7

DISCUSSION STIMULATORS

Right-Left Hemisphere Differences

The finding, described in the text, that conversion symptoms are more likely to occur on the left side of the body than the right (leading to the hypothesis that they relate to the functioning of the right hemisphere and emotional arousal), may be used in a discussion of right vs. left hemisphere differences. A simple demonstration of the differential functioning of the hemispheres can be done by having students briefly interview one or two people outside of class. The question asked should be a problem which most college students could accomplish with concentration. For instance: "How many letters are there in the word Washington?" or "Multiply 12 by 13." The interviewer's task is to record the direction of the subject's eye movements when he or she pauses to think about the question. It has been reported that when people concentrate on a reasoning problem, their eyes tend to shift up and to the right. Some people will shift the other way, but most people are consistent in their movements (Bakan, P., 1971, _Psychology Today_, _4_ (11), 64 ff.). It is thought that these eye movements reflect unequal activation of the hemispheres. When asked to reason, the left (dominant) hemisphere--the verbal, analytic half--is activated, and the eyes drift to the right.

Distinguishing Multiple Personality and Schizophrenia

Students (and the popular media) frequently confuse the concepts of multiple personality and schizophrenia. It is worthwhile to spend some time at this point in the course explaining the difference. Pointing out the derivation of the term "schizophrenia" will help to clarify the source of confusion: "Schizo" means split and "phrenia" means mind, thus the interpretation that schizophrenia means split personality. The term was coined by Bleuler, however, and indicates his view that the central problem in schizophrenia is the "breaking of associative threads" or the loss of connections between thoughts (see Chapter 14). In fact, schizophrenia and multiple personality are two very different disorders.

Demonstrating Hypnotic Suggestibility

Many theorists and researchers have reported that individuals with multiple personality disorder are more susceptible to hypnosis, making them more likely to dissociate as a means of coping with trauma. Hypnotic suggestibility may have other, less pernicious, associations with creativity, imagination, and ability to relax. People who are able to vividly imagine may be better candidates for systematic desensitization. Students may be interested in finding out how susceptible to hypnosis they are; try the following demonstration with the class (from Hadley, J. & Staudacher, C., 1985, Hypnosis for Change, Oakland, CA: New Harbinger Press, pp. 22-23).

Make sure you are completely comfortable. Stretch your legs, your arms. And now begin to relax. Close your eyes and take a deep breath . . . and exhale . . . and relax. Completely relax. Relax your legs, lower back, relax your shoulders. Relax your shoulders, your arms, your neck, your face. Relax your whole body, just relax. Take another deep breath . . . and exhale . . . let go, and relax. Become aware of the rhythm of your breathing. Begin to flow with the rhythm of your breathing, and as you inhale, relax your breathing and begin to feel your body drift and float into relaxation. The sounds around you are unimportant, let them go, and relax. Let every muscle in your body completely relax from the top of your head to the tips of your toes. As you inhale gently, relax. As you exhale, release any tension, any stress from any part of your body, mind, and thoughts.

Now stretch your arms in front of you at a level even with your shoulders. Imagine you are holding a bucket in each hand. Curl your fingers around the handles of the buckets, hold onto those two buckets. The bucket in your left hand is made of paper, it is made of paper. It is empty and feels very light, the bucket in your left hand feels very, very light. The bucket in your left hand is very, very light because it is made of paper. You hold that light bucket in your left hand. The bucket in your right hand is made of iron. It is made of iron, it is made of heavy, heavy iron, and the bucket has a few rocks in it. As you hold the heavy iron bucket, more and more rocks are dropped into the bucket until the bucket is completely full of heavy rocks. The bucket is completely

full of heavy rocks, the rocks are heaped up to
the top of the bucket. The bucket is so very
heavy, it is pulling your right arm down. The
bucket of rocks pulls your arm down and your arm
goes down because the heavy iron bucket is so
heavy, so very heavy.

In this exercise, the students' arms will begin to move some
distance from their original position at shoulder level.
The further the distance between the left and right arms,
the greater their suggestibility. Discuss students'
experiences.

NOTES

INSTRUCTIONAL FILMS

1. <u>Hypochondriasis and Health Care: A Tug of War</u>. (Workshop Films, 38 min., color, 1978) A lecture illustrated with simulated interviews on hypochondriacs and ways of dealing with them. "Most fascinating . . . very interesting . . . very informative" (Mental Health Materials Center review).

2. <u>Case Study of a Multiple Personality</u>. (PCR-2049K, 30 min., 1957) Interesting case study of dissociative reaction in a woman (Eve White, Eve Black, and Jane). A mimeographed transcript may be ordered because the sound is poor in some instances.

3. <u>Left Brain/Right Brain, Part I: The Great Ravelled Knot;</u> <u>Part II: The Split Brain; Part III: The Whole Brain</u>. (AVNA, color, filmstrips with record, cassette, or script, 71-81 frames, 1977) Part I is an overview and history of the brain. Part II discusses the animal experiments on split brain functioning and questions whether split brain humans have a divided consciousness. Part III discusses split brain humans and the differential functions of the hemispheres.

CHAPTER 8

Psychophysiological Disorders

CHAPTER SYNOPSIS

Psychophysiological disorders, previously called psychosomatic problems, are characterized by genuine physical symptoms that are caused or can be worsened by emotional factors. Unlike conversion disorders, psychophysiological disorders involve actual physical damage to the body. These disorders are not listed in DSM-IIIR because virtually all diseases are now viewed as potentially related to psychological stress.

Stress and Illness

The fields of behavioral medicine and health psychology focus on the study and treatment of psychophysiological disorders. Measures of the number and stressfulness of life events have been shown to be related to a number of illnesses and physiological symptoms. Recent prospective research demonstrates an increase in undesirable and a decrease in desirable daily life events in the days before onset of symptoms of infectious illness.

The quality and quantity of a person's social supports has been shown to be related to both mortality and disease onset. Higher levels of social support may increase the occurrence of health behaviors or have a direct effect on biological processes. The effects of stress on the immune system offer another explanation of the relation between stress and illness.

Theories of the Stress-Illness Link

Various physiological theories have been offered to explain how stress causes illness. Somatic-weakness theory suggests that the weakest bodily organ is likely to be affected by stress. Specific-reaction theory hypothesizes that individuals respond to stress in their own idiosyncratic way, with the most responsive body system being the likely candidate for disorder. Evolution theory assumes that the body's once adaptive response to physical danger is now triggered by psychological phenomena, thus increasing the frequency of autonomic arousal.

Psychological theories of stress include Alexander's psychoanalytic theory that different stress-related illnesses result from different unconscious emotional states. Conditioning theories focus on how stress may exacerbate an illness, and assume that a physiological diathesis must be present in addition to operant or classical conditioning.

Cardiovascular Disorders

Essential Hypertension

High blood pressure without an evident organic cause is called __essential hypertension__. Stressful conditions such as loss of employment and holding anger in have been linked to hypertension. Harburg explained high rates of the disease in urban blacks by a combination of environmental stress and anger-in.

Among animals several powerful diatheses to hypertension have been identified, including rearing in social isolation, emotionality, and salt sensitivity. Some evidence suggests that blood pressure reactivity is related to hypertension in humans.

Coronary Heart Disease

CHD takes two principal forms--__angina pectoris__ (chest pains) and __myocardial infarction__ (heart attack). Both diseases are caused by an insufficient supply of oxygen to the heart, but in myocardial infarction, the shortage is so severe that the muscle is damaged.

Traditional factors such as cigarette smoking and hypertension have been estimated to explain about half the etiology of CHD. Psychological factors hypothesized to cause CHD include __type A behavior pattern__. Type A persons, reliably identified by means of a structured interview, are intense, competitive, time-urgent, and hostile. Prospective evidence has indicated that type As are more than twice as likely to develop CHD and more than five times as likely to have a recurrence. However, more recent studies have failed to replicate the original findings, and some current researchers suggest that a narrower construct (perhaps focusing on hostility or cynicism) will prove more useful than global type A ratings (see box).

Asthma

Somewhere between 2 and 5 percent of the population has asthma, about one third of them children and two-thirds boys. Contrary to popular beliefs, research indicates that most cases do not have psychological factors as a dominant cause. However, psychological stress can precipitate attacks, as documented by several laboratory studies. Some research suggests that parent-child interactions play a role in asthma, but it may be that they help to maintain the illness, not cause it. No personality characteristics have been found to be related to asthmatic children more than to those with other chronic illnesses. Physiological predispositions implicated in asthma include a history of respiratory infection, genetic transmission, and a less responsive sympathetic nervous system.

Therapies for Psychophysiological Disorders

Since psychophysiological disorders are true physical dysfunctions, consultation with a physician is necessary. Therapists agree that reducing anxiety is the best way to alleviate the disorders, as drug interventions treat only the physical symptoms, not the psychological stress. Behavioral medicine devises treatments to lessen habits known to contribute to illness. Biofeedback provides information about heart rate, blood pressure, and other autonomic functions; a box discusses the treatment of migraine headaches using biofeedback.

Nonpharmacological treatment of hypertension usually involves relaxation training; recent research indicates that such treatment might be most helpful for those hypertensives with high sympathetic arousal. In treating type A behavior, the Recurrent Coronary Prevention Project demonstrated that the behavior pattern could be altered, and that this change reduced the likelihood of a second heart attack. However, trying to change type A is difficult since it is so readily rewarded in our society. The new field of "stress management" uses techniques such as arousal reduction, cognitive restructuring, behavioral skills training, and environmental change to reduce the stress implicated in psychophysiological disorders.

STUDENTS SHOULD KNOW . . .

Key Points

1.   Psychophysiological disorders are distinct from conversion disorders in that they involve genuine physical symptoms made worse by psychological factors.

2.   There is no listing of psychophysiological disorders in DSM-IIIR because virtually all physical illnesses are now viewed as potentially related to psychological stress.

3.   The relation found between stress and illness is not perfect, in part because of problems in measuring stress and mediating factors.

4.   Students should know the various theories linking stress and illness, both physiological and psychological.

5.   Holding anger in is a predisposing factor in hypertension, and relaxation has been shown to reduce high blood pressure.

6.   The type A behavior pattern has been linked to coronary heart disease, although recent evidence casts some doubt on the usefulness of the type A construct.

7.   Psychological factors are not the cause of a large percentage of cases of asthma, but parent-child relationships do appear to play a role in its onset or maintenance.

8.   Therapists of various persuasions agree that reducing anxiety is the best way to alleviate the suffering from psychophysiological disorders.

9.   Psychological techniques are used in consultation with physicians to treat problems such as hypertension and type A behavior pattern, and the field of stress management has developed widely used methods for relieving stress.

New Terms
(key terms underlined)

psychophysiological disorders, psychosomatic, general adaptation syndrome, Life Change Unit, social support, somatic-weakness theory, specific-reaction theory, evolution theory, cardiovascular disorders, essential hypertension, anger-in, coronary heart disease, angina pectoris, myocardial infarction, type A behavior pattern, asthma, stress management

New Names
(key figures underlined)

Rene Descartes, Franz Alexander, Meyer Friedman and Ray Rosenman

NOTES

LECTURE LAUNCHERS

Hardiness and Health

The fact that illness and stress are imperfectly correlated has led to a search for mediators which may ameliorate the effects of life events. In this vein, Kobasa, Maddi, and Kahn (1982, Journal of Personality and Social Psychology, 42, 168-177) test their theory of "hardiness"--a constellation of personality characteristics that protect one from stressful life events. Included in this constellation are three personality dispositions: commitment, control, and challenge.

Commitment refers to the tendency to involve oneself in whatever one is doing, rather than experience alienation from one's activities. Control involves experiencing oneself as influential, rather than helpless, in handling life events. Finally, challenge refers to acceptance of and welcoming of change rather than stability.

In a prospective, longitudinal test of the theory that such hardiness mediates the relationship between stress and illness, Kobasa and colleagues had 259 male management personnel report on stressful life events and illness symptoms over a period of several years, and personality characteristics relating to the three dimensions of hardiness. The authors found both concurrently and prospectively that hardiness decreased the likelihood of illness symptoms, and that this health-preserving effect was particularly strong under highly stressful life conditions.

The authors suggest future research which might be done, including ruling out third variable effects, such as social support and health practices, exploring the interaction between hardiness and other resistance resources, and studying how this personality constellation develops.

Integrating the Effects of Hardiness, Life Events, and Health Behavior

In line with research directions suggested by Kobasa and colleagues (above), Roth, Wiebe, Fillingim, and Shay (1989, Journal of Personality and Social Psychology, 57, 136-142) explored the combined and interactive effects of stressful life events, fitness, and hardiness on physical illness. The investigators studied 373 undergraduate students, collecting information on physical illness, stressful life events, fitness and exercise participation, and hardiness. Confirming earlier studies, the authors found that both fitness and hardiness were directly associated with physical health. However, regression analyses indicated that hardiness did not independently predict health. Structural equation analyses suggested that the effect of hardiness on health may be mediated by stressful life events. Hardy individuals may experience fewer stressful life events, or they may interpret such events differently, rendering them less stressful. No interaction effects were found for the three predictor variables (fitness, stress, and hardiness) and exercise was found to have no direct effect on health (its effect is apparently indirect, through its relationship to fitness).

Muscle-Tension and Chronic Back Pain

Flor, Turk, and Birbaumer (1985, Journal of Consulting and Clinical Psychology, 53, 354-364) presented evidence that would appear to support a specific reaction theory in the etiology of chronic back pain. These investigators studied the muscle tension reactions of chronic back pain patients, general pain patients, and healthy subjects in response to stress (discussions of personally-relevant stressful experiences). While the subjects discussed stressful experiences, the investigators monitored heart rate, skin conductance, frontalis EMG (electromyogram) and, most importantly, paraspinal EMG. These same physiological recordings were also monitored during discussions of emotionally neutral subjects. No between group differences were found during the discussions of the neutral topics, nor were any differences noted in heart rate, skin conductance, and frontalis EMG during the discussion of personal stress. However, the following data were obtained for the paraspinal EMG during the personal stress discussions:

	left back		right back	
	M	SD	M	SD
back pain	3.63	6.80	2.48	2.21
general pain	1.33	1.21	1.57	0.98
healthy	1.23	0.63	1.47	0.88

Differences in EMG (which reflects muscle tension) were significant between the chronic back pain group and the other two groups, which did not differ significantly from each other. Moreover, the chronic back pain group returned to baseline muscle tension levels more slowly than did the other groups. Finally, abnormal muscular reactivity was better predicted by measures of depression and coping than by measures of organic functioning. While the investigators point to a number of possible methodological problems with the study, it is intriguing to speculate that chronic back pain might be characterized and perhaps caused by a specific reaction to stress.

AIDS and the Immune System

A timely issue which might be discussed in conjunction with this chapter is Acquired Immunodeficiency Syndrome, or AIDS. The November, 1988 issue of American Psychologist is devoted to Psychology and AIDS, and an article by Kiecolt-Glaser and Glaser (Psychological influences on immunity: Implications for AIDS) is particularly useful in relation to the chapter on psychophysiological disorders. The authors review psychosocial and behavioral variables which have been shown to influence immune function. For example, commonplace, transient, stressful events, such as taking exams, have been shown to adversely affect the immune system. Disruption of interpersonal relationships through divorce or separation, bereavement, or marital conflict is consistently related to poorer immune functioning. Finally, chronic stressors such as those involved in providing care to a person with a severe, long-term illness affect immune functioning.

Diseases such as mononucleosis and other herpesviruses have been shown to be linked to psychosocial stressors. For example, one study followed cadets entering the military over a four-year period, and found that those who with a triad of psychosocial risk factors (high motivation for a military career, poor academic performance, and "over-achieving" fathers) were more likely to develop Epstein-Barr virus infections and were hospitalized longer in the infirmary. Even mild herpesvirus symptoms such as cold sores are more common in people under stress. Conversely, interventions designed to reduce stress, such as visits to lonely older adults by college students, relaxation training, and even writing about traumatic experiences, have been shown to improve immune functioning.

Kiecolt-Glaser and Glaser relate their review of psychological influences on immunity to the AIDS epidemic. Since people infected with the human immunodeficiency virus (HIV) have poorer immunological defenses, they are at greater risk for the adverse consequences of stress: smaller immune changes could have more important effects on their health, including development of full-blown AIDS. In addition, there are psychosocial stressors unique to those individuals in AIDS high-risk groups: perceiving oneself to be in a high-risk group for AIDS is stressful; HIV-positive individuals often lose social supports because of friends and family's fear of the disease or disapproval of their membership in a high-risk group; and losses of friends to AIDS-related deaths become a frequent experience. Recent research findings suggest a relationship between such psychological variables and HIV progression, suggesting an important role for psychology in helping with the AIDS crisis.

Does Meditation Reduce Autonomic Arousal?

Is meditation an effective intervention in the treatment of hypertension and other psychophysiological disorders? David Holmes examined this question in a recent review (1984, American Psychologist, 39, 1-10).

First, Holmes argues that it is necessary to examine studies that contain experimental controls, and not to focus solely on studies that use subjects as their own controls. Own-control studies have compared autonomic functioning of subjects during periods of sitting quietly with periods of meditation, consistently finding significant differences in arousal. According to Holmes, however, such a design does not adequately account for the effects of resting, which alone might produce the quieting of autonomic functioning. This possibility is better controlled for in experimental research in which subjects are asked at random to either engage in meditation or to rest. A second important point is that Holmes limits his review to outcome measures regarding psychophysiological responding and does not consider the effects of meditation on psychic states. Third, he examines the small number of studies in which the reactions of meditators and nonmeditators have been compared during times of stress.

The conclusions of this careful review are not very optimistic regarding the effectiveness of meditation. Experimental studies generally indicate no differences between meditators and people who simply rest. In 16 studies in which heart rate was examined, none showed a reduction due to meditation. In 13 studies examining electrodermal activity, only one found a significant difference. Similarly, few consistent findings were demonstrated for measures of respiration rate, blood pressure, EMG activity, or biochemical factors. Moreover, Holmes finds no evidence that meditators respond to stressful situations with lower autonomic arousal than do nonmeditators. While it is possible that meditation produces important psychic effects or that it leads to consistent somatic changes that have not yet been examined, Holmes concludes that the effectiveness of the technique has not been demonstrated and that there is no justification for its clinical use based on existing research.

Laughter as Medicine

It is widely believed that stress and the negative emotions which follow from it cause or exacerbate disease. But what about the converse? "Is it possible that love, hope, faith, laughter, and the will to live have therapeutic value?" This was the question Norman Cousins (1976, New England Journal of Medicine, 295, 1458-1463) posed as he pondered how to help himself recover from a rare, degenerative disease of the connective tissues of the joints. He was in the hospital, barely able to move or even speak. Gravel-like substances were growing under his skin, forming nodules on his body. But when doctors told him that his chances for recovery were 1 in 500, Cousins took the news not as cause for despair, but as word that he was in a fight for his life. He would become personally and actively involved in his treatment in order to survive.

Drawing on the work of Cannon and other pioneers of psychosomatic medicine, Cousins reasoned that stress, by exhausting his endocrine system, had predisposed him to react as he did to some mild heavy metal poisoning. Consequently, he believed that if he could reactivate his endocrine system the body's natural processes would begin to work toward health rather than disease. He hypothesized that as negative emotions impair endocrine system function, positive emotions might activate it to its fullest, maximizing its healing powers. Therefore, Cousins prescribed himself a program of affirmative emotions. A movie projector was set up in his room and instead of taking sleeping pills, he would watch "Candid Camera" re-runs or have nurses read to him from humor books. "I made the joyous discovery that ten minutes of genuine belly laughter had an anesthetic effect and would give me at least two hours of pain-free sleep" (p. 1461). Before and after measurements of certain blood characteristics also suggested that the laughter was having beneficial physiological effects.

Positive emotions were only part of his self-prescription: believing that the drugs he was given were toxic to his endocrine system, he persuaded his doctor to administer extraordinarily high doses of absorbic acid. (These were not delusional ideas; Cousins was very well read in medicine and his ideas, if unconventional, did have some basis in the literature.) Also believing that hospitals were a poor place to be sick, he checked into a hotel instead, where he could sleep undisturbed and laugh without waking others. His recovery began soon after his self-treatment was implemented. Three weeks later he was jogging on the beach in Puerto Rico, although joint pain and range of motion limitations bothered him for many years to come. Luck? Chance? Placebo effect? Cousins acknowledges each of these possibilities. But for him it was an affirmation of the tremendous capacity of the human mind and body to regenerate. Scientists could do well, he says, to turn their attention to "the chemistry of the will to live." It is to this realm that psychotherapeutic interventions are directed.

NOTES

DISCUSSION STIMULATORS

Demonstrating the Stress-Illness Connection

Several rating scales have been constructed to measure life stress by asking subjects to identify typical life stressors that people often experience. These experiences are then given estimated stress values by another sample. Studies attempting to correlate such life stressors with the number of illnesses suffered during a specific period of time have usually found low positive correlations ranging from .2 to .4 (In the Kobasa et. al., 1982, study described above, the correlation was .24).

Below is a health checklist and a life events scale with the corresponding values in Life Change Units, modified from Cline and Chosy (1972, Archives of General Psychiatry, 27, 51-53). Present the health checklist to the class first; you can have it mimeoed or simply read it to the class and have them check off any illnesses that apply to them, then totalling the number of items checked. Present the life events scale next and have the class total up the values of points that they awarded themselves. You can leave the exercise at that, or for a more interesting demonstration, choose 10 students at random, ask them for their scores, and do a quick correlation on the board. Alternatively, find out the range of scores on the life events scale, then pick five or ten students from the upper and lower ends and record their health checklist scores; the means for each group can then be compared.

In discussing the results, emphasize that correlation does not prove causation, although here the assumption is that it is the life stress that causes the illness. Additionally, be aware that correlations done in class may not be particularly high because the rating scales were not constructed with a student sample. You might discuss with students the possible mediators that limit the impact of the life events, such as social support, hardiness, and the like.

Health Checklist

minor accident	injuries	cut
bruises	blisters	boils
pimples	eye strain	headache
toothache	muscle strain	coughing
sneezing	running nose	bloody nose
allergic reaction	nausea	vomiting
diarrhea	constipation	shortness of breath
skin rash	athlete's foot	hoarse voice
dizziness	painful joints	sinusitis
running ear	hearing loss	hay fever
skin disease	asthma	chest pain
indigestion	rupture	appendicitis
piles	painful urination	kidney stones
blood in urine	lost finger or toe	recurrent back pain
trick or locked knee	trouble sleeping	depression/anxiety
nervous trouble	other (specify)	

Life Events Scale

Event	Life Change Unit Value
1. Death of a spouse	100
2. Divorce	73
3. Getting into debt beyond means of repayment	66
4. Immediate family member attempts suicide	66
5. Marital separation	65
6. Jail term	63
7. Death of a close family member	63
8. Immediate family member starts drinking heavily	63
9. Abortion	63
10. Immediate family member sent to prison	56
11. Personal injury	53
12. Break up with steady boy- or girlfriend	51
13. Marriage	50
14. Fired at work	47
15. Marital reconciliation	45
16. Change in health of family member	44
17. Increase in number of family arguments	43
18. Pregnancy	40
19. Sex difficulties	39
20. Gain of new family member	39
21. Change in financial status of parents	38
22. Death of a close friend	37
23. Change in number of arguments with spouse	35
24. Trouble with in-laws	29
25. Outstanding personal achievement	28
26. Wife begins or stops work	26
27. Begin or end school	26
28. Change in living conditions	25
29. Change in personal habits	24
30. Change in work hours or conditions	20
31. Change in residence	20
32. Change in schools	20
33. Change in recreation	19
34. Change in church activities	19
35. Change in social activities	18
36. Loan less than $10,000	17
37. Change in sleeping habits	16
38. Change in number of family get-togethers	15
39. Change in eating habits	15
40. Vacation	13
41. Minor violations of the law	11

Measuring Stress

The life events scale above can be used not only to demonstrate the link between stress and illness but as a jumping off point for discussing the measurement of stress. One controversial point concerns the weighting of the various stressors. Do the students agree with the weights that have been assigned? How would they weight items differently? Do they think averaging subjective ratings is a valid way of measuring the intensity of a stressor? What other methods might be used? Another point of controversy is the inclusion of positive events on the list of stressors. Is an outstanding personal achievement really nearly as stressful as the death of a close friend? As discussed in the text, more recent measures focus on unpleasant stressful events. Finally, the inclusiveness of the list can be discussed. What significant stressors are not on the list, and what stressors would the students eliminate? Should chronic stressors be distinguished from short-term ones?

Identifying Risk Factors for Cardiovascular Problems

Students may be interested in filling out brief self-report measures which may inform them about psychological risk factors for cardiovascular problems. Spielberger's Anger Expression Scale (Spielberger, C. D., Johnson, E. H., Russell, S. F., Crane, R. J., Jacobs, G. A., & Worden, T. J. (1985) In M. A. Chesney and R. H. Rosenman (Eds.) Anger and Hostility in Cardiovascular and Behavioral Disorders, New York: Hemisphere Publishing Company) identifies anger-in and anger-out as modes of anger expression. The student version of the Jenkins Activity Survey (Krantz, D. S., Glass, D. C., & Snyder, M. L., 1974, Journal of Experimental Social Psychology, 10, 284-300) is used to assess the Type A Behavior Pattern. Students may enjoy discovering whether they would be considered Type A or Type B and refuting or confirming the assessment, as well as discussing the reinforcement of Type A behavior in our society.

"Reengineering" to Alter Type A Behavior

Finding that they are "Type A," some of your students may be interested in learning how they can reduce their Type A behavior. Friedman and Rosenman's book, Type A Behavior and Your Heart (1974, New York: Fawcett Columbine Books), available in most bookstores, offers practical suggestions for reducing Type A behavior. The following drills to reduce "hurry sickness" might be presented in class:

"Each morning, noon, and midafternoon, remind yourself--preferably while looking at yourself in a mirror--that life is always an unfinishedness."

"Begin in your avocational hours to listen quietly to the conversation of other people. Quit trying to finish their sentences. . . Seek out a person who stutters and then deliberately remain tranquil."

"Whenever you catch yourself speeding up your car in order to get through a yellow light at an intersection, penalize yourself by immediately turning to the right at the next corner. Circle the block and approach the same corner and signal light again" (p. 206-208).

Biofeedback Demonstration

If you have access to biofeedback equipment, students might enjoy trying out this technique themselves. Simple measures to try include galvanic skin response, heart rate feedback, and skin temperature. If no equipment is available, an inexpensive cardboard-backed thermometer can be used to measure skin temperature: cut off the cardboard back just above the bulb and tape the thermometer to the finger. (Students can try this at home and report on their experiences.) Higher temperatures indicate more relaxed states and colder temperatures indicate more tense states. Students can practice trying to increase and decrease their skin temperature voluntarily. To help relax, they can say to themselves: "I am very quiet . . . My feet are heavy and warm . . . My hands, my arms, and my shoulders feel heavy, relaxed, and comfortable . . . My hands are warm . . . Warmth is flowing into my hands; they are warm, warm . . . My thoughts are turned inward and I am at ease" (from Danskin, D. G. & Crow, M. A., 1981, Biofeedback: An Introduction and Guide, Palo Alto, CA: Mayfield Publishing Co., p. 34). Alternatively, students can try visualizing their hand being lowered into a bucket of warm water, or holding their hands over a warm fire.

Physician-Patient Relationship

Given the increasing focus on psychological influences on health and health behavior, the impact of the physician-patient relationship on illness has become an increasing area of interest. The dramatic increase in interest in family medicine among medical school students is one reflection of this trend. Did the old family doctor know something that has been forgotten during the technological boom in medicine? One interesting observation in this regard is that, before the advent of effective treatments by modern medicine, the history of medicine is considered to be a documentation of the effectiveness of the placebo effect. Perhaps the "placebo effect" is something that physicians want to capitalize upon more than they have in their recent, technological history.

NOTES

INSTRUCTIONAL FILMS

1. <u>Learn to Live with Stress: Programming the Body for Health</u>. (DOCUA, 20 min., color, 1975) Discussions with Hans Selye and Herbert Benson regarding stress and its effects on brain and body systems: heart problems, hypertension, ulcers, and so on.

2. <u>Stress</u>. (CM, filmstrips in 8 parts, approximately 14-19 min. each, color) Part I: Stress: A Fact of Life; Part II: Sources of Stress; Part III: Stress: The Body's Response; Part IV: Stress: A Nursing Concern; Parts V and VI: Stress and Disease; Parts VII and VIII: Managing Stress.

3. <u>Stress</u>. (SF, 1975, color) "Examines the concept of stress in conjunction with a variety of people and lifestyles." Monitors the activities of a businessman equipped with a device which monitors his body's stress reactions.

4. <u>Stress, Health, and You</u>. (AMEDLF, also available as a 3/4" video cassette from Time-Life Films, 18 min., color, 1978) "Focuses on the causes and effects of stress and shows how dramatic changes affect the human body."

5. <u>Stress: A Disease of Our Time</u>. (BBC-TV, available from Time-Life Films, 35 min., color) Experiments with rats, soldiers, and children in classrooms illustrate the concept of stress.

6. <u>Mind Over Body</u>. (Time-Life Films, 49 min., color, 1972) Shows the influence of a person's psychological state on routine illnesses and body injuries; includes discussion of autonomic conditioning.

7. <u>Dialogue on Biofeedback</u>. (VACO or USDA, 50 min., color, 1973) History, research, and clinical applications of biofeedback to a variety of medical problems including asthma, migraine, and hypertension. "Fascinating trip through a variety of laboratories and clinical facilities where biofeedback experimentation is being carried on" (Mental Health Materials Center review).

8. <u>Involuntary Control</u>. (WILEYJ, 20 min., color, 1971) Introduces research on biofeedback as rats are trained to alter their heart rates and humans learn to control brain waves.

CHAPTER 9

Mood Disorders

CHAPTER SYNOPSIS

General Characteristics of Depression and Mania

The most common symptoms of depression are generally agreed upon: depressed mood, appetite changes, sleeping difficulties, changes in activity level, loss of interest, fatigue, negative self-concept, difficulty concentrating, and thoughts of death or suicide. Some people who suffer from periods of depression also experience mania, which is characterized by elevated mood, increased activity level, talkativeness and racing thoughts, decreased need for sleep, inflated self-esteem, distractibility, and involvement in reckless activities. The manic's flight of ideas is demonstrated in speech that rapidly changes topics. Mania usually comes on suddenly and may last from a few days to several months.

Formal Diagnostic Listings

Two major mood disorders are listed in DSM-IIIR, major depression and bipolar disorder. Bipolar disorder refers to both mood swings between depression and mania and mania alone, while major depression, also called unipolar disorder, does not include mania. Heterogeneity exists within each category; some patients experience both depression and hypomania, a less severe form of mania. Current subclassifications of major depression include psychotic depression, involving delusions and hallucinations, a melancholic subtype, in which individuals find no pleasure in any activity, and seasonal mood disorder, in which episodes of mood disturbance coincide with the seasons of the year. Two chronic mood disorders listed in DSM-IIIR are cyclothymic disorder, involving frequent periods of depression and hypomania, and dysthymic disorder, involving chronic depression.

144

Psychological Theories of Depression

Psychoanalytic Theory

Freud and his student Abraham hypothesized that the process leading to depression begins with fixation at the oral stage which leads to excessive dependency. Following the loss of a loved one, the mourner introjects the lost person into him or herself and through mourning work, separates again by reliving memories. For an overly dependent person, the mourning work might fail, and the anger felt at the loved one for dissertion might turn inward to become depression. Since not every depressive episode is preceded by a real loss, Freud suggested that a symbolic loss could trigger depression. Little evidence is available to support this influential theory.

Cognitive Theories

Aaron Beck has suggested that people become depressed because they commit logical errors when evaluating themselves, their world, and their future. The principal cognitive distortions include arbitrary inference, selective abstraction, overgeneralization, magnification and minimization. While a number of investigations have demonstrated that such cognitive errors do accompany depression, researchers have yet to demonstrate whether the cognition is a cause or a consequence of depression.

Martin Seligman's learned helplessness theory of depression suggests that depression results from a person believing that he or she is unable to control a situation. Beginning as a noncognitive learning theory based on observations that dogs exposed to inescapable shock fail to learn avoidance, the theory has since taken a more cognitive bent. Depression is now seen to arise from helpless experiences that are attributed to internal, global, and stable causes. While evidence supports this new formulation, questions about the theory remain: Which type of depression is being modeled? Can college student populations provide good analogues? Are the findings specific to depression? Are attributions relevant? Two boxes discusses the hypothesis that the higher incidence of depression in women may be due to learned helplessness, and the link between life stress and depression.

Interpersonal Aspects of Depression

Interpersonal aspects of depression may be relevant to both its etiology and its course. Reduced social support contributes to depression, although evidence suggests that the depressed person plays a role; they tend to be low in social skills and their interpersonal style may elicit negative reactions from others.

Psychological Theories of Bipolar Disorder

Few psychological theories of mania have been offered; most view mania as a defense against depression. Viewed as a defense, one would not expect the low self-esteem that is postulated to lie behind mania to be readily acknowledged in self-report data. However, evidence using a subtle pragmatic inference test has suggested that manics have lower self-concepts.

Physiological Theories of Mood Disorders

The Genetic Data

Evidence from both family and twin studies strongly supports a heritable component to bipolar disorder. For unipolar disorder, the genetic data are less compelling. While genetics apparently contributes to both disorders, the heterogeneity of unipolar disorder may account for the weaker evidence for a genetic link in depression. Recent evidence using linkage analysis has identified two genetic markers which may predispose individuals to mood disorders.

Biochemistry and Mood Disorders

Two major theories have been proposed relating depression to neurotransmitters. One theory suggests that depression results from low levels of norepinephrine (with an excess causing mania); the other points to low levels of serotonin. Evidence supporting these theories comes from the effectiveness of the tricyclics and monoamine oxidase inhibitors in the treatment of depression and from research on neurotransmitters and their metabolites. However, more recent findings about the action of antidepressant medication cast doubt on the theory that they cause a simple increase in neurotransmitters. It is currently thought that the medications work by increasing the sensitivity of postsynaptic receptors.

Chapter 9

The Neuroendocrine System

The limbic area of the brain and the hormones of the hypothalamus and pituitary, have also been implicated in depression. Evidence from the dexamethasone suppression test and from Cushing's syndrome supports the hypothesis that the hypothalamic-pituitary-adrenal cortical axis may be overactive in depressives. While such biological data suggest a physiological basis for mood disorders, the interaction of such factors with psychological processes is of great importance for understanding these disorders.

Therapy for Mood Disorders

Psychoanalytic treatment attempts to help the patient achieve insight into the inward anger believed to cause depression, but little evidence supports its effectiveness. Beck's cognitive therapy focuses on altering thought processes through verbal techniques, along with more behavioral components such as encouraging patients to be more active. Research has demonstrated this treatment to be superior to medication. While no therapy has grown out of learned helplessness theory, logotherapy, an existential approach described in a box, may reduce helplessness by helping people find meaning in their suffering. A recent study demonstrated that matching patients to type of treatment may achieve the best results.

Somatic treatments for mood disorders include electroconvulsive therapy (ECT); despite side affects such as memory loss, confusion, and possible brain damage, ECT may be the optimal treatment for severe depression. Antidepressant drugs, including tricyclics and MAO inhibitors, have demonstrated effectiveness, although patients often relapse after the drug is withdrawn. Lithium can prevent the mood swings of bipolar disorder; it must be monitored carefully because of the possibility of dangerous side effects.

Suicide

Many depressives have suicidal thoughts and more than half of suicide attemptors are depressed. A number of facts about suicide are presented in the text, and a box discusses myths about suicide.

Freud proposed two theories of suicide: an act directed against and introjected lost person, and the death instinct turned inward. Durkheim offered a sociological theory of suicide, distinguishing egotistical suicide, altruistic suicide, and **anomic suicide**. Schneidman proposed a psychological approach to suicide, in which the act is seen as a conscious effort to seek a solution to a problem that is causing intense suffering.

Psychologists have attempted to predict suicide on the basis of scores on psychological tests. Investigations have found that people who attempt suicide are more hopeless than those who have not; others have found them to have more constricted thinking. Such research compares patients after the suicide attempts, however, making interpretation tenuous. Suicide prevention centers (discussed further in Chapter 20) often rely on demographic indicators to predict suicide. Psychological autopsies are studies of people who have committed suicide. A box discusses clinical and ethical issues in handling suicide.

NOTES

Key Points

1. The two major mood disorders listed in DSM-IIIR are major depression and bipolar disorder. In addition, cyclothymic and dysthymic disorders are two chronic but less severe mood disorders.

2. Freud viewed depression as resulting from a complex process including fixation at the oral stage, real or symbolic loss, and incomplete mourning work.

3. Aaron Beck's cognitive theory suggests that depression results from making certain logical errors.

4. Martin Seligman suggests that learned helplessness is a cause of depression; that is, depression is a consequence of experiencing failure to control events in your life and attributing this failure to internal, global, and stable causes.

5. Interpersonal relationships play a role in depression; depressed people often lack social support, possibly because of their own aversive interpersonal style.

6. There are very few psychological theories of mania, but most of those that exist propose that mania is a defense against depression.

7. Genetic data indicate there is a heritable component to both bipolar disorder and major depression, although evidence demonstrates that genetics are more prominent in bipolar disorder.

8. Biochemical theories of depression indicate that a depletion of certain neurotransmitters, particularly norepinephrine and serotonin, may underlie the psychic state of depression.

9. The neuroendocrine system in the brain has been suggested to be overactive in depression.

10. Empirical work indicates that Beck's cognitive therapy appears to be the most effective psychological treatment for depression, and in fact, it may be superior to medication.

11. That there are a number of somatic treatments for depression, including electroconvulsive therapy and antidepressant drugs--tricyclics and MAO inhibitors. Lithium is useful in the treatment of bipolar disorder.

12. While all people who commit suicide are not depressed, many people who are depressed think about or attempt to take their own lives.

New Terms
(key terms underlined)

manic-depressive illness, depression, mania, flight of ideas, mood disorders, major depression, bipolar disorder, unipolar depression, hypomania, seasonal mood disorder, cyclothymic disorder, dysthymic disorder, introjection, mourning work, symbolic loss, arbitrary inference, selective abstraction, overgeneralization, magnification, minimization, learned-helplessness, attribution, neurotransmitters, norepinephrine, serotonin, tricyclics, monoamine oxidase inhibitors, neuroendocrine system, logotherapy, electroconvulsive therapy, lithium, egoistic suicide, altruistic suicide, anomic suicide, anomie, suicide prevention center, psychological autopsy

New Names
(key figures underlined)

Martin Seligman, Victor Frankl, Durkheim, Schneidman

LECTURE LAUNCHERS

Rose-Colored Glasses?

An assumption made by Beck's cognitive theory of depression is that depressives have a negative schema through which they filter their experiences. An analogy to the theory might suggest that depressives see the world through "grey-colored" glasses. But it may not be depressives who have a distorted view of the world.

Lewinsohn, Mischel, Chaplan, and Barton (1980, <u>Journal of Abnormal Psychology</u>, <u>89</u>, 203-212) presented evidence that would seem to be both compatible with and contradictory to Beck's theory. These investigators compared normals, depressives, and nondepressed psychiatric patients on various dimensions of their behavior in a group setting. Each individual's behavior was self-rated and rated by an independent observer. The depressives were rated as less socially competent both by themselves and by outside observers. Of more interest, however, depressives and outside observers were in closer agreement in their ratings than were observers and either the normals or the psychiatric controls. In short, depressives were more likely to view themselves as the raters viewed them, whereas the other two groups overestimated their social effectiveness.

Is it possible that it is nondepressives who distort the view of the world by seeing things through rose-colored glasses? This study and other experimental research suggests such a possibility. It may be that depressed people see the world and the turmoil that exists in it with all too acute accuracy. Existentialists would hardly quibble with such a conclusion. Moreover, we are reminded that Freud argued that the defenses are healthy adaptations despite the fact that they involve distortion of reality.

Is it therefore the job of clinicians to teach depressives to view the world through rose-colored glasses? Perhaps. Lewinsohn and his colleagues found that treatment (which was designed to create illusory perceptions) resulted in depressives developing less accurate but more favorable views of themselves.

Depressive Self-Schemas and Life Stress

The interaction of cognitive schemas and life stress have been explored in the vulnerability model of depression proposed by Hammen, Marks, Mayol, and deMayo (1985, _Journal of Abnormal Psychology_, _94_, 308-319). The authors suggest that knowledge of a person's self-schema and stressful life experiences may enable us to predict which individuals become depressed in which stressful circumstances.

To test their theory, the investigators used a behavioral recall measure to classify student subjects as possessing primarily a _dependent_ self-schema (involving particular sensitivity to negative events affecting interpersonal _relationships_) or a _self-critical_ self-schema (in which negative _achievement_ events are particularly upsetting); subjects rated as having a self-critical schema, for example, were those who recalled more examples of negative experiences involving achievement than involving relationships. In addition, students level of depression was rated using the Beck Depression Scale and the SADS.

Once a month for four months after the above measures were taken, participants reported on their stressful life experiences through questionnaires and interviews, and their depression status was re-evaluated. The authors hypothesized that schema-consistent negative life events would be associated with depression, whereas schema-inconsistent negative events would not be. For example, a person with a self-critical schema would be more likely to become depressed following an academic failure (schema-consistent) than following an interpersonal rejection (schema-insconsistent).

The results supported the hypotheses for the dependent self-schematics, and provided some support for the hypotheses about self-critical groups. For example, interview-elicited (but not questionnaire-elicited) interpersonal life-events were more strongly associated with depression for those with dependent self-schemas than were achievement life-events. The authors suggest that combining the research on life stress with theories of cognitive vulnerability may be useful for predicting the interaction between life events and depression in particular individuals.

Evidence for the Effectiveness of Beck's Cognitive Therapy

Dobson (1989, _Journal of Consulting and Clinical Psychology_, _57_, 414-419) presents results from a meta-analysis of studies testing the effectiveness of Beck's cognitive therapy for treating depression. The review covers all studies published from January, 1976 to December, 1987 involving an analysis of the efficacy of cognitive therapy, explicitly referring to Beck's method, targeting depression as the focus of treatment, and using the Beck Depression Inventory as an outcome measure (resulting in the review of 28 studies). In comparing cognitive therapy groups with no-treatment or wait-list control groups, the average cognitive therapy client did better than 98% of the control subjects (mean effect size = -2.15, indicating the experimental groups showed decreases in depression scores over 2 standard deviations greater than control groups). Compared to behavioral treatments, cognitive therapy also fared better (effect size = -0.46). In relation to nonbehavioral psychotherapy treatments (a varied category), cognitive therapy was also more effective (effect size = -0.54). Finally, cognitive therapy was shown to be superior to medication treatment (effect size = -0.53).

The length of treatment and proportion of women in the sample were not related to the change in depression in the cognitive therapy condition. (The average length of therapy was 14.9 weeks, indicating a fairly rapid effect of cognitive therapy.) There was a trend for younger clients to improve more with cognitive therapy than older clients; however, the samples were limited in their age range, making these findings tentative.

NIMH Depression Awareness, Recognition, and Treatment Program

The National Institute of Mental Health launched a program in May, 1988 to educate the public about major depression, bipolar disorder, and dysthymic disorder (Regier, D. A. et al., 1988, _American Journal of Psychiatry_, _145_, 1351-1357). Noting that although 80% to 90% of people with major depression can be treated successfully, only one in three sufferers seek treatment, the goal of the NIMH Depression, Awareness, Recognition, and Treatment Program is to disseminate the message that depressive disorders are common, serious, and treatable. Audiences targeted include primary care providers, mental health specialists, and the general public.

In the first phase of the project, grants were awarded to set up programs for training primary care physicians and mental health providers in the diagnosis and treatment of depressive disorders. The public education campaign has included surveying the public about their knowledge of depression and its treatment, and will result in preparing and disseminating print and electronic educational materials throughout the country. The basis for these materials includes the following information: (1) epidemiological studies indicate that 3% of the population has depression at any one time; the life-time prevalence is 5.8%. Manic-depression has a 0.8% prevalence rate, and dysthymia, 3.3%. The rate of affective disorders is twice that in men; the highest risk is between ages 22 and 44. (2) Highly effective treatments are available for the depressive disorders, including pharmacotherapy and other somatic treatments, psychotherapy. The NIMH Treatment of Depression Collaborative Research Program (Elkin, I., Parloff, M. B., et al., 1985, Archives of General Psychiatry, 41, 305-316) is currently studying the comparative and combined effectiveness of a variety of treatment approaches.

Suicide on T.V.: Imitation Effects?

Studies reported in the text suggest that suicide rates increase following depiction of suicide in the media; these findings have raised public concern about imitation effects. We might hypothesize that youths would be particularly prone to such effects, and indeed, some research has demonstrated an increase in imitative youth suicides following both news stories of suicide and television movies about suicide. However, more recent evidence raises doubt about the suggested negative effects of depicting suicide on T.V.

Berman (1988, American Journal of Psychiatry, 145, 982-986) reviews research on youth suicide following made-for-television movies depicting suicide, and conducted a study to improve methodological problems identified in previous research. Their re-analysis found a significant decrease in the number of suicides following the broadcast of three films depicting suicide in 1985 and 1986; the decrease was nonsignificant for youth age 24 and younger. However, their findings did suggest that films which depict a specific method of committing suicide may result in selection of that method over another in subsequent suicides. The authors conclude that a complex interplay of the person, the stimulus, and the environment affect the impact of media suicide, and further suggest that beneficial effects of the depiction of suicide have not be ruled out.

In a second analysis of imitation effects, Kessler, Downey, Milavsky, and Stipp (1988, American Journal of Psychiatry, 145, 1379-1383) examine the evidence linking news stories about suicide to subsequent suicide in

adolescents. Their research replicated previous findings
indicating that between 1973 and 1979, teenage suicides
increased after newscasts about suicide. However, this
trend was reversed in the period from 1980-1984, when teen
suicides actually decreased (though nonsignificantly)
following such newscasts. Moreover, they predicted that if
teens were imitating news-depicted suicide, the prediction
of teen suicide following news stories should improve when
the number of teenagers exposed to such broadcasts (using
Neilson ratings) is considered. This hypothesis was not
supported, as models of prediction taking into account
exposure to the news broadcasts did not improve over the
model omitting that information. These authors also
conclude that a beneficial impact of media depiction of
suicide is a possibility; for example, the increase in
stories about youth suicide in the past 10 years (documented
in their study) may give today's teenagers a more realistic
and less glamorous perception of suicide. In addition, it
is possible that more discussion of suicide may lead more
teenagers to seek help when feeling suicidal.

NOTES

DISCUSSION STIMULATORS

Biochemical vs. Psychological Theories: An Either/Or?

Students are often confused by the "levels of analysis" suggestion that biochemical explanations of the mood disorders are not incompatible with psychological theories. In our reductionist world, we tend to discard more molar explanations for a phenomenon when more molecular theories are offered. Thus, when support is found for a biochemical theory of depression, the immediate (but not necessarily correct) conclusion is that a somatic treatment is called for.

The levels of analysis concept can be conveyed to students with the following example: You are a Martian who has been sent to Earth in order to discover why these peculiar metal vehicles with four wheels move about the surface at varying speeds. Which would be the correct explanation?

(1) There are black surfaces of various widths, lengths, and curvature that contain signposts with symbols on them; these determine the speed of the vehicles.

(2) There are peculiar creatures who occupy these vehicles. Something about their leg movement determines the vehicle's speed, although different creatures appear to prefer to travel at very fast speeds.

(3) These vehicles contain an energy-consuming device which generates the motion of the vehicle. Some vehicles contain larger or smaller devices in proportion to their total weight, and this influences the speed.

All three explanations would be correct, of course, each at a different level of analysis. Psychologists make use of explanations at different levels of analysis, but the concept could be broadened to include the more molecular chemist or physicist and the more molar sociologist, economist, or historian.

Relating Activity to Mood

Lewinsohn and his colleagues have identified an important factor in depression: engagement in pleasant activities. While it is not clear which is cause and which is effect, the relationship between depression and a low level of pleasant activities is well-documented. An exercise which students find both interesting and helpful is having them chart their engagement in pleasant activities and their mood over a one-week period. For this purpose, students can be asked to keep a little notebook with them and list throughout the day the pleasant activities they engage in, adding up the total number at the end of each day. The Pleasant Events Schedule may be passed out or read to give students an idea of the kinds of events to monitor (Lewinsohn, P. M. & MacPhillamy, D. J., 1972, Journal of Abnormal Psychology, 79, 291-295). In addition, students should rate on a scale from 1 to 10 their mood for that day (1 being extremely depressed, and 10 being elated). At the end of the week, students can chart their daily mood on one axis and the number of activities engaged in on the other. Most people find a strong association between the number of pleasant events they engage in and their mood--this can be a real eye-opener and of practical value, particularly for those students who feel depressed.

Clinical, Ethical, and Philosophical Issues in Handling Suicide

The topic of suicide is likely to raise personal issues in an abnormal psychology class; at least one student in your class has probably had personal experience with suicide: a friend's or family member's ideation or attempt, personal grappling with suicidal ideas, or the ubiquitous question among adolescents: "How would you do it?" Discussion of the issue in class might focus on debunking the myth that people who talk about suicide don't try it, and describing the practical steps that clinicians take to prevent suicide, including establishing a no-suicide contract, making oneself more available during times of stress, and even involuntary commitment to a psychiatric hospital.

The latter course of action might be discussed in conjunction with an article by Thomas Szasz, "The case against suicide prevention" (Szasz, T., 1986, American Psychologist, 41, 806-812). Szasz, viewing suicide as a fundamental right, places responsibility for decisions about suicide in the hands of the patient, not the therapist; he opposes the use of coercive means of preventing suicide in adults. Students might be encouraged to debate the pros and cons of mental health workers taking on the responsibility of preventing suicide.

Psychological Autopsies: Suicide Notes

Suicidologists have been interested for some time in studying the suicide notes left by successful suicides in hopes of discovering the motivations or other characteristics that might provide a basis for predicting and therefore preventing suicides. In the course of such studies, they discovered that suicide notes typically differ from the popular stereotype of what a suicide note should be; actual suicide notes and simulated ones (written by normal subjects asked to write a suicide note as if they were going to take their own lives) can be differentiated (cf. Schiedman, E., Farberow, N., & Litman, R. (Eds.), 1970, The Psychology of Suicide. New York: Science House. Chapters 9, 13, & 14). Below are real and simulated suicide notes. First, read the notes in random order to the class and have them rate which they believe are real and which simulated.

REAL NOTES:

To whom it may concern: I live at 400 Oak Drive, Cincinnati, Ohio. You will find on the kitchen table a letter with instructions to my wife on the disposition of my estate. Please notify all of my friends. Do not mourn me. H. Smith.

I can't stand it any longer. Tell Jack he can have my golf clubs. Harry.

Dear Susan, Please take care of your mother and your brother. They won't be able to get along without you. I've made a list of things that have to be done and bills to be paid. See if you can take care of things for me. I want you to be sure I'm cremated and my ashes scattered over the ocean. Daddy.

SIMULATED NOTES:

To whom it may concern: I have looked and found that life is not worth living. What meaning is there anyway? Better this way. H. Smith.

Everything is so depressing. People talking, no one listening. One day comes, another day comes and goes, and still we're running in the rat race. Maybe some day people will understand why. Until then, goodbye. Harry.

I thought things would work out between us, but now I see that they won't. I thought you were the only one for me, but now I see differently. Couldn't you have understood my unhappiness. Why didn't you care? Perhaps we'll meet together in the next world. Bill.

Discuss with students the findings about differences between real and simulated notes (either after you tell them which notes were which, or giving them another chance to guess after they hear the following findings): Real suicide notes are usually more specific and concrete than simulated notes. They contain specific information, use names of people, places and things, make frequent mention of women and sexual themes, and give instructions specific enough to be carried out. In contrast, simulated notes were less specific and contain a number of "thinking" words. You might discuss the implications of these findings for predicting suicide.

INSTRUCTIONAL FILMS

1. <u>Depression: The Shadowed Valley</u>. (IU, 1975, 57 min., color) An overview of the forms of depression, including suicide as the most extreme form. Depressed persons discuss symptoms and their origins. Forms of treatment are also examined.

2. **Biochemistry of Depression**. (CM, 29 min., color) Presents a wide range of technical material including: the biogenic amine theory, the catecholamine hypothesis, indolamine, permissive and two-disease hypothesis, neurotransmitters, the endocrine theory, and the electrolyte theory. Discusses and negates the hormone imbalance, increased cortisol, and oral contraceptives theories of depression. Explains sex differences in the incidence of depression by showing the correlation between sex hormone levels and mood disorders.

3. <u>Depression: Recognizing It, Treating It</u>. (HRM, 1980, 42 min.) Presents biochemical theories, cognitive and psychoanalytic viewpoints, and treatment of depression.

4. <u>Depression: A Study in Abnormal Behavior</u>. (CRM Films, 1973, 26 min.) Follows a young housewife and teacher through the course of her depressive disorder. Various approaches to treatment are discussed and the use of drugs, ECT, and group therapy illustrated. The film also touches on the issue of life in a mental institution.

5. <u>Grief Therapy</u>. (Carousel Films, 1977, 19 min.) Originally part of a "60 minutes" television program, this film illustrates a therapeutic interview with a woman who lost her mother and daughter in a fire. "Grief therapy is a strikingly impressive film, wonderfully filmed and narrated, dealing with Ronald Ramsey's approach to traumatic grief" (<u>Contemporary Psychology</u> review).

6. <u>On Death and Dying</u>. (FI, 1974, 40 min., color) A discussion with Elizabeth Kubler-Ross focuses on the stages through which a dying person passes and the means by which the process can be made more humane.

7. <u>One Man's Madness</u>. (BBC, 1976, 31 min., color) Documentary of a writer who became a manic depressive. Swinging in mood from ecstasy to severe depression, his symptoms of alienation and withdrawal are shown and his treatment in the hospital is portrayed. Guaranteed to provoke discussion.

8. <u>Do I Really Want to Die?</u> (PF, 1978, 31 min.) Film consists of a series of interviews with people who have attempted suicide. They discuss their reasons, current feelings, and sense of hopelessness at the time of the attempt.

9. <u>The Suicide Clinic</u>. (NET, AVC, Indiana University--CS-2148, 1969, 28 min.) Illustrates work of suicide clinic, and discusses psychological characteristics of suicides.

10. <u>Depression and Suicide: You Can Turn Bad Feelings Into Good Ones</u>. (PCR, 1975, 26 min., color) Explores some of the causes of depression in teenagers and ways to prevent such feelings of loneliness or sadness from becoming overwhelming. Simulates discussion about physical and emotional pleasures, as several teenagers discuss their own struggles with depression.

NOTES

CHAPTER 10

Personality Disorders and Sociopathy

CHAPTER SYNOPSIS

Personality disorders, based on a trait approach to personality, are diagnosed on Axis II to ensure that their presence or absence is considered whenever a diagnosis is made. Problems with diagnosing personality disorders include low reliability and the difficulty of classifying individuals into a single, specific personality disorder. Since personality traits exist on a continuum, some researchers have suggested using a dimensional approach to classification instead. The specific personality disorders listed in DSM-IIIR include:

Paranoid Personality Disorder--an overly suspicious, secretive, and sensitive individual.

Schizoid Personality Disorder--a person with difficulties in relationships, who is aloof, indifferent, but basically in good contact with reality.

Schizotypal personality disorder--similar to schizoid personality, but more eccentric; illusions and magical thinking may be present, but not severe enough to be diagnosed as schizophrenic.

Borderline personality disorder--a person with unstable relationships, mood, and self-image, who has no clear sense of self; not the same as borderline schizophrenia; a controversial diagnosis.

Histrionic personality disorder--an overly dramatic, manipulative, and superficial individual.

Narcissistic personality disorder--a person with a grandiose view of their own uniqueness and abilities. A box discusses Kohut's views on this disorder.

Avoidant personality disorder--characterized by low self-esteem and fear of rejection.

Dependent personality disorder--distinguished by low self-confidence and an over-reliance on others.

Obsessive-compulsive personality disorder--perfection-ists who are preoccupied with details and work rather than pleasure-oriented.

Passive-aggressive personality disorder--characterized by passive but hostile resistance toward others.

Antisocial Personality Disorder (Sociopathy)

The terms sociopath and psychopath are used inter-changeably with antisocial personality, a diagnosis which is not limited just to certain criminals but which may also apply to those who have used others while climbing the ladder of success. According to Cleckley, sociopaths are characterized by a number of features including superficial charm, absence of anxiety, lack of remorse, planned antiso-cial behavior, and a failure to learn from experience. These features are reflected in the DSM-IIIR criteria. Lack of shame or guilt seems essential for distinguishing the disorder from criminal behavior.

The family has been implicated as playing a role in the development of antisocial behavior, with such factors as in-consistent discipline, lack of affection, parental rejec-tion, and antisocial behavior in the father being identified as important. Twin and adoption studies suggest a genetic component to antisocial behavior, though most are conducted with criminals.

Sociopaths have been found to differ from controls in terms of their EEG activity in that more slow-wave activity and positive spikes have been found. (The EEG is discussed in a box.) Evidence also suggests that psychopaths have a deficit in learning from experience, particularly avoidance learning. However, when salient punishment is used, or when impulsive behavior is blocked until after feedback has been presented, sociopaths do appear to learn from experience.

It has been suggested that psychopaths seek excitement because they are chronically underaroused. Evidence indi-cates that their pattern of physiological responses differs from controls. The skin conductance of psychopaths is at a lower resting level and reacts less to aversive stimuli; their heart rate, on the other hand, is more reactive when a stressful stimulus is anticipated. Researchers conclude that sociopaths are able to ignore aversive stimuli, show almost no anxiety, and seek arousal.

<u>Therapies for Personality Disorders</u>

There is little research-based information on treating personality disorders; most guidelines come from clinical case reports. The borderline personality disorder has attracted most attention recently. For example, Kernberg has developed a modified, more directive psychoanalytic approach which seeks to strengthen a borderline patient's weak ego through such techniques as analyzing the defense of "splitting," or dichotomizing persons into all good or all bad. Behavior therapists, consistent with their attention to situations rather than traits, have no specific treatments for personality disorders.

As for treatment of antisocial personality disorder, there is unusual consensus: therapists of varying theoretical persuasions find it virtually impossible to treat. Since a primary problem in sociopathy is an inability to form relationships, the lack of therapeutic effectiveness is not surprising. Moreover, there is little evidence that somatic treatments help, although very tentative evidence suggests that anxiolytics may reduce their hostility, and those who had attention-deficit hyperactivity disorder as children may be helped by Ritalin. Since many sociopaths spend time in prison, the discouraging results of imprisonment as rehabilitation are traced at least in part to the inability to modify sociopathic behavior. An interesting argument in favor of incarceration is that sociopaths often "settle down" in middle age.

<u>NOTES</u>

Chapter 10

Key Points

1. Personality disorders are characterized by inflexible and maladaptive traits that interfere with functioning. The diagnoses, made on Axis II, are more controversial and less reliable than many other diagnostic categories.

2. Students should know names and basic characteristics of the 11 personality disorders listed in DSM-IIIR.

3. Antisocial personality disorder, or sociopathy, is characterized by antisocial behavior which occurs with no sense of responsibility or shame.

4. Evidence suggests that family factors, including inconsistent discipline, lack of affection, and parental rejection, are important in the development of antisocial behavior.

5. Evidence also indicates that genetic factors play a role in the etiology of antisocial personality.

6. Sociopaths do not seem to learn from experience or to be responsive to punishment, as indicated by both clinical experience and laboratory studies. This is not a general deficit, however, as they will respond to certain types of situations or rewards.

7. A number of theorists suggest that sociopaths are underaroused, ignore aversive stimuli, and engage in antisocial behavior to obtain stimulation.

8. Attempts at treating antisocial personality disorder have been notably ineffective.

Chapter 10

New Terms
(key terms underlined)

personality disorders, paranoid personality, schizoid personality, schizotypal personality, illusions, magical thinking, borderline personality, histrionic personality, narcissistic personality, avoidant personality, dependent personality, obsessive-compulsive personality, passive-aggressive personality, antisocial personality, sociopath, psychopath, electroencephalogram, slow-wave activity, positive spikes, alpha, beta, theta, and delta rhythms

New Names
(key figures underlined)

Heinz Kohut, Hervey Cleckley, Otto Kernberg

NOTES

LECTURE LAUNCHERS

Psychological Perspectives on Personality Disorders

Psychiatry and psychology have distinct and largely independent traditions in the study of personality. While psychiatrists have focused primarily on the categorical classification of clinical populations, psychologists have devoted their major efforts to the dimensional description of the normal personality. In an effort to bridge these two traditions, Widiger and Frances offer several perspectives from psychology regarding the classification of personality disorders in DSM-III (1985, Archives of General Psychiatry, 42, 615-623).

One suggestion offered by Widiger and Frances concerns that nature of the classification model itself. They argue that psychiatry in particular and medicine in general have relied on a classical model of classification, one in which one or more defining features are essential for defining the classification. These monothetic classifications indicate that, for example, a patient can be classified as having an avoidant personality disorder if, and only if, he or she is hypersensitive to rejection. The classification model is monothetic because a single theme (or combination of themes) defines the class. Widiger and Frances prefer a prototypical classification scheme to a classical one. Prototypical classifications are polythetic; they are based on the presence of a designated number of different defining characteristics, no one of which must be present in order to make a given classification. (Many of the diagnostic criteria in DSM-III are polythetic in that they suggest that a given number of a listing of symptoms must be present in order to make a certain diagnosis.) Different individual cases may be more or less representative of the prototype. For example, a robin is a better prototype of the class "bird" than is a penguin. It is argued that the use of a prototype theory of classification fits better with the classification schemes that people ordinarily use, it allows for multiple diagnoses to be given, and the model can also permit the differential weighting of more or less essential symptoms.

Widiger and Frances extend their arguments about prototypic classes to the use of prototypic acts as defining features of different diagnostic criteria. For example, the failure to obtain medical help for a seriously ill child may be a prototypical act that is characteristic of the irresponsibility found in antisocial personality disorder. Such a listing would help with the behavioral anchoring of the DSM-IIIR diagnostic criteria and may well improve the reliability of personality disorder diagnoses. A related point is that, given the assumption of temporal consistency that is implicit in the personality disorder diagnoses, diagnostic criteria should include evidence of stability of behavior over time. The criteria for antisocial personality disorder, for example, indicate that antisocial behavior should be continuous from adolescence through early adult life.

The final suggestion offered by Widiger and Frances is to include a dimensional rating scheme of central personality characteristics in the diagnosis of personality disorders. They argue that such a scheme allows for more flexible, specific, and comprehensive information to be rated, and it avoids many of the dilemmas involved in making categorical decision. Their later attempts to devise such a scheme are described in the text.

A recent article by Widiger and colleagues (1988, American Journal of Psychiatry, 145, 786-795) reviews the changes made in the diagnoses of personality disorders from DSM-III to IIIR, some of which are in line with the suggestions outlined above. For example, while several of the DSM-III categories were monothetic, all the DSM-IIIR diagnoses use polythetic criteria sets. The authors note that while monothetic classifications result in too many false-negatives, being overly restrictive, the new polythetic diagnoses may prove too heterogeneous. Future improvements could include weighting items, including one necessary item along with several polythetic criteria, and basing cutoff scores for the number of required characteristics on research findings about validity.

Validity of Borderline Personality Disorder

Tarnopolsky and Berelowitz (1987, British Journal of Psychiatry, 151, 724-734) review over 60 studies of borderline personality disorder published mainly between 1980 and 1986 to determine the status of the disorder's validity. Their mainly positive findings are summarized here:

First, the authors report that the newer diagnostic interviews, including Gunderson and colleagues' Diagnostic Interview for Borderlines and Spitzer's DSM-III structured interview, yield reliable diagnoses and concur largely with one another. Evidence for validity is focused mainly on the differentiation of borderline personality from other disorders. The link once proposed between borderline personality and schizophrenia has been disproved; as discussed in the text, schizotypal disorder has been found to relate to schizophrenia, while borderline personality appears to be a separate entity. The distinction between borderline and affective disorders is less clear; as many as 50% of borderline patients have been found to have depression as well. The authors suggest that there may be two types of borderline personality, one which is "pure" and one which coexists with affective disorder. Some validity for this distinction comes from findings that "pure" borderlines are unlikely to develop affective disorders over time (while most of those with mixed diagnoses have depression at follow-up), and there is a higher prevalence of affective illness only in the relatives of the mixed group._ The most difficult distinction to make is that between borderline and other personality disorders, particularly histrionic. This finding may reflect a multidimensional component to personality disorders which deserves further study.

Personality Disorders and the Ego Defenses

Vaillant and Drake have recently presented data on a subject infrequently subjected to empirical study--the use of ego defense mechanisms (1985, Archives of General Psychiatry, 42, 597-601). In a longitudinal follow-up evaluation of the Glueck's delinquency sample, these two investigators provide information on the relationship between ego defenses, personality disorder, and health functioning. They also analyze early predictors of adult functioning.

It is important to understand Vaillant's classification of the ego defenses in order to comprehend the data obtained in this investigation. Defenses are classified into three groups: mature, intermediate, and immature. Mature defenses include suppression (postponement of impulse gratification without repression), altruism, mature humor, sublimation, and anticipation (affective rehearsal of future stressful events). Intermediate defenses are those that are typically associated with neurosis in psychoanalytic theory, including reaction formation, isolation, displacement, and repression. Finally, immature defenses are thought to be associated with personality disorder and include hypochondriasis (magnifying somatic complaints), dissociation (the denial of inner feelings), autistic schizoid fantasy, projection, and acting out.

In the present investigation, ego defense diagnoses were made from independent ratings of a two-hour semi-structured interview. Data obtained in this investigation revealed a strong association between defensive maturity and DSM-III diagnoses of personality disorder. 67% of the men in the sample who used immature defenses were judged to have a personality disorder as compared to 15% of the intermediate group and 0% of the mature group. Defensive maturity was also strongly associated with ratings on the Health-Sickness Rating Scale, with socioeconomic status, and with stage of adjustment according to Erikson's psychosocial model. Defensive maturity was not predicted by childhood family environment, contrary to what might be expected based on psychoanalytic theory, but was related to earlier ratings of emotional problems, to grades in school, and to IQ measures.

Vaillant and Drake offer several conclusions based on their investigation. First, they suggest that the correspondence between defensive maturity and personality disorder is so great that it is justifiable to replace the former classification with the latter. Nevertheless, they do argue for a routine assessment of the ego defenses in psychiatric diagnosis. Second, they suggest that others who have studied the ego defenses may have found primarily negative results because they have focused on the wrong defenses. In general, the intermediate defenses were not found to be strongly related to other measures, but these "neurotic" defenses have received the greatest attention among psychodynamic investigators. More primitive defenses were found to have considerably greater predictive power in this study. Finally, the authors note the lack of association obtained between ego defense maturity and childhood experience. They suggest that ego defense style, however it is produced, may be a stable characteristic of the "invulnerable" child.

Sociopathy and Arousal

Arousal theory suggests that people's (and animals') responsiveness to their environment is dependent on the sensitivity of their arousal system, and that people with a lower than normal level of arousal (most likely inherited) are particularly "insulated" from the environment, leading them to seek stimulation and be more prone to endure pain. This theory has been used to explain both criminality and psychopathy, as evidence (reviewed in the text) suggests that these groups have sub-optimal levels of arousal, or are able to ignore incoming stimuli.

Ellis (1987, _Personality and Individual Differences_, _8_, 905-925) asserts that, if arousal theory is appropriate for explaining criminal behavior, other behaviors associated with sub-optimal arousal should be associated with criminality and psychopathy. His review of the literature reveals eight behavior patterns which have been explained using arousal theory: (1) resistance to punishment, (2) academic performance below intellectual potential, (3) impulsiveness, (4) childhood hyperactivity, (5) risk taking and sensation seeking, (6) recreational drug use, (7) preference for active social interaction, and (8) preference for broad-ranging sexual experiences. (It should be noted that some of these characteristics, including impulsiveness, risk taking, and preference for varied sexual experiences, are included in the DSM-IIIR criteria for antisocial personality disorder, making them inappropriate for independent validation of the theory.)

Ellis documents consistent evidence supporting an association between criminality and sociopathy and the eight behavior patterns listed above. Arousal theory may be seen as a parsimonious explanation for the high intercorrelation between these behaviors. In discussing this correlational design, students might be asked to think of other third variables (besides sub-optimal arousal) which may account for the observed relationships.

A Neuropsychological Explanation for Sociopathy

Another important theory of a biological etiology of sociopathy lies in the analysis of neuropsychological findings. Miller (1987, Aggressive Behavior, 13, 119-140) reviews evidence demonstrating that aggressive psychopathic adolescents and adults have deficits in verbal ability, as well as impaired impulse control and other signs of frontal lobe deficits. Pointing out that the frontal lobe has the role of regulating behavior, particularly social behavior, and that the left hemisphere uses language (particularly inner speech) to organize and inhibit behavior, Miller hypothesizes that the aggressive psychopath, less able to use inner speech to modulate affect and behavior, resorts to the use of more primitive aggressive strategies to handle social frustration or ambiguity. Interestingly, both Ellis (see above) and Miller suggest that testosterone levels in the developing fetus (higher in males) may underlie low arousal (Ellis) and left hemisphere deficits (Miller), explaining the greater prevalence of sociopathy in males.

Mental Illness and Criminality

The link between sociopathy and criminality is only part of the broader question of the relationship between mental illness and criminality. Certainly the perception of the mentally ill or retarded person as dangerous is very common, as witnessed by the violent (sometimes literally so) struggles of many communities against efforts to locate halfway houses or hostels for the retarded in their areas. One reason for this may be a tendency for people to label unusual, dangerous, or destructive behaviors as "insane." Using the same circular reasoning psychopathologists often display, citizens may reason that the murderer must be insane because a sane person could not murder, and the reason he murders is that he is insane. Another may be the intensive media coverage given the particularly gruesome crimes committed by a few disturbed people. There is also historical tradition; it appears that the Romans guarded the mentally ill so that they would not harm others, and Benjamin Franklin, in arguing for the first mental hospital in the colonies, cited the idea that the mentally incapacitated were a terror and threat to their neighbors.

Despite this persistent association of criminality and psychopathology in the public mind, there is little evidence of a genuine association. The question can be asked in two ways. First, what is the prevalence of mental illness among criminals? Since only criminals who are caught are generally studied, the available data consist of prison surveys. In general, these studies have concluded that mental illness is no more prevalent among inmates than in the general population. It is certain that only a minority of inmates have psychotic, major affective, or anxiety disorders. Substance use disorders (which are not what people usually think of in referring to mental illness) and sociopathy are probably more common among prisoners than among community residents. Thus, prison surveys suggest that with the exception of alcoholism, drug abuse, and sociopathy, having a psychological disorder does not increase the probability of criminal behavior. (Another exception would appear to be the paraphilias, where the act defining the disorder is itself illegal.)

A second form of this question is, what is the prevalence of criminal behavior among the mentally ill? Most of the relevant data here come from the study of arrest records of former mental patients. Interestingly, up until 1960 such studies consistently found that former mental patients were _less_ likely than community controls to be arrested, while studies done in the 1960s and 1970s show former patients to be _more_ likely to be arrested. The explanation for this shift appears to be the changing admissions practices at the state hospitals. Of patients hospitalized in New York State in 1947, 15% had an arrest prior to hospitalization, but in 1975, 40% of the patients had been arrested. It may be that with the advent of psychotropic medications and the emphasis on deinstitutionalization, potential dangerousness as measured by an arrest record became a more important factor in the decision to hospitalize.

For all persons, the best single predictor of future criminal behavior is past criminal behavior. Statistics back up the idea that it is an arrest record, rather than mental patient status, which predicts future criminality. For instance, in a large scale survey of former mental patients, Coczza, Melick, and Steadman (1978, cited in J. Monahan, _Predicting violent behavior: An assessment of clinical techniques_. Beverly Hills: Sage, 1981) found that the arrest rate among the general population was 32.5/1000,

among patients with no prior arrest record 22.1/1000, among
patients with one prior arrest 138/1000, and among patients
with two or more arrests 413/1000. The finding that
patients without an arrest record were less likely than community residents to be arrested also held true for violent
crimes, potentially violent crimes, and sex crimes. When
patients' arrests were examined by diagnosis, it was found
that the high risk disorders were alcohol and drug abuse and
personality disorder (probably mainly sociopathy); 18% of
the substance abusers and 28% of those with personality
disorders were arrested within 19 months of release.

Answers to the two questions fit together rather
nicely. Most mental disorders do not seem to carry any elevated risk of criminal behavior. Substance abuse and
sociopathy do. It should be noted, though, that even these
relationships may be exaggerated since substance abuse in
itself is often illegal, and criminal behavior has been used
as a major part of the definition of sociopathy by some
researchers.

NOTES

DISCUSSION STIMULATORS

Evaluating and Refining Diagnoses

To expose students to the finer points of attempting to devise reliable and consistent diagnostic criteria, try presenting them with the diagnostic criteria for one of the personality disorders in DSM-II. Antisocial, obsessive-compulsive, paranoid, passive-aggressive, and schizoid personality disorders were all included in both DSM-II and IIIR, making them candidates for comparison. Passive-aggressive personality might be an especially good one to choose, since the DSM-II version focused on such hard-to-define psychoanalytic concepts as the "oral-sadistic" character. Students could be divided into groups and asked to come up with better operational definitions of the criteria listed. Following an attempt at group consensus in this exercise, give the students the DSM-IIIR criteria for the same disorder; this will give them an opportunity to see how diagnostic classification has changed and to compare their attempts to those of the "experts."

Personality Disorders: Mental Disorders?

If personality disorders are maladaptive personality traits that interfere with functioning, should they be considered to be "mental disorders"? Are they disorders in the same sense as agoraphobia or bipolar disorder? Or are they instead just the individual's personality? Does calling such behavior a disorder excuse it and allow the individual not to take responsibility for their behavior (as some have asserted regarding the controversial proposed diagnosis, sadistic personality disorder)? What trait, if it was maladaptive and interfered with functioning, wouldn't qualify as a personality disorder?

Sociopaths and Society

Given that sociopaths are by definition people who repeatedly engage in antisocial behavior, and given also that they do not seem to learn from experience or respond to therapy, how should society treat sociopaths? Should they be punished the same as other law breakers? Would students consider the death penalty for sociopaths more appropriate (given that rehabilitation may be less likely) or less appropriate (given that they have a mental disorder) than for other criminals. Should they be considered insane and committed to treatment?

Criminal Justice

What is the purpose of the criminal justice system? Is it our society's responsibility to rehabilitate those who break the law, or is punishment the only goal that we need to concern ourselves with? The issue is complicated by the facts that many criminals, particularly younger ones, are not sociopaths but are people who in some senses seem to be victims of poverty or other unfortunate life experiences. It is complicated further by the observation that, in fact, the system does not do much of a job of rehabilitating; if anything, the criminal justice system seems to produce criminals. This observation is so keen that some have suggested that the best thing the criminal justice system can do in order to facilitate rehabilitation is to keep offenders out of the system--divert them into restitution programs, community service, or some form of therapy.

Adopt a Sociopath

Should adoptive parents be told if the child they are about to adopt is the offspring of a sociopath? As an adoptive parent, would you want to know this information? If you were told, what steps would you take to maximize the likelihood of the child growing up to become a normal adult? Students might also be asked to propose ways to prevent sociopathy by intervening in childhood, as preparation to the material on conduct disorder discussed in Chapter 15.

NOTES

INSTRUCTIONAL FILMS

1. <u>Descriptions and Interventions</u>.   (CM, 17-25 min., filmstrip) One film in this series covers personality disorders; other topics in the series include origins of abnormal behavior, anxiety disorders, and schizophrenia.

2. <u>Psychopath</u>.   (PCR-2121, 30 min., 1961)   Case history reconstructed through interviews with the patient, a detective, a director of a rehabilitation service, the deputy warden of a federal training center, and a psychiatrist.

3. <u>Commitment Evaluation</u>.   (ASC, 20 min.)   This film explores issues of jail vs. psychiatric hospitalization through an interview with a patient being evaluated for commitment to a hospital.

4. <u>In Cold Blood</u>.   (Swank, b & w, 1967)   Truman Capote's account of the murder of a family by two psychopaths.

5. <u>Violent Youth: The Unmet Challenge</u>.   (HR, 23 min., 1976) Features a discussion with three juveniles in jail; they describe their feelings about themselves, society, and their crimes.

6. <u>Shotgun Joe</u>.   (UCEMC-7910, 25 min., color, 1970)   A teenager in a reformatory talks flippantly about his crimes. Casually explains that he got his nickname from his tendency to club people with a sawed-off shotgun.   He dreams of becoming a successful criminal.   People who know him describe his good humor, outgoing nature, and leadership qualities.

7. <u>Little White Crimes: A Question of Ethics</u>.   (NYU, 28 min., b & w, 1967) "Depicts various behavior patterns and situations of ethical conflict that exist in the business world. Follows the adventures of a young advertising executive on the way up, who is intent on building an image to match his ambitions. In doing so, he leaves a trail of hurt feelings among those he uses as he steps toward his goal."

CHAPTER 11

Psychoactive Substance Use Disorders

CHAPTER SYNOPSIS

The Psychoactive Substance Use Disorders fall into two categories. Substance dependence involves the following symptoms: the substance is used excessively and interferes with work responsibilities, health, and social relation-ships, tolerance develops (larger doses of the substance are needed to reach the desired effect), and withdrawal symptoms occur when substance use is reduced. While DSM-III defined addiction as physiological, requiring tolerance and withdrawal as necessary symptoms for the diagnosis of dependence, DSM-IIIR does not require physiological symptoms for the diagnosis. Substance abuse is a less severe version of dependence. Polydrug use refers to the use of more than one drug at a given time, which can create synergistic effects when the interaction of the two drugs produces an especially strong reaction. Chapter 11 also discusses substance-induced organic mental disorders, covered in a separate section of DSM-IIIR.

Alcoholism

Alcoholism is a serious problem, linked with medical costs, highway deaths, hospital admissions, suicide, and family violence. Symptoms of alcohol dependence include tolerance and withdrawal, blackouts, social and occupational difficulties, and arrests for intoxication or traffic accidents. Polydrug use is common in alcoholics.

Short-term Effects of Alcohol

Alcohol is not digested, but is absorbed into the bloodstream and metabolized by the liver. The drug acts as a depressant; initially stimulating, it reduces tension and inhibitions. Larger amounts interfere with motor coordination and thought processes and may lead to depression and withdrawal, sedation and sleep. Alcohol interferes with cognitive performance, but drinkers who are becoming sober outperform those who are becoming drunk. In addition, expectations about the effects of alcohol on aggression, anxiety, and sexual arousal seem to have an important impact on behavior, beyond the direct physiological effects.

Long-term Effects of Prolonged Alcohol Use

Frequently cited, Jellinek's (1952) work describes four phases of alcoholism: (1) prealcoholic, including social drinking and drinking to alleviate tension; (2) prodromal, including furtive drinking and blackouts; (3) crucial, wherein control over drinking is lost, social adjustment deteriorates, and one drink after a period of abstinence can set off a repeat of the pattern; and (4) chronic, characterized by continual drinking, benders, and loss of concern about family, friends, and work. While this descriptive model has been useful, many alcoholics do not experience blackouts, questions have been raised about the one drink notion, the progression described by Jellinek is not always followed, and the description may not apply well to women.

Severe physiological damage is also a serious consequence of chronic drinking. Because alcohol provides calories, food intake is often reduced and malnutrition can result. A deficiency of B-complex vitamins is believed to cause severe memory loss (Korsakoff's psychosis). Cirrhosis of the liver is the eighth leading cause of death. Heavy alcohol consumption during pregnancy can result in fetal alcohol syndrome, a retardation in mental and physical growth of the fetus. Delirium tremens (DTs) is a severe physiological withdrawal from alcohol.

Theories of Alcoholism

Most psychoanalytic accounts of alcoholism point to fixation at the oral stage of development as the precipitating cause. Two personality characteristics, hyperactivity in childhood and antisocial behavior, have been linked with alcoholism. Epidemiological studies reveal great cross-national variation in alcohol consumption, suggesting that cultural attitudes and patterns of drinking influence the likelihood of abusing alcohol. Learning views suggest that the consumption of alcohol reduces distress. The delay of reward gradient is one explanation for why the immediate beneficial consequences of drinking may outweigh the deleterious long-term effects: a small but immediate reward can be more powerful than a larger but delayed one. Recently, it has been suggested that the tension reduction produced by alcohol may be cognitive in nature; it may decrease self-awareness and thereby help individuals cope with failure and negative thoughts. Finally, evidence points to a physiological predisposition toward becoming alcoholic, one which may be stronger in men than in women. The inherited diathesis may be the ability to tolerate alcohol; some individuals may be at a decreased risk for becoming alcoholic because they react adversely to the drug.

Therapy for Alcoholism

The withdrawal from alcohol--<u>detoxification</u>--can be painful both mentally and physically and is often supervised in a hospital setting. Treatments to prevent subsequent drinking include Antabuse, a drug which causes violent vomiting if alcohol is ingested, and Alcoholics Anonymous, a self-help program with a spiritual emphasis which has helped many problem drinkers but has been subjected to little scientific scrutiny. Aversion therapy involves punishment for drinking, either directly or through <u>covert sensitization</u>. A box describes recent scientific and ethical issues involved in aversion therapy. <u>Controlled drinking</u> is a controversial procedure which does not prohibit all drinking but instead aims to teach appropriate alcohol consumption. A general problem with attempts to treat alcoholism has been the assumption that one approach will work for all individuals; a more appropriate approach is to assess the role that alcohol occupies in the person's life in developing a treatment plan. Finally, it is important to note that "spontaneous recovery" occurs in up to 40% of alcoholics; social support for their efforts appears to be a crucial component in their success.

Sedatives and Stimulants

The major <u>sedatives</u> slow the activities of the body and reduce its responsiveness. The <u>stimulants</u> increase alertness and motor activity.

Sedatives

<u>Opium</u> has been known since 7000 B.C., but <u>morphine</u> and <u>heroin</u>, its more powerful derivatives, were only developed in the 1800s. While commonly available at first, their addicting properties became apparent and they were outlawed in the early 1900s. Opium and its derivatives produce euphoria, drowsiness, and reverie; heroine produces a "rush" as well. <u>Endorphins</u>, the body's natural pain relievers, may play a role in addiction; ingesting an exogenous opiate may halt the normal production of endorphins. Heroin is associated with serious physical withdrawal symptoms and social consequences, including illegal activity to obtain money for the drug.

<u>Barbiturates</u> were synthesized as aids for sleeping and relaxation, but their frequent prescription has been questioned because of their addictive nature. Barbiturates are depressants, relaxing the muscles and producing a mildly

euphoric state. Physical and emotional control are lost with large doses, however. Withdrawal effects are particularly severe and long lasting, and barbiturates are frequently chosen as a means to commit suicide.

Stimulants

The first amphetamines were synthesized in 1927, and the drug has been used to control mild depression, suppress appetite, and ward off fatigue. Amphetamines produce effects similar to those of norepinephrine (wakefulness, appetite reduction, increased autonomic activity) and can be addicting. Large doses taken over a period of time can produce a state similar to paranoid schizophrenia. Tolerance develops rapidly.

Cocaine is a pain-reliever that is used as a local anesthetic; it also heightens sensory awareness and induces a brief state of euphoria. An overdose can produce chills, nausea, and hallucinations, and may lead to death due to heart attack. Chronic use may lead to changes in personality and disturbances in eating and sleeping. Cocaine is ingested in many ways, including sniffing, smoking, swallowing, and injecting. Especially potent forms of the drug include "freebase," purified cocaine made by heating the drug with ether and then smoking it, and "crack," a new, less expensive form of freebase. Recent data indicate that cocaine is addicting, inducing a particularly strong withdrawal syndrome.

Theories of the Origins of Drug Addiction

Physiological theories portray addicts as unwitting victims of physiological reactions, continuing to use drugs to ward off the distress of withdrawal. This notion has been challenged by those who point out that withdrawal reactions of heroin, for example, are not that severe. Psychological theories usually emphasize reduction of distress, and some also attempt to explain why particular kinds of people seem to need these effects.

Therapy for the Use of Illicit Drugs

Detoxification is central to the treatment of those who use illicit drugs, yet withdrawal is the easiest part of the treatment process: long-term abstinence is often not achieved. Methadone is a heroin substitute which converts the addiction to a legally available drug with less severe withdrawal symptoms. Heroin antagonists prevent addicts from experiencing a high when heroin is taken. AIDS--transmitted through sharing needles--has made opiate dependence particularly serious. Drugs are now being sought which will alleviate the withdrawal symptoms of cocaine; clonidine, discussed in a box, is one promising medication for this purpose.

While the major types of psychotherapy are all used to treat drug abuse, their relative efficacy is not known. Self-help residential homes involve a total drug-free environment, charismatic role models, direct confrontation in group therapy, and separation of the addict from previous social contacts. Finally, prevention is considered the best way to deal with drug abuse.

Nicotine and Cigarette Smoking

Smoking is a well-documented health hazard, although smoking rates finally appear to be on the decline. There is growing evidence that nicotine is a powerful addictive drug, at least as powerful as dependency on heroin.

Three-quarters of those who attempt to quit smoking return to the habit within a year. Of the thirty million people who have quit since 1964, 95% did so without professional help. Rapid-smoking treatment, involving rapid smoking of successive cigarettes in a poorly ventilated room, is a promising behavioral technique. Focused smoking (smoking for a sustained period of time at a normal rate) and rapid puffing (like rapid smoking but without inhaling) are newer techniques which may avoid some of the health risks of rapid smoking. A box describes the use of nicotine gum in withdrawing from smoking.

Prevention of smoking is a top priority among health researchers; school-based programs include peer pressure resistance training, correction of normative expectations about the prevalence of smoking, inoculation against mass media messages, information about parental influences, peer leadership, affective education and self-image enhancement.

Marijuana

Marijuana consists of the dried and crushed leaves and flowers of the hemp plant, and hashish is produced by removing resin from high-quality plants. Marijuana use has declined in recent years, but it remains popular because of its pleasurable effects.

Marijuana interferes with a wide range of cognitive functions, more so as its potency is increasing. Short-term memory and state-dependent learning are particularly affected, and the skills involved in driving are also impaired. Marijuana smoking may also interfere with fertility in both males and females, and it appears to pass the placenta barrier. The drug also elevates heart rate, posing a danger to people with abnormal heart functioning. Long-term use may seriously impair lung structure and function. There is debate as to whether marijuana is addicting and whether it is a stepping stone to harder drugs. On the positive side, marijuana can be used therapeutically to treat nausea in cancer patients and is useful in treating glaucoma.

LSD and Other Psychedelics

LSD, mescaline, psilocybin, and other psychedelics or hallucinogens were originally thought to produce effects similar to a psychotic state. They produce a marked slowing of time, a feeling that bodily boundaries are lost, detachment from reality, affective lability, heightened visual experience, and hallucinations. The effects last from six to twelve hours, and are influenced by the attitudes and expectancies of the user. There is no evidence that these drugs are addicting, though "bad trips" can occur. Flashbacks are the transient recurrence of the drug symptoms after the pharmacological effects have worn off, and occur in 15 to 30% of users. The reasons for flashbacks are not well understood, although some evidence supports the idea that expectations may play a role in their occurrence.

Phencyclidine or PCP, described in a box, produces variable and often very unpleasant effects, including physical side effects and delusions and hallucinations. Users may become agitated and combative, and high doses can lead to coma, seizures, and sometimes death. Chronic use can lead to severe cognitive disruptions and personality changes.

NOTES

Chapter 11

Key Points

1. **Psychoactive substance dependence** involves maladaptive use of a drug, interference with social, familial, or occupational functioning, and may involve physiological dependence as well. **Substance abuse** is a milder form of dependence.

2. Alcohol is an addicting drug which exacts a high cost from individuals and from society.

3. Alcohol has direct short-term physiological effects which are also mediated by cognitive expectancies. Long-term use can have severe psychological and physiological consequences.

4. Sedatives, including narcotics and barbiturates, slow the activities of the body and reduce its responsiveness.

5. Narcotics--opium, morphine, and heroin--are highly addicting and have important social consequences, including criminal behavior.

6. Stimulants, including amphetamines and cocaine, heighten alertness and increase autonomic activity. They have recently been shown to be addicting.

7. A variety of treatments have been used for alcoholism and illicit drug use, including self-help methods, psycho-therapy, medications, and behavioral treatments such as aversion therapy.

8. Cigarette smoking poses a tremendous health problem; nicotine is highly addicting. Prevention may be the best treatment, as the habit is extremely difficult to stop.

9. Marijuana use has declined somewhat but remains prevalent. The drug interferes with cognitive functioning and appears to have some adverse physical effects with long-term use.

10. LSD and other psychedelics produce a state that was once thought to mimic psychosis and is characterized by sometimes dramatic changes in perception and cognition.

New Terms
(key terms underlined)

polydrug abuse, <u>psychoactive substance use disorders</u>, <u>psychoactive substance dependence</u>, <u>tolerance</u>, <u>withdrawal symptoms</u>, <u>psychoactive substance abuse</u>, <u>alcoholism</u>, fetal alcohol syndrome, delirium tremens, delay of reward gradient, detoxification, Alcoholics Anonymous, aversion therapy, covert sensitization, controlled drinking, <u>sedatives</u>, <u>narcotics</u>, opium, morphine, heroin, endorphins, <u>barbiturates</u>, <u>stimulants</u>, amphetamines, cocaine, heroin substitutes, heroin antagonists, methadone, clonidine, <u>nicotine</u>, rapid-smoking treatment, focused smoking, rapid puffing, <u>marijuana</u>, <u>hashish</u>, synergistic effect, <u>LSD</u>, <u>psychedelics</u>, mescaline, psilocybin, <u>hallucinogen</u>, flashback, PCP

New Names

NOTES

LECTURE LAUNCHERS

The Self-Medication Hypothesis of Addiction

Khantzian has recently elaborated on an intriguing hypothesis concerning the etiology of substance use disorders (1985, _American Journal of Psychiatry_, _142_, 1259-1264). He argues that commonly held notions about the cause of substance use--peer group pressure, escape, or self-destruction--are simplistic in their formulation. He suggests instead that there is considerable psychopathology associated with the heavy reliance on and continuous use of illicit drugs. Moreover, he proposes that the choice of dependence on a given illicit drug is not random. Rather, he sees drug choice as a form of self-medication. A drug is selected based on the underlying psychopathology that has caused the substance abuse in the first place. Narcotic addiction, for example, is thought by Khantzian to be an attempt to repress feelings of aggression and rage. He argues that many of the narcotics addicts that he has treated come from backgrounds characterized by extreme forms of violence, and he suggests that narcotic drugs effectively combat feelings of rage and violence. Khantzian offers the following vignette as an example of clinical evidence for this hypothesis:

> A successful 35-year-old physician described how defensive and disdainful he had become since his early adulthood as a consequence of his mother's insensitivity and his father's cruel and depriving attitude toward the patient and his family, despite their significant affluence. He said he became dependent on opiates when his defense of self-sufficiency began to fail him in a context of disappointing relationships with women and much distress and frustration working with severely ill patients. More than anything else, he became aware of the calming effects of these drugs on his bitter resentment and mounting rage. He stressed how this effect of the drugs helped him to feel better about himself and, paradoxically, helped him to remain energized and active in his work.

As a contrast to his hypothesizing about opiate addiction, Khantzian suggests that cocaine addiction may be an attempt to combat depression. Based on this hypothesis, he reports the successful treatment of some cocaine addicts by prescribing a stable, long-acting amphetamine. While there are few data available on the self-medication hypothesis, it provides for some interesting speculation on substance use and drug selection.

Chapter 11

Hypnosis: A Treatment for Substance Dependence?

Hypnosis is a treatment which is probably applied to addiction--particularly smoking and drinking--quite often, at least if one were to judge from the frequency with which advertisements appear for hypnosis clinics in various newspapers. What is the evidence for the effectiveness of hypnosis for this purpose? Research evidence is almost nonexistent, and the evidence that is available is quite contradictory. In a review of the topic, Katz (1980, Addictive Behaviors, 5, 41-47) finds reported success rates that range from 0% to almost 100% for smokers undergoing hypnosis. For alcohol, reported success rates range from 40% to 70%.

Like other forms of treatment, careful research is needed to overcome the many obstacles which block the sound evaluation of hypnotic treatments of drug abuse. A paradox exists for hypnosis in particular, however. One of the best predictors for a successful outcome in hypnosis is the expectancy of success. Perhaps finding that hypnosis was successful for, say, 40% of all smokers would serve to decrease the chances for the further success of hypnosis, since expectancies about outcome might be diminished by research findings. In any event, given the low success rates of other treatments for addictions, it is hard to believe that, if hypnosis is dramatically more successful, there would not have been some empirical demonstration by this time.

"Designer Drugs"

A recently evolving drug problem is the development of new "designer drugs"--synthetic analogs of organically found drugs, prepared by underground chemists to mimic the effects of other drugs (1986, U.S. Department of Health and Human Services, Public Health Service memo). Up to 3,000 times stronger than the drugs they mimic, designer drugs are less expensive to manufacture and, until recently, were legal because they were not structurally identical to their parent compounds. A heroin analog, Fentanyl, became widely available in 1979 and has caused numerous overdose deaths. Another narcotic analog, MPPP, has been found to contain an impurity (MPTP), a potent neurotoxin which has caused irreversible brain damage, similar to Parkinson's disease, in several individuals. Given its widespread use on college campuses, students may be familiar with MDMA, an amphetamine analog known as "Ecstasy." Psychological difficulties associated with MDMA

186

include confusion, depression, anxiety, and paranoia; physical symptoms include muscle tension, nausea, blurred vision, chills or sweating, and increased heart rate and blood pressure. Research has demonstrated that this drug destroys serotonin-producing neurons in animals, neurons which regulate aggression, mood, sexual activity, sleep, and sensitivity to pain. In addition, recent evidence indicates degeneration of dopamine following chronic use (or even a single high dose). Although immediate impairment may not be noticeable, researchers hypothesize that with aging and exposure to other toxic elements, Parkinsonian symptoms will develop (1985, ADAMHA News, 11 (6), p. 8). One particularly serious problem with designer drugs is their potential for overdose; "in animal studies, the doses of MDMA which produce neurotoxicity are only 2 to 3 times more than the minimum dose needed to produce a psychotropic response" (1986, U.S. Department of Health and Human Services).

AIDS and Intravenous Drug Use

Acquired immunodeficiency syndrome (AIDS) has greatly increased the urgency of modifying behaviors associated with drug addiction; sharing needles for intravenous drug use results in an exchange of contaminated blood and is a leading mode of transmission of the AIDS virus. In addition, IV drug users infected with the AIDS virus can transmit the disease to non-drug-users through sexual contact, and infected pregnant women can pass the disease to their children.

Psychologists have an important role to play in preventing AIDS among IV drug users: Des Jarlais and Friedman (1988, American Psychologist, 43, 865-870) review studies of AIDS risk reduction among IV drug users that were conducted through early 1988. Several studies demonstrate that almost all IV drug users have heard of AIDS and are aware that it is transmitted through sharing needles; about half report changing their needle-sharing activities to reduce the risk of AIDS. While much of this knowledge has been spread by informal means, educational programs have been developed as well; for example, a program in New Jersey uses ex-addicts to educate users about sterilizing equipment. While these programs also encourage users to enter drug-treatment programs, extended waiting lists (approximately 1,000 people in New York City) and fees ($50 for detoxification in New Jersey) preclude this option for many users. Several cities outside of the United States (for example, Amsterdam) have needle exchange programs which have been shown to reduce both needle sharing and, contrary to fears, IV drug use. Similar programs are beginning to be implemented in the major U.S. cities, although controversy surrounds their implementation. Little success has been demonstrated thus far in changing the sexual behavior of IV drug users to reduce transmission of the AIDS virus.

From the studies reviewed, the authors derive three principles for AIDS risk reduction among IV drug users: (1) IV drug users need basic information about AIDS virus transmission before they change their needle-sharing behavior; (2) information is not sufficient; means for behavior change (such as sterilized needles or bleach for sterilizing) must be readily available for change to occur; and (3) sustained reinforcement for risk reduction behaviors, especially new peer norms favoring safer behavior, may be necessary for change to occur.

NOTES

DISCUSSION STIMULATORS

Pre-Test on Alcohol Expectations

Before the students read the chapter, discuss their impressions about the effects of alcohol and other drugs on aggression, sex, and anxiety, or have them write out answers on a questionnaire and compile the results. After reading the chapter, these impressions can be discussed in terms of the impact that _expectations_ about drug effects have on the behavior of those under the influence of a drug. How might expectancies influence other responses to alcohol or to other drugs? What are the expectancies about the effects of cigarette smoking, marijuana use, or psychedelics?

Chapter 11

Effects of Alcohol

Please answer the following questions before reading the chapter on Substance Use.

1) How does alcohol affect aggression? Does drinking make people less aggressive, more aggressive, or have no effect on aggressiveness? Why do you think this occurs?

2) How does alcohol affect sexual responsiveness and arousal? Why do you think these effects occur?

3) How does alcohol affect anxiety? Why do you think these effects occur?

4) What other short-term effects does alcohol have?

Controlled Drinking vs. Abstinence

Organizations like Alcoholics Anonymous assert that the only way to insure that a substance will not be abused in the future is to never again partake of the substance. Is it true that once you are an alcoholic, you always are an alcoholic? Is one drink sufficient to begin binging? Can alcoholics be taught to become social drinkers? What are the consequences of AA's stance, and what are the consequences of challenging that stance? While these appear to be straightforward questions, scientific evidence regarding their answers is equivocal and certainly controversial.

Personal Experiences with Smoking

How did the smokers in the class get started? Do their parents smoke? Did they begin smoking with friends? Was it "cool" to smoke? How did the nonsmokers resist peer pressure? You might break the class into groups, including both smokers and nonsmokers in each group, and ask them to come up with a smoking prevention program based on their own experiences. The following questions could be addressed: (1) What age group should be targeted? (2) In what setting(s) should the program be implemented? (3) Who should convey the message to the target group (mental health professionals, paraprofessionals, ex-smokers, peers, parents)? (4) How could the mass media be used to help in the prevention program? (5) How would you measure the effectiveness of your program?

Drug Use and the Law

What are the social consequences of making a drug illegal when there is a continuing market for the drug despite the possibility of prosecution? At least three examples can be discussed in connection with this question. First is the experiment with the prohibition of alcohol in the United States in the 1920s, which resulted in prevalent law breaking, a rise in gangsterism, and eventual repeal of the constitutional amendment. Second is the continuing illegality of marijuana which, at least in the 1960s, may have alienated young marijuana users from the law. Third is the different status of heroin in the United States, where it is illegal, and Britain, where heroin can be obtained in clinical settings. Some have argued that the British treatment of the drug has greatly reduced the profit available to underworld heroin dealers, and thus explains the lesser incidence of heroin addiction in Britain as compared to the United States. In a similar vein, students might debate the pros and cons of making sterilized needles easily available to IV drug users to prevent the spread of AIDS. While many people have expressed concern that such a practice would increase drug use and make it appear that the government is condoning illegal activity, research (see above, in lecture material) indicates that IV drug use has actually declined when sterile needles have been made more available.

Drug Testing

Recent concern about drug abuse has led to wide-spread drug testing, at work, in athletics, and even within the home, as parents test their children. What do students think of this approach to the drug problem? Ask students to discuss the following case:

You are a counselor in a mental health clinic connected with a hospital. A man brings his 15-year-old son to see you because he suspects him of using drugs. The father insists that you arrange for drug testing, to confirm his suspicion. The son denies using drugs and insists that his only problems occur in relation to his father. He has refused to comply with his father's requests to take a drug test. What would you do? Would you agree to the father's request? If so, how would you get the son to comply with the plan? What would you propose as a treatment plan?

NOTES

INSTRUCTIONAL FILMS

1. **A Man With a Problem**. (PCR-2160, 17 min., 1967) "Shows admission of alcoholic to clinic, describes etiology, follows diagnosis, treatment, and team approach by psychiatrists and psychologists. Demonstrates the treatment of alcoholism by aversion and relaxation techniques, and illustrates the learning of new habit patterns based on system of operant conditioning."

2. **Calling the Shots**. (CDF, 30 min., color, 1983) Reviews the way that alcohol is advertised and how we are encouraged to drink.

3. **An Ounce of Prevention**. (HR, 20 min., 1976) Examines the causes of alcoholism, the damage to individuals and families, and treatment and prevention programs.

4. **The Distant Drummer: Flowers of Darkness**. (PCR-21280, 22 min., color, 1969) "Traces history of opium to present day use of heroin. Examines Asian usage, methods and procedures of organized crime trafficking drugs to U.S. Addicts talk about the compulsion for drugs; experts describe methods of combatting the problems. Narrated by Paul Newman."

5. **Methadone: Escape from Heroin**. (UCEMC-8599, 28 min., color, 1971) "Former drug addicts, medical specialists, clinic directors, and ghetto drug-fighters examine the strengths and weaknesses or New York City methadone treatment program for heroin addicts."

6. **ACID**. (UCEMC-8128, 26 min., color, 1971) Reviews history of LSD, human and animal research. Shows effects of drug on artistic creation, use in therapy with alcoholics. Warns against poor quality street acid.

7. **LSD: Lettvin vs. Leary**. (UCEMC-7454, 51 min., 1968) Drug advocate Timothy Leary, former psychology professor at Harvard, debates Jerome Lettvin, professor of physiology at MIT. Exciting film.

8. **The Perfect Drug Film**. (AVC, Indiana University, HSC-910, 31 min., color, 1971) "Dramatizes the effects that a cheap, nonaddictive, socially acceptable pill that eliminates the need to cope with problems and tensions, would have on society . . . Recounts a history of drug usage from antiquity to modern times, pointing out that each new drug was supposedly safer and more improved than its predecessors."

CHAPTER 12

Sexual Disorders: Gender Identity Disorder and the Paraphilias

CHAPTER SYNOPSIS

Gender Identity Disorders

Our sense of ourselves as male or female is called gender identity; while firmly linked to biological gender in most people, some people, most often men, are certain that they are of the opposite sex, despite anatomical evidence to the contrary. Previously classified with the other sexual disorders, gender identity disorders are grouped with the childhood and adolescent disorders in DSM-IIIR because they are considered to almost always begin in childhood.

A transsexual is an adult who has a persistent sense of discomfort with his sex, wants to be rid of his genitals and acquire those of the opposite sex, and has felt this way for at least two years. The question has been raised whether it is delusional for a man to believe he is a woman, with arguments hinging on whether the man truly believes this or recognizes he is not a woman, yet feels like a woman.

Gender identity disorder of childhood refers to profoundly feminine boys or profoundly feminine girls. While this diagnosis seems based on value judgments or stereotypes, there is evidence for a hormonal basis. Other research points to the role of family attention for opposite-sex-typed behavior. Research indicates that by the age of three children have obtained a gender identity that is virtually impossible to change. However, most children with gender identity disorder do not become transsexual in adulthood, and large numbers of children engage in cross-gender behavior without experiencing any gender conflicts.

Therapies for Gender Identity Disorders

In sex-change surgery, anatomical sex is surgically altered. The outcome of such operations is controversial, as some findings suggest that it does not lead to better life adjustment. Whether transsexuals use sex-change surgery or not, psychotherapy is usually recommended to help them through their conflicts, anxiety, and depression.

Apparently successful procedures for altering gender identity through behavior therapy have been reported. Not surprisingly, such treatments are very controversial. The measurement of sexual arousal, which is sometimes used in behavioral treatments, is discussed in a box.

194

The Paraphilias

The term _paraphilia_ means a deviation in what the person is attracted to. A DSM-IIIR diagnosis is made only if the person acts on their unconventional fantasies or is distressed by them. A _fetishist_ is almost always male and is sexually enthralled by some inanimate object. _Transvestistic fetishism_ or transvestism refers to a man who is sexually aroused by dressing in opposite-sex clothing, while still regarding himself as a member of his own sex. Transvestites are usually heterosexual; few homosexuals ever "go in drag."

The taboo against _incest_ seems virtually universal. However, it is now acknowledged to occur much more often than previously believed; one study found 19% of women and 8.6% of men to have been sexually victimized as children, with a quarter of the cases involving incestuous relations. Incest has been shown to have long-term adverse psychological impact.

Pedophiles are adults, usually men, who derive sexual gratification through physical and often sexual contact with prepubertal children. Pedophilia has been difficult to prosecute because of the problems of obtaining testimony from a child without causing further psychological damage.

Voyeurism is recurrent "peeping" at unsuspecting people for the purpose of sexual excitement. The element of risk seems important, and peeping may give a sense of power these men otherwise lack in their social lives. _Exhibitionists_ are frequently arrested for their behavior. They rarely come into contact with their observers, and generally feel remorse for their actions.

Forcible rape is the fastest growing violent crime in the United States. In addition, reports indicate that men frequently subject women to sexual contact short of rate. _Statutory rape_ refers to sexual intercourse with any female who is a minor. Rape is considered as much an act of aggression as a sexual act. Victims are often physically and mentally traumatized by the experience, and rape may give rise to posttraumatic stress disorder. Four main motivations for rape have been identified: opportunistic, pervasively angry, sexual, and vindictive; a box discusses the sadism of rape. Some theoreticians view rape as based on the cultural stereotypes of masculinity and femininity, and research suggests that violent pornography may dispose some men to act aggressively toward women in sexual situations. A box discusses a psychophysiological analysis of rape.

The majority of <u>sadists</u> establish relationships with <u>masochists</u> to derive mutual sexual gratification. Sexual practices involving pain or humiliation are estimated to be quite common, although not to the degree to warrant a diagnosis of sadism or masochism. The shared activities of a sadist and masochist are highly "scripted," involving themes of submission and domination.

A number of <u>atypical paraphilias</u> are listed, all of which involve gaining sexual gratification from unconventional activities such as feces, a corpse, or an enema.

Therapies for the Paraphilias

Aversion therapy, either presented directly or through <u>covert sensitization</u> has been shown to have some beneficial effects on pedophilia, transvestism, exhibitionism, and fetishism. <u>Orgasmic reorientation</u> involves pairing sexual arousal with more conventional sexual stimuli. Treatment should include consideration of other aspects of the person's life, such as a lack of social skills or the abuse of drugs or alcohol.

Incest is increasingly viewed as involving the whole family, and thus treated with <u>family therapy</u>. Drugs have been used to control pedophilia, with equivocal results. Confrontational group therapy as well as hormonal and surgical treatments have been used with rapists, with questionable effectiveness. As discussed in a box, punishment for the sex offender is more popular than treatment. Victims of rape are helped through crisis centers and hot lines, as well as counseling focused on alleviating their feelings of responsibility and guilt. The ongoing personal relationships of the victim need to be considered in these interventions as well.

Homosexuality

Until 1973, the DSM listed <u>homosexuality</u> as one of the sexual deviations, but under pressure the diagnosis was replaced with the term <u>sexual orientation disturbance</u>. The DSM-III category, <u>ego-dystonic homosexuality</u>, referred to a person who is homosexually aroused but finds this distressing and wants to become heterosexual; such distress was seen as caused primarily by societal prejudice. Few clinicians used this diagnosis in practice, however. Currently, the DSM-IIIR contains no specific mention of homosexuality, although "persistent and marked distress about one's sexual orientation" is listed as a Sexual Disorder Not Otherwise Specified. A box discusses problems in logic and theory in the study of homosexuality, making the following points: (1) <u>homophobia</u> may actually encourage exclusive homosexuality, by not tolerating bisexuality; (2) many homosexuals have no signs of problems with gender identity; and (3) finding differences between homosexuals and heterosexuals does not demonstrate that homosexuality is pathological.

NOTES

STUDENTS SHOULD KNOW . . .

Key Points

1. Gender identity disorders, including transsexualism and gender identity disorder of childhood, refer to believing oneself to be the opposite of one's anatomical sex.

2. The two major treatments for gender identity disorders--sex-change surgery and alterations of gender identity--are quite controversial.

3. The term paraphilias denotes a deviation in the object of sexual arousal, including nonhuman objects (fetishism), nonconsenting partners (incest, rape, pedophilia, voyeurism, exhibitionism) or suffering and humiliation (sexual sadism and masochism).

4. Rape is typically more a crime of aggression and dominance than of sex. Incest, pedophilia, and rape all often have a tremendously adverse impact on the victim.

5. Little is known about the specific etiology or the most effective treatments of the paraphilias.

6. There has been a history of debate as to whether homosexuality should be considered to be abnormal. Currently, it is not directly listed as a disorder in DSM-IIIR.

New Terms
(key terms underlined)

gender identity disorders, paraphilias, ego-dystonic homosexuality, transsexualism, hermaphroditism, gender identity disorder of childhood, sex-change surgery, penile plethysmograph, genital plethysmograph, fetishism, transvestistic fetishism, incest, pedophilia, voyeurism, exhibitionism, forcible rape, statutory rape, sadism, masochism, orgasmic reorientation, homosexuality, sexual orientation disturbance, homophobia

New Names
(key figures underlined)

Susan Brownmiller, Kinsey

LECTURE LAUNCHERS

Transsexuals in Indian Tribes

The role of cultural values in defining abnormality has perhaps been most emphasized with respect to sexual behavior. In transsexualism, though, two aspects of human sexuality which are closely linked in the minds of most people--anatomy and gender identity--are juxtaposed. This perhaps makes it appear a more "culture free" disorder. To point out how cultural values affect transsexualism, it is helpful to consider how another culture treats this phenomenon.

An interesting contrast to the modern Western approach is that of the North American Plains Indians. Many of the plains tribes had a few "berdaches," men who lived in the tribe as women. These people were occasionally hermaphrodites, but more often unambiguously anatomic males who dressed as women, did the work of women, and did not participate in male activities. Some were homosexual, some heterosexual, and others were celibate. The Indians clearly recognized these men as being deviant, but they did not take the further step of labeling them criminal or sick. Instead, they viewed the condition as one of nature or as a result of divine will and gave them socially acceptable roles within the tribe. In some tribes the berdaches were of low status, but in others they were very important and highly esteemed. Among the highly aggressive Cheyenne, for instance, berdaches were respected as doctors and thought to possess great powers which could give men victory in war and love (Forgey, D. C., 1975, _Journal of Sex Research_, _11_, 1-15). Would modern-day transsexuals feel the same despair and desperate desire for sex-change operations if there were well-defined, respectable roles for them in our society?

Gender Identity Disordered Children and Adult Sexuality

Recently, Green gathered data pertaining to the adult sexual preferences of children with gender identity disorders (1985, _American Journal of Psychiatry_, _142_, 339-341). In a follow-up evaluation of 66 clinic-referred boys with gender identity disorder and a matched comparison group of 56 boys, there were dramatic differences in terms of adult sexual preferences. Fully 68% of the gender identity boys expressed sexual preferences that were either homosexual or bisexual, as compared to none of the boys in the comparison sample. Interestingly, 12 of the boys in the gender identity group were involved in some form of formal psychotherapy during the course of the study, but they did not differ from the nontreated boys in terms of adult sexual preferences. These prospective data provide support for the retrospective reports of adult homosexuals who remember having cross-sex interests and engaging in cross-sex activities as children. As in much of the literature on precursors to homosexuality, controversy exists as to the significance of these findings. Carrier (1986, Archives of Sexual Behavior, 15, 89-93) points out that most studies find a minority of homosexuals reporting having engaged in cross-sexed behavior as children, and many gender-identity disordered children do not become homosexual. Furthermore, if we no longer consider homosexuality to be pathological, should we continue to consider cross-sexed behavior in childhood as a disorder?

Transsexual Surgery at Age 74

Docter (1985, Archives of Sexual Behavior, 14, 271-277) presents an interesting case report of a man who underwent transsexual surgery at age 74. While "Marty/Mary Ann" reported lifelong weak fantasies of being a woman, he had only occasionally cross-dressed (in private) and was happily married for 37 years. Ten years after the death of his wife, Marty realized that he could experiment with his fantasies of being a woman without hurting his wife, and he contacted a club for transsexuals. Finding others who felt as he did, Marty became more comfortable cross-dressing, and in fact began speaking to college classes about transvestism. After becoming friends with a female-to-male transsexual, Marty (now Mary Ann) lived for a year as a woman (a requirement in preparing for transsexual surgery) and underwent surgery at the age of 74. For the remaining three years of his life, he reportedly enjoyed a more active and satisfying social life than he had experienced as an isolated widower, and was treated as somewhat of a celebrity in the neighborhood he had lived in for 20 years.

An Exhibitionist's Account

The following description comes from a 31-year-old married engineer with an eleven year history of exhibiting. He first exposed himself at age 20, about six months after his "forced" wedding. Thereafter he exposed himself about every six months with particular incidents being apparently linked to marital or job stress. Prior to this incident he had been arrested four times for exhibiting. His behavior was destroying his marriage and he had once attempted suicide in despair over his compulsion. The description illustrates the irrational, driven, uncontrollable quality of the exhibitionist's behavior. This particular incident took place in New York City, shortly after he and his wife arrived to celebrate their anniversary.

> "As I drove by some stores, I saw a lot of good-looking females walking around in their scanty summer clothing and I started having sexual fantasies. I got extremely tense and keyed up and pulled my pants down . . . and started playing with myself. I was in my '67 Chevy and had the windows down so that it was easy to see inside. I was extremely tense and scared but couldn't talk myself out of driving slowly down the fire lane with my genitals exposed. I continued this for about 10 minutes and finally stopped after exposing myself to a particularly good-looking woman as she got out of her car. I never really had a complete erection and was very shook up throughout the entire ordeal. After exposing myself to this woman, who reacted with disbelief and disdain, I put myself back together and started to leave. As I was driving across the parking lot, a police car came into the driveway through which I was going to exit. The officer motioned for me to pull over and came over to my car. He asked me to get out of the car and as I did, I passed out." (From Daitzman, R. J. & Cox, D. J., 1980, An extended case report: The nuts and bolts of treating an exhibitionist. In D. J. Cox & R. J. Daitzman (Eds.), _Exhibitionism: Description, Assessment, and Treatment_. New York: Garland (pp. 258-259).

The Child Sexual Abuse Accommodation Syndrome

Through his extensive clinical experience with victims of child sexual abuse, Roland Summit (1983, _Child Abuse and Neglect_, _7_, 177-193) has developed a widely cited theory, the child sexual abuse accommodation syndrome, to describe the experiences of these children in the aftermath of abuse and its disclosure. The five characteristics of the syndrome are briefly presented here, providing a helpful organization of the consequences of molestation and an understanding of the phenomenology of its victims.

Secrecy. First, child sexual abuse is almost always a secret act, very often accompanied by threats or intimidation which make clear to the child the importance of keeping the secret. Numerous retrospective studies have found that the majority of victims never told anyone about the abuse during their childhood. Unfortunately, many adults assume that "real" victims of abuse would naturally report it, leading them to distrust the validity of non-immediate disclosures.

Helplessness. By far the majority of sexual abuse is perpetrated by a recognized, trusted adult; while children are usually taught to distrust strangers, they are generally not prepared to repel the advances of an adult entrusted with their care. Given that children always have less power in relationships with adults, they should not be seen as "consenting" to the abuse when they do not forcibly resist. As Summit vividly describes, "Children generally learn to cope silently with terrors in the night. . . The normal reaction is to `play possum,' that is to feign sleep, to shift position and to pull up the covers. . . Bed covers take on magical powers against monsters, but they are no match for human intruders" (p. 183).

Entrapment and Accommodation. When children feel helpless to resist and compelled to keep the secret of abuse, the only healthy option left to them is to accommodate to the situation in order to survive. Often the safest view for the child to adopt (safer than believing their parent could be self-serving and ruthless) is self-blame and self-hate. Young children are often incapable of seeing their parents as bad; even in the face of molestation, they are more likely to see themselves as being at fault, and this sense of responsibility may be actively encouraged by the molester. In the face of threats of disintegration of the family, "in the classic role reversal of child abuse, the child is given the power to destroy the family and the responsibility to keep it together" (p. 185). The accommodation takes many forms, including submission and even seeking of sexual contact, altered consciousness (even to the extreme of multiple personality disorder), delinquency, self-mutilation, and victimization of other children when the child becomes an adult.

Delayed, Conflicted, and Unconvincing Disclosure. When disclosure does occur, it is usually only after years of ongoing abuse, after the accommodation mechanisms have finally broken down and the child is beginning to individuate. Disclosure often occurs, then, in adolescence, and often after open family conflict when the child is angry-- the very time when the victim is least likely to be believed. The adults' reactions to the disclosure can be as damaging to the child as the abuse itself; the disclosing child may experience humiliation, scapegoating, and even punishment. Most adults simply cannot believe that a child would not have reported the abuse when it first occurred, or cannot believe that the adult they trust and respect was capable of the acts disclosed. And since even when the child is believed, the response of the adults is usually removal of the child from the home and no prosecution of the perpetrator, "protection" usually is experienced as punishment by the child.

   <u>Retraction</u>. In the aftermath of disclosure, the child
learns that the threats about revealing the secret were
real; her family is destroyed, her father abandons her, she
is placed in custody and blamed for the disintegration of
the family. Bearing the responsibility for the chaos in the
family, the <u>normal</u> course, when adult support is lacking,
is for the victim to retract her complaint.

NOTES

DISCUSSION STIMULATORS

"Tomboys" and "Sissies"

The terms "tomboy" and "sissy" denote similar concepts:
children of one sex who engage in behaviors that are
stereotyped as being appropriate for the opposite sex.
Interestingly, however, the two terms have very different
connotations. A sissy is much more likely to be viewed
negatively than a tomboy. What does this tell us about our
social attitudes toward sex roles? We often think of
females as having the more narrowly defined cultural sex-
role, but is that really the case?

Demonstration of Sex-Conditioning

An effective demonstration of sex-conditioning,
homophobia, and proxemics (the study of personal space) can
be done as follows: Ask two men to come to the front of the
class. Position them to face each other at opposite sides
of the room and ask them to walk toward each other and stop
when they feel comfortable. Note the distance, then ask
them to approach each other as closely as they are able.
Question them about how comfortable they feel. Ask them to
hug each other. Have them sit down, then repeat the
procedure with two women and then a man and a woman. Even
though the class will anticipate your purpose during the
first demonstration, the subsequent demonstrations should
still work. Point out to the class how reluctant the males
were to get close to each other, but how easily the females
and mixed pair were able to do so.

Sex Roles

Material in this chapter can lead to considerable discussion about male and female roles. Try reading the following hypothetical case history to the class and telling them that it is an example of a liberated male:

"When my wife and I both got our Ph.D.'s, I turned down a terrific job at a prestigious university in an out-of-the-way place and took a job teaching at a lesser school in a larger city so that my wife could get a part-time clinical psychology position at a clinic. We moved close to the clinic rather than live in the country as I preferred, so that my wife could more easily send the children off to school in the morning and meet them in the afternoon. Since we both get paid well, my wife can afford to hire a maid to do most of the housework. As I believe in equality in marriage, I wash the dishes and do the laundry while my wife prepares the meals. I spend as much time as I can with the children on weekends and sometimes during the week. I have a lot of respect for my wife who can be a mother and also have a career, so I try to help as much as possible."

Students should be nodding their heads in approval of how liberal the husband rightly is. Now read to them the following case history to see how deeply ingrained sex-role stereotypes are:

"When my husband and I both got our Ph.D.'s, I turned down a terrific job at a prestigious university in an out-of-the-way place and took a job teaching at a lesser school in a larger city so that my husband could get a part-time clinical psychology position at a clinic. We moved close to the clinic rather than live in the country as I preferred, so that my husband could more easily send the children off to school in the morning and meet them in the afternoon. Since we both get paid well, my husband can afford to hire a maid to do most of the housework. As I believe in equality in marriage, I wash the dishes and do the laundry while my husband prepares the meals. I spend as much time as I can with the children on weekends and sometimes during the week. I have a lot of respect for my husband who can be a father and also have a career, so I try to help as much as possible."

(Idea after Bem, S. L. & Bem, D. J., 1970, In D. J. Bem, **Beliefs, Attitudes, and Human Affairs**. Belmont, CA: Brooks/Cole.)

Homosexuality and Psychotherapy

Davison has argued that therapists should not help homosexuals who want to change their sexual orientation to do so, for in acquiescing to this request the therapist is reinforcing society's prejudice that homosexuality is abnormal. Instead, the therapist should help the homosexual overcome the problems and distress he faces, just as he or she would help a heterosexual--that is, without making the client's sexual orientation an issue. Students may be interested in reading and discussing Davison's article presenting his views (1982, <u>American Behavioral Scientist</u>, <u>25</u>, 423-434), which is followed by commentary by Bieber, Halleck, and Sturgis and Adams.

Lesbian Parenting

Lesbian women can become mothers in a variety of ways: through adoption, artificial insemination, or heterosexual intercourse. In the courts, lesbian mothers experience considerable difficulty gaining custody of their children; estimates suggest that only 50% succeed. Falk (1989, <u>American Psychologist</u>, <u>44</u>, 941-947) discusses and refutes the assumptions made by the family law courts about the ability of lesbian women to be good mothers, citing evidence from social science research. Assumptions made about lesbian mothers include the idea that all homosexuals are mentally ill, and that lesbians are less maternal than other women. Regarding the parent-child relationship, the courts assume that children of lesbian mothers are more likely than other children to be sexually molested, have impaired gender role development, become homosexual, and be traumatized and stigmatized by their peers or society in general. Since many members of your class may hold these assumptions as well, it may be worth reviewing the evidence Falk marshalls to refute them.

Regarding the mental health of lesbian women, numerous studies have found that gay women have either the same or a lower incidence of psychiatric disorders than heterosexual women. In addition, lesbian and heterosexual women have been found to be more alike than different in their self-concept and maternal attitudes, and in fact, lesbian mothers have been found to be more child-oriented. Only one study has compared the psychological health of children raised by lesbian vs. heterosexual parents, finding no differences between the groups. While there is no controlled research on rates of sexual molestation of children in gay vs. heterosexual households, researchers point out that the vast majority of cases of molestation are heterosexual, and no incidents of sexual assault between lesbians and minor female children have ever been reported in the U.S..

Several studies have examined the gender role development of children raised by lesbian parents. No evidence suggests a differential influence of lesbian parenting on children's gender roles; this is not surprising given the many influences on children's gender identity other than the mother, particularly peers. Although the fear that children raised by homosexual parents will become homosexual is widely cited by the courts to justify denying custody to lesbian mothers, research on the sexual orientation of such children finds no evidence to support such an assumption. Finally, many courts have denied custody to lesbian mothers on the assumption that the children may be victims of stigmatization by society. Falk argues that this basis for a decision is unjust, and notes that it is not applied to cases of interracial custody disputes, or other situations where parents seeking custody are different from the traditional white middle-class parent.

Presentation of this material is likely to elicit lively discussion in class. Students who have seen Tracey Ullman's television skits involving a girl being raised by two gay men may enjoy discussing this rare portrayal of the issue in the popular media. Most states now allow homosexuals to be foster parents (usually of gay adolescents)--what do students think of this policy?

NOTES

INSTRUCTIONAL FILMS

1. <u>Sex differences in Children's Play</u>. (PCR, 16 min., color, 1976) A documentary record of a research study, this film demonstrates sex differences in the play of young children.

2. <u>Sexuality--The Human Heritage</u>. (AVC, 59 min., color, 1976) Points out various factors influencing the development of sexual identity, including hormones, family, and society. Presents discussion of teenagers and homosexuals on how they view themselves in regard to society's standards.

3. <u>Killing Us Softly</u>. (CDF, 30 min., color, 1981) A narrated film about the portrayal of women in advertising. Interesting, engaging, and provocative. Very useful for beginning a discussion of sex roles.

4. <u>Rape Culture</u>. (CDF, 35 min., color) Examines the relationship between men and women as portrayed in the popular media. Suggests that there is a connection between social attitudes and rape, and questions our society's views about rape.

5. <u>Normalcy--What is it?</u> (PUBTEL, 29 min., 2" color videotape) Uses person-on-the-street interviews to illustrate a variety of definitions of normalcy, and Dr. Milton Diamond discusses ideas of normalcy in sexual behavior.

6. <u>Pink Triangles</u>. (CDF, 35 min., color, 1982) A documentary film about attitudes toward lesbians and gay men. Particularly emphasizes social homophobia.

7. <u>Homosexuality: What About McBride?</u> (CRM, 10 min., color, 1975) Friends on a raft trip argue over their questions and anxieties about homosexuality.

8. <u>The Boys in the Band</u>. (Swank, b & w) Based on the Broadway play, this film depicts the various roles and conflicts experienced by gay men in the 1960s.

CHAPTER 13

Sexual Dysfunctions

CHAPTER SYNOPSIS

The Sexual Response Cycle

DSM-IIIR distinguishes four phases in the human sexual response cycle, which is quite similar in men and women: (1) appetitive (sexual desire), (2) excitement (sexual pleasure and accompanying physiologic changes such as tumescence), (3) orgasm (the peak of sexual pleasure), and (4) resolution (relaxation following orgasm).

Masters and Johnson's work served to dispel some myths about sex, finding that (1) continuous direct stimulation of the clitoris during intercourse may be painful, (2) there is no distinction between vaginal and clitoral orgasm, contrary to Freud's theorizing, (3) having simultaneous orgasms is not a mark of superior sexual achievement, (4) most women enjoy intercourse during menstruation, (5) most pregnant women desire sexual stimulation, and (6) the size of a man's penis is not a factor in his or his partner's sexual enjoyment.

The Sexual Dysfunctions

Since problems with sexual activity are extremely common, such dysfunctions must be recurrent and persistent before they are classified as disorders in DSM-IIIR. Each sexual dysfunction is related to one or more phases of the sexual response cycle.

In hypoactive sexual desire disorder, the person is lacking in sexual fantasies and urges. A more extreme form of the disorder is sexual aversion disorder, in which the person actively avoids genital contact. Sexual desire disorders are difficult to define since it is unclear what normal desire should be. It is known that certain drugs dull sexual desires, and a partner's sexual dysfunction or interpersonal problems between a couple may be implicated in the lowered desire.

Two sexual arousal disorders, female sexual arousal disorder and male erectile disorder, are diagnosed only if adequate sexual stimulation is provided without arousal occurring. Consideration is given to subjective experiences of excitement as well as physiological signs. This disorder may occur in women who have not learned what they find sexually arousing. A variety of causes are likely in men, including performance anxiety and organic factors.

Three kinds of <u>orgasm disorders</u> are described in DSM-IIIR: <u>Inhibited female orgasm</u> refers to absence of orgasm after a period of normal sexual excitement. It may be that orgasm in women is a learned response; those who have not masturbated are more likely to be nonorgasmic. Fear of losing control and problems in the relationship are other possible causes. <u>Inhibited male orgasm</u> and <u>premature ejaculation</u> are orgasm disorders in men. The former is rare, while the latter is quite common, present in 30% of men at any given time.

Two pain disorders associated with sex are <u>dyspareunia</u> (persistent or recurrent pain before, during, or after sexual intercourse, which is not due to lack of vaginal lubrication or vaginismus) and <u>vaginismus</u> (involuntary spasms of the outer third of the vagina which make intercourse impossible). Dyspareunia is almost always caused by a medical problem.

Theories of Sexual Dysfunctions

Psychoanalytic views have linked sexual dysfunction to repressed conflicts--particularly anger toward the partner--but there is little to support this view. A box describes the <u>bioenergetic approach</u>, in which sexual dysfunctions are seen as resulting from chronic tension and relieved by relaxing the body's musculature through insight and physical exercises. Most sex therapists now recognize the need for direct behavioral techniques.

Contemporary Views

Masters and Johnson identify the adoption of a <u>spectator role</u> and <u>fears of performance</u> as the primary current variables maintaining sexual dysfunctions. Important historical antecedents include religious ortho-doxy, psychosexual trauma, homosexual inclinations, inadequate counseling, excessive intake of alcohol, part-ner's vaginismus, physiological causes, and sociocultural factors.

Other theorists have pointed to factors not emphasized by Masters and Johnson, including marital conflict, irrational thinking, lack of knowledge or skill, poor communication between partners, and fear of acquiring sexually transmitted diseases. A box discusses the epidemic of Acquired Immune Deficiency Syndrome, or AIDS.

Behavioral and Cognitive Therapies for Sexual Dysfunctions

Behavioral and cognitive therapies have been particularly successful in treating sexual dysfunctions. Masters and Johnson's pioneering work is discussed in a box: The intensive two week program begins with a ban on sexual activity and a discussion of the couple's <u>sexual value system</u>. On the third day, <u>sensate focus</u>, or pleasurable touching without intercourse, begins, and couples are encouraged to communicate their desires to their partner. Finally, specific instructions for approaching intercourse are given, according to particular dysfunctions.

The following techniques are frequently used by sex therapists: sex education, anxiety reduction techniques, directed masturbation, skills and communication training, procedures to change attitudes and thoughts, shifts in routines, marital therapy, psychodynamic therapy, and medical and physical procedures.

NOTES

STUDENTS SHOULD KNOW . . .

Key Points

1. The human sexual response cycle includes four phases: appetitive, excitement, orgasm, and resolution.

2. Students should know the sexual myths dispelled by Masters and Johnson.

3. The sexual desire disorders include hypoactive sexual desire disorder and its more severe form, sexual aversion disorder.

4. The sexual arousal disorders include female sexual arousal disorder and male erectile disorder.

5. The orgasm disorders include inhibited female orgasm, inhibited male orgasm, and premature ejaculation.

6. Dyspareunia and vaginismus are the two sexual pain disorders.

7. Adopting a spectator role and fears of performance are the primary current variables maintaining sexual dysfunctions.

8. Students should know the historical antecedents thought to be causes of sexual dysfunctions.

9. Acquired Immune Deficiency Syndrome (AIDS) is a fatal disease transmitted through introduction of infected bodily fluids into the blood stream, usually through sexual relations or sharing of needles by IV drug users. Psychologists play a role in prevention of AIDS and treating the psychological problems of its victims.

10. Behavioral and cognitive therapies are particularly effective for treating sexual dysfunctions, and are used by most sex therapists.

New Terms
(key terms underlined)

sexual dysfunctions, appetitive, excitement, orgasm, and resolution phases, tumescence, clitoris, vaginal barrel, sexual desire disorders, hypoactive sexual desire disorder, sexual aversion disorder, sexual arousal disorders, female sexual arousal disorder, male erectile disorder, orgasm disorders, inhibited female orgasm, inhibited male orgasm, premature ejaculation, sexual pain disorders, dyspareunia, vaginismus, spectator role, bioenergetic approach, in vivo desensitization, sensory-awareness procedures, Acquired Immune Deficiency Syndrome, sexual value system, sensate focus

New Names
(key figures underlined)

Havelock Ellis, Helen Singer Kaplan, William Masters, Virginia Johnson, Wilhelm Reich

NOTES

Denslow Lewis: The First Sexologist?

In 1983, the Journal of the American Medical Association published an article entitled "The Gynecological Consideration of the Sexual Act," by Denslow Lewis, M.D., which reached the conclusion that women were capable of having orgasm. What is remarkable about the article is that it was written 84 years earlier--and the editor of JAMA refused to print it at the time (and the president of AMA refused to allow a reprint of it to be circulated at the annual convention). Comments about the paper at the time included remarks by a leading contemporary figure in gynecology, Dr. Howard Kelly of John Hopkins: "Its discussion is attended with more or less filth and we besmirch ourselves by discussing it in public."

Lewis' paper was remarkable primarily for his frank discussion of a topic which was not to be discussed at the time. He reached conclusions such as: "Sexual matters should be taught the young at an early age. It is only fair for the girl to understand that there is no immodesty in her active participation." He argued, "The instinct that determines self-preservation is almost equaled in importance and in its control of the individual by the instinct that dictates the perpetuation of the species. It is therefore proper for medical men in their deliberations to take cognizance of this great factor in human life." Medical authorities of the time obviously disagreed, but times have changed sufficiently that JAMA published the paper as a part of its "landmark" reports that served as a celebration of the journal's centennial anniversary.

Hormones and Sex Drive

Research suggests that there is a complicated relationship between hormones and sex drive. Hormone-behavior relationships are notoriously difficult to research, so the findings to date should be considered to be tentative. Among the problems are that sex drive is difficult to measure, and that sexual behavior is affected by many factors other than hormones which are themselves difficult to measure (e.g., partner receptivity). Most of the data are from abnormal cases and the data base is small because until recently there was no accurate way to assess levels of many hormones, including androgens. Another point is that the endocrine system is a very complex, dynamic system, making it difficult to change levels of one hormone without affecting levels of others. Finally, it is clear that behavior can change hormone levels, and specifically, there is some evidence that sexual activity in males can boost male hormone levels.

A safe generalization is that the sex hormones do affect sexual behavior. Children of either sex, who through disease or defect do not have enough hormones, will not undergo the normal changes at puberty. If a man is deprived of androgens (the male sex hormones) from before puberty, it is unlikely that he will develop a sexual interest. If, however, the deprivation occurs in adulthood, its effects are variable. Studies of castrated males show that while most report significantly reduced interest and activity within a year, some continue to have desire and to function sexually for decades. Antiandrogenic drugs also seem to reduce sexual desire and activity in males. However, giving additional androgens to males with normal levels does not seem to raise sexual desire. And there is tremendous variability in the normal level; a group of sexually normal males may show differences of 100% in blood testosterone levels. The most reasonable conclusion is that a minimum level of androgens is very important to normal sexual function, but that beyond this threshold, other factors are dominant.

Interestingly, androgens may have even stronger effects on _female_ sexual desire than on males'. Experimental and clinical evidence suggests that increasing androgen levels will increase female sex drive and that reducing androgen levels will reduce sex drive. Androgen therapy is not indicated in most cases of female low sex drive because of its marked masculinizing side effects, including clitoral enlargement, body and facial hair growth, and voice changes. Variations in estrogen levels do not seem to affect sexual desire in females. (Summary based on Crooks, R. and Baur, K., 1980, _Our Sexuality_. Menlo Park, CA: Benjamin/ Cummings.)

The "PLISSIT" Model of Sex Therapy

Describing the techniques of therapy for sexual dysfunction may be enhanced by presentation of the "PLISSIT" model, which contains the following elements:

Permission
Limited Information
Specific Suggestions
Intensive Therapy

The model suggests that sex therapy proceeds from one level to the next depending on the couple's (or individual's) needs and the likely etiology of the presenting problem. For some people, permission and limited information may be enough to overcome their sexual dysfunction; more lengthy or "in-depth" therapy is often unnecessary.

Permission involves giving the individual explicit permission to be sexual, without making judgments. This may be an important step for someone whose sexual dysfunction is rooted in religious or parental prohibitions which have prevented them from finding sex enjoyable and relaxing.

Limited information refers to giving the person basic facts about human sexuality which they may never have learned, such as the importance of clitoral stimulation for women to reach orgasm. This is the level of "therapy" that Dr. Ruth employs, and which is quite helpful for many people.

Specific suggestions are the meat of behavioral sex therapy, involving teaching techniques known to help alleviate particular sexual dysfunctions; the suggestions are tailored for the individual presenting problem.

While the vast majority of sex therapy cases involve only the first three levels, intensive therapy may be necessary in some cases. For example, some couples find themselves unable to follow the specific suggestions (homework assignments), and the therapist needs to find out why. A person with deep ambivalence about sexual pleasure, for example, may be unable to enjoy sensate focus exercises. A person who was sexually molested as a child may find intercourse frightening and threatening, and be unable to complete the homework assignments with his or her spouse.

Treatment of Premature Ejaculation

Description of the specific technique used in treating premature ejaculation will help students get a better picture of the way sex therapy works (and, in the process, may educate them further about a common sexual problem which they or their partner may be experiencing). The following account comes from Kaplan's The New Sex Therapy (1974, New York: Brunner/Mazel), an invaluable source.

While distracting oneself from the sensations being experienced during intercourse (thinking about garbage) is probably the most common folk remedy for premature ejaculation, in fact the most effective technique for this problem involves focusing the man's attention on the sensations preceding orgasm. Kaplan sees the primary factor in premature ejaculation to be the absence of voluntary control over orgasm, not simply a rapid ejaculatory reflex, and as in biofeedback, sensory feedback about orgasm is essential to learning voluntary control.

The most common technique prescribed for this purpose is the "stop-start" method, in which the man stimulates himself (or has his partner stimulate him), while focusing exclusive attention on the sensations he experiences. As soon as he feels that orgasm is near, he is to instruct his partner to stop stimulating him, and then wait for the sensation to subside (usually in a few seconds). This procedure is repeated numerous times, enabling the man to learn to recognize the sensations which precede orgasm, and postponing it by stopping stimulation before it occurs. The same approach is then used during intercourse. Cure rates have been reported from 98% to 100% with men using this technique under the guidance of a sex therapist, and the benefits appear to be permanent in most cases.

Sexuality and Aging

As Kaplan writes, "The potential for erotic pleasure seems to begin with birth and does not need to end until death" (1974, The New Sex Therapy, New York: Brunner/Mazel, p. 104). An understanding of the changes in sexual response which occur with age are important to convey to students, elucidating the complex interplay of physiological and psychological factors in human sexuality.

Male sexual functioning with age: Boy infants have erections from birth, and masturbation is a normal phase of development, as is sex play with peers. Puberty brings with it a sudden and dramatic increase in sexual desire, and the peak of sexual potency and reactivity occurs at age 17 to 18 in men. In the 30s, sexual urgency becomes less pressing.

The quality of sexual pleasure changes noticeably by the mid-40s, becoming less genitally-oriented and more diffuse and generalized. After the 50s, the frequency of orgasm has decreased significantly, and the refractory period has lengthened. In addition, longer and more intense stimulation is necessary to reach erection. While the sexual drive is diminished in older men, a man in his 80s is still perfectly capable of experiencing orgasms and can have erections given enough stimulation. Kaplan writes, "freed of the intense need for fast orgastic release and of the inhibitions of his youth, more satisfying and imaginative love play is often enjoyed by the older man and his partner. For the secure man, age need never be a barrier to sexual pleasure providing good health and opportunity exist" (p. 109).

  <u>Female sexual functioning with age</u>. Girls also experience diffuse sexual pleasure in childhood, masturbate (though while all boys masturbate, a third of girls do not), have sexual fantasies, and engage in sex play (if not prevented). While sexual desire increases with adolescence, the orgastic urge appears to be less intense than in boys, and purely physical aspects of sex are less important than relationships with boys. (Of course, we cannot know whether this difference is due to biology or culture.) The first coital experiences of girls are often disappointing, without orgasm and sometimes even painful. Women in our culture reach their sexual peak in their late 30s and early 40s, characterized by rapid and intense responsiveness. After menopause, female sexual functioning is highly variable; while some women's sexual desire decreases, others experience an <u>increase</u> in desire. Women who have regular sexual opportunity later in life maintain their sexual responsiveness, though a gradual physical decline does occur, leading to less preoccupation with sex, slower vaginal lubrication, and less vigorous contractions during orgasm.

DISCUSSION STIMULATORS

Sex Survey

If the class is large enough, a survey of students taken and tabulated before the lecture can provide an interesting backdrop and a spring-board for discussion. Obviously, special efforts to insure anonymity need to be taken and its completion should be entirely optional.

NOTES

Anonymous Sex Survey

Sex: M   F

1) How often do you (does your male partner) ejaculate before it is desired? (circle one)

   never   rarely   occasionally   often   always

   not applicable

2) How often do you (does your female partner) not climax during sexual relations? (circle one)

   never   rarely   occasionally   often   always

   not applicable

3) How often do you (does your male partner) have difficulties achieving or maintaining an erection when wanted? (circle one)

   never   rarely   occasionally   often   always

   not applicable

4) How often do you (does your female partner) have difficulty becoming sexually aroused when it is desired?

   never   rarely   occasionally   often   always

   not applicable

5) How long should intercourse last?

6) How often should two people with a normal level of sexual desire have intercourse (assuming they have an available partner)?

7) Should both partners reach orgasm at the same time?

Sensate Focus Exercise

To help students "get a feel" for what sex therapy techniques are like, you might suggest they try a simple sensate focus exercise outside of class, the "hand, face, foot caress." Students will need to ask a friend to participate in the exercise. They will take turns caressing their partner's hand, face, or foot, moving very slowly and gently. The person doing the caressing is to focus only on the sensation of touching, experimenting with different kinds of touches, not thinking about what the partner is experiencing. The person being caressed should likewise focus on the experience of being touched. As an exercise in communication, the person being caressed can try telling their partner what feels especially good, including what type of touch, how light or hard, how fast or slow. After the exercise, partners can talk with each other about what it felt like to caress and to be caressed.

Self-Help Books on Sexuality

Two popular books available in most bookstores are extremely helpful to men and women who are interested in their sexuality; you might want to tell the class about them and encourage your students to read them in conjunction with this chapter of the text. For Yourself (Barbach, L. G., 1976, Garden City, NY: Anchor Books) is about female sexuality and of particular interest to pre-orgasmic women. Male Sexuality, by Bernie Zilbergeld (1978, New York: Bantam Books), contains comprehensive coverage of male sexuality and sexual dysfunction, containing many practical exercises for overcoming common problems and enhancing sexuality.

Case Studies

Helen Singer Kaplan's Disorders of Sexual Desire (1979, New York: Brunner/Mazel) contains numerous case examples of inhibited sexual desire and other sexual dysfunctions, complete with descriptions of therapeutic approaches and complex problems which sometimes develop during treatment. You might want to pass out copies of one or two cases and have the class discuss Kaplan's analysis of the problem and treatment approach.

Adolescent Sexuality

An article by Brooks-Gunn and Furstenberg in __American Psychologist__ (1989, __44__, 249-257) raises many topics about adolescent sexuality which may provoke interesting discussion in class:

__Age at first intercourse__. Dramatic changes in the age at first intercourse have occurred in the last 50 years. Approximately 7% of white females had intercourse by age 16 in the 1940s and 50s; by 1982, the figure had risen to 44%. Interestingly, similar data for boys have not been collected, suggesting that our society sees fertility control as a female, not a male issue. What age do students think is appropriate for first intercourse? What factors affect their decision? What do they see as the most important factors determining when a person becomes sexually active: Parents' values? Peer behavior? Religious beliefs?

__Antecedents to sexual experiences in adolescence.__ Research indicates that most adolescents do not consciously plan to become sexually active. Important antecedent factors identified include hormonal changes associated with puberty, contextual effects (what is considered normal sexual behavior in the peer group), development of secondary sexual characteristics, parental influences, including communication and supervision, and school functioning (teens who are not doing well in school are more likely to begin sexual activity during adolescence).

__Contraceptive use.__ About one half of all teenagers do not use contraceptives when they first engage in sexual relations, and many continue to have unprotected intercourse for years. Why do students think this problem exists? Research indicates that teenagers put off coming to a family planning clinic because of procrastination, ambivalence about their sexual behavior, and fear of their parents finding out. What would make adolescents more likely to use contraception? Factors found to be associated with irregular contraceptive use include lower social class, nonattendance of college, fundamentalist Protestant affiliation, lack of a steady partner, never having been pregnant, infrequent intercourse, and no access to free, confidential family planning. In addition, teenagers who have little communication or have conflict with their parents, and those who do not know about their parents' contraceptive experience, are less likely to use birth control. Again, these findings are all concerning girls; very little is known about male contraceptive use.

Students might be asked to design a program for increasing the use of contraception among sexually active adolescents: What approaches would they recommend? What age-group would they target? How might approaches differ for boys vs. girls? How would they present their ideas to parents? What problems do they foresee with implementing such a program?

NOTES

INSTRUCTIONAL FILMS

1. <u>Sexes: Breaking the Barriers</u>. (UCEMC-8408, 22 min., color, 1971) "Dr. William Masters and Virginia Johnson discuss their research and treatment programs, and express hope that more freedom of sexual expression will result from their work. Also shows a nude encounter and therapy group in which participants discuss their sexual and emotional problems, and a group of New York college students in a coeducational dormitory talk about their attitudes toward sex, marriage, and monogamy. Includes scenes of a homosexual wedding of two men, and a brief description of gay liberation movement activities."

2. <u>Sex in Aging and Disease</u>. (Network for Continuing Medical Education, New York, 19 min., 3/4" color video cassette, 1974) "This program discusses various aspects of sex in aging and disease. Sexual response in both the female and male is reviewed as a basis for dispelling various myths such as erection is necessary for ejaculation. Causes of impotency and dyspareunia are identified and factors to consider when counseling patients about these problems are discussed. Sexual problems which can be associated with such conditions as malnutrition, diabetes, and heart disease are described. The effects of drugs on sexual functioning are also mentioned. Positions which may help to compensate for physical limitations imposed by disease or age are illustrated clinically."

3. <u>Lowen and Bioenergetic Therapy</u>. (PSYCD, 48 min., color, 1973) "Features Dr. Alexander Lowen describing his key ideas of bioenergetic therapy and demonstrating them in his work with a young female patient."

CHAPTER 14

Schizophrenia

CHAPTER SYNOPSIS

History of the Concept

Emil Kraepelin first presented his concept of <u>dementia praecox</u> in 1898, emphasizing the progressive intellectual deterioration (dementia) and the early onset (praecox) of the disorder that would come to be known as <u>schizophrenia</u>. Eugen Bleuler focused on the "breaking of associative threads" as the core of the disorder, rather than onset and course. Kraepelin's view led to a narrow definition of schizophrenia; Bleuler's led to a broad one with a much greater theoretical emphasis on "core symptoms."

Bleuler had a great influence on the American conception of schizophrenia, as evidenced by the increased use of the diagnosis. Diagnostic terms such as "schizo-affective psychosis" and "pseudoneurotic schizophrenia" are further examples of the broadened concept. The <u>process-reactive</u> distinction also maintained the broad concept; reactive schizophrenics were said to have a <u>good</u> <u>premorbid</u> history and prognosis, having become psychotic following some life stressor.

The current DSM-IIIR definition of schizophrenia narrows the concept in several ways: (1) specific diagnostic criteria are given; (2) patients with symptoms of affective disorder are excluded; (3) the disturbance must last at least six months, excluding those patients with acute psychotic reactions to stress; and (4) mild forms of schizophrenia are now seen as personality disorders. Debate over the best definition of the disorder continues, however.

Clinical Symptoms of Schizophrenia

Disorders of Thought

<u>Thought disorders</u> can occur in the form or content of thoughts. <u>Disorders of thought form</u> include <u>incoherence</u>, <u>neologism</u>, <u>loose associations</u>, poverty of speech, poverty of content, perseveration, and blocking; all reveal problems in the organization of ideas. While considered the principal symptom of schizophrenia by Bleuler, evidence suggests that thought disorder may not discriminate well

between schizophrenia and other disorders. __Disorders of thought content__ include lack of insight and __delusions__, or beliefs that are misinterpretations of reality. Important delusions include __persecutory__ delusions, a delusional percept, somatic passivity, thought insertion, thought broadcast, thought withdrawal, "made" feelings, "made" volitional acts, and "made" impulses.

Disorders of Perception and Attention

Schizophrenic patients frequently report that the world seems different or unreal. The most dramatic distortions of perception are __hallucinations__--sensory experiences in the absence of any stimulation from the environment. Particularly important hallucinations include audible thoughts, voices arguing, and voices commenting.

Motor Symptoms

Disturbances in motor activity are obvious and bizarre, ranging from wild gestures and expressions to __catatonic immobility__, a rigid posture with lack of movement for long periods of time. __Waxy flexibility__ occurs in some catatonic patients; they will maintain strange positions which their limbs have been placed in by another person.

Affective Symptoms

__Flat affect__, or the absence of emotional response, and __inappropriate affect__, or emotional responses occurring out of context, are the major affective abnormalities found in schizophrenics.

Impairments in Life Functioning

Schizophrenics typically have impairments in social relationships, work, and self-care in addition to the symptoms described above.

Subcategories of Schizophrenia

Three of the types of schizophrenic disorders in DSM-IIIR were initially proposed by Kraepelin. __Disorganized__ (hebephrenic) schizophrenia is characterized by profuse delusions an hallucinations, absurd and silly behavior, and neglect of self-care. __Catatonic__ schizophrenia is characterized by motor disturbance; it is rarely seen today. _Paranoid_ schizophrenia is the most common diagnosis, and includes prominent delusions which are usually persecutory but may be _grandiose_. _Delusional jealousy_ or _ideas of reference_ also may be present. As is discussed in a box, Freud believed that paranoid delusions stemmed from repressed homosexual conflicts, but this commonly held assumption is, in fact, highly speculative.

Positive and Negative Symptoms

The subtypes of schizophrenia, including those listed above as well as the _undifferentiated_ and _residual_ types, exhibit low diagnostic reliability, considerable overlap between types, and limited predictive validity. A current system attracting much interest distinguishes between positive and negative symptoms. _Positive symptoms_ consist of excesses, such as hallucinations, delusions, and bizarre behavior. _Negative symptoms_ consist of behavioral deficits, including affective flattening, alogia, avolition-apathy, and anhedonia-asociality.

Research on the Etiology of Schizophrenia

Broad theoretical views, which have had little impact on research, are discussed in a box. Psychoanalytic theory views schizophrenia as a regression to a state of "primary narcissism," _labeling theory_ suggests that schizophrenia is a learned social role, and experiential theory views schizophrenia as one way of coping with extreme stress.

The Genetic Data

There now exists a convincing body of evidence indicating that a predisposition for schizophrenia is transmitted genetically. Family studies reveal an increased risk for schizophrenia in relatives of schizophrenic patients. Concordance rates for identical twins are much greater than for fraternal twins, while not reaching 100% (indicating that some nongenetic factors play a role). Studies of adopted children demonstrate a high rate of schizophrenia among the biological children of schizophrenics, even when they are reared by healthy adoptive parents. Overall, it is clear that genetic factors do play a role in the etiology of schizophrenia without explaining the whole picture. A diathesis-stress model appears to be the best fit.

Biochemical Factors

The theory that schizophrenia is brought on by excess activity of the neurotransmitter dopamine is based principally on the mode of action of the <u>phenothiazines</u>, drugs which alleviate some symptoms of schizophrenia but also produce side effects similar to Parkinson's disease, a disease caused by low levels of dopamine. The literature on amphetamine psychosis supports the theory of <u>excess dopamine activity</u>. Other evidence suggest that the theory may apply only to those schizophrenics with positive symptoms. To date, the excess-dopamine hypothesis, while promising, has not been proven conclusively.

Neurological Findings

A percentage of schizophrenics, particularly those with chronic, negative symptoms, have been found to have observable brain pathology. CAT scan images reveal that some have enlarged ventricles, particularly in the frontal lobes, suggesting a deterioration or atrophy of brain tissue. Some evidence supports the hypothesis that a viral infection occurring during fetal development may cause this brain damage.

Social Class and Schizophrenia

Numerous studies have shown a relation between lower social class and schizophrenia. This correlation has been interpreted in both directions. The <u>sociogenic hypothesis</u> suggests that low social class causes schizophrenia, whereas the <u>social-drift hypothesis</u> argues that schizophrenics become poor because of their life difficulties. Evidence on the social class of fathers of schizophrenics supports both views--there are a disproportionate number of fathers from the low social classes, but schizophrenic children tend to drift even lower in occupational status.

Schizophrenia and the Family

The term <u>schizophrenogenic mother</u> was coined to describe the supposedly cold and dominant, conflict-inducing parent who was said to produce schizophrenia. <u>Double-bind</u> theory is another prominent family view, emphasizing mixed messages the parent sends to the child. However, neither of these two theories have been supported by controlled studies. Recent evidence does suggest that deviant communication patterns are predictive of future pathology. Most importantly, high <u>expressed emotion</u> in the post-hospital environment has been found to predict relapse.

High-Risk Studies of Schizophrenia

Mednick and Schulsinger conducted the first high-risk study of schizophrenia, following 207 young people with schizophrenic mothers and 104 low-risk subjects. Predictions of schizophrenia in the high-risk group included separation from parents early in life and being brought up in an institution (for boys), and early onset of the disorder in the mothers of girls. Other high-risk studies have found attentional dysfunction, low IQ, and poor neurobehavioral functioning to predict schizophrenia.

Therapies for Schizophrenia

Somatic Treatments

<u>Insulin coma therapy</u>, <u>prefrontal lobotomy</u>, and electro-convulsive therapy were early treatments for schizophrenia which are no longer used in treating the disorder because of dangerous side effects and ineffectiveness. The most important development in the treatment of schizophrenia was the use of <u>neuroleptics</u>, anti-psychotic medications which are the most effective means of treating the positive symptoms of schizophrenia and reducing the need for long-term hospital treatment. However, the drugs must be taken consistently over long periods to prevent relapse, and serious side effects make maintenance difficult.

Psychological Treatments

Harry Stack Sullivan pioneered the treatment of schizophrenics with psychotherapy. He focused on helping patients achieve insight and learn adult forms of communication. While Sullivan and Fromm-Reichman, another psychoanalyst, advocate a gentle approach to treatment, Rosen's <u>direct analysis</u> involves an extremely confrontational method. A box discusses evidence that such intrusive interaction can actually be quite harmful to schizophrenic patients. Existential and humanistic therapies have made little impact on schizophrenia, although empathic skills are important for working with these individuals. In general, there is little evidence to support the use of insight-oriented approaches to treating schizophrenia.

Family therapy is currently aimed at helping to reduce the expressed emotion that has been demonstrated to predict relapse in schizophrenics. Evidence for this type of treatment has been quite positive, and a recent study indicated that the combination of family therapy and social skills training resulted in no relapses, even when expressed emotion remained high.

Operant conditioning techniques have been used in hospital settings. There is consistent evidence that such therapy helps schizophrenics to function better, although like the other therapies described, it is not a cure.

The most effective treatment package for schizophrenia probably includes educating the family and patient about current scientific knowledge, working to reduce the stress experienced by the patient on discharge, and encouraging networking among affected families. The integration of somatic and psychological interventions is essential; somatic treatments are limited by their serious side effects, lack of effect on negative symptoms, lack of improvement in some individuals, and the difficulty getting patients to continue their medication.

NOTES

STUDENTS SHOULD KNOW . . .

Key Points

1. Students should know the history of the diagnosis of schizophrenia, including Kraepelin's dementia praecox, Bleuler's associative threads, and the broadened American concepts such as the process-reactive distinction.

2. The major clinical symptoms of schizophrenia include disordered thought, disorders of perception and attention, motor behavior, affective abnormalities, and problems in life functioning.

3. The three major subcategories of schizophrenia are disorganized, catatonic, and paranoid.

4. Positive symptoms (hallucinations, delusions, bizarre behavior) are now distinguished from negative symptoms (flat affect, language deficits, apathy, anhedonia).

5. Evidence from family, twin, and adoption studies indicates that a predisposition for schizophrenia is transmitted genetically.

6. Biochemical research suggests that excess dopamine may play a role in schizophrenia.

7. Some schizophrenics have been found to have enlarged ventricles, demonstrating atrophy in the frontal lobes. Viral infections during fetal development have also been associated with the illness.

8. The link between schizophrenia and lower social class status has been explained by both the sociogenic and the social-drift theories.

9. There is little strong evidence that the family plays an etiological role in schizophrenia, although recent evidence indicates that high expressed emotion can predict relapse.

10. High-risk studies of schizophrenia may shed light on factors which cause the illness in children with a biological disposition.

11. Neuroleptic medication is the most effective method of controlling the positive symptoms of schizophrenia and reducing long-term hospitalization.

12. There is little evidence that insight-oriented psychotherapy is helpful in treating schizophrenia.

13. Family therapy has been found to be helpful in reducing expressed emotion and relapse in schizophrenics.

14. Behavior therapy, including social skills training and operant conditioning techniques, has been shown to improve the functioning of schizophrenics.

15. The best treatment package is an integration of medication with psychological treatments, particularly education of the family and patient and reduction of stress in the post-hospital environment.

New Terms
(key terms underlined)

schizophrenia, dementia praecox, process-reactive dimension, premorbid adjustment, schizoaffective disorder, schizophreniform disorder, thought disorder, incoherence, neologism, loose associations, poverty of speech, poverty of content, blocking, delusions, persecutory delusions, delusional precept, somatic passivity, thought insertion, thought broadcast, thought withdrawal, "made" feelings, "made" volitional acts, "made" impulses, hallucinations, catatonic immobility, waxy flexibility, flat affect, inappropriate affect, hebephrenic, catatonic, paranoid, and disorganized schizophrenia, undifferentiated and residual types, delusions of persecutions, grandiose delusions, delusional jealousy, ideas of reference, positive and negative symptoms, alogia, avolition-apathy, anhedonia-asociality, labeling theory, phenothiazines, excess dopamine activity, sociogenic hypothesis, social-drift theory, schizophrenogenic mother, double bind, expressed emotion, insulin coma therapy, prefrontal lobotomy, neuroleptics, direct analysis

New Names
(key figures underlined)

Eugen Bleuler, Adolf Meyer, Harry Stack Sullivan, Kurt Schneider, Scheff, Ronald Laing, Paul Meehl, Gregory Bateson, Sarnoff Mednick, Frieda Fromm-Reichman, John Rosen

Chapter 14

LECTURE LAUNCHERS

A First Person Account: Problems of Living with Schizophrenia

The following is an anonymous account of the personal problems of living with schizophrenia. The article appeared in the Schizophrenia Bulletin (1981, 7, 196-197). It is a good piece to read to students at the beginning or end of the lecture(s) on schizophrenia as it reviews many of the issues outlined in the chapter from a very human perspective.

"Living with schizophrenia creates problems for me that are not obvious or easy to explain. I am not entirely comfortable with the label 'schizophrenia' because it implies that I am different in some basic way from other people, when I feel I am not. The label has helped me, though, to feel less guilt about my inability to 'conquer' my problems, and to learn to make some allowances for my difficulties in handling situations. Unfortunately, other people often do not recognize the difficulties I face or make any attempt to make allowances for me.

"The largest problem I face--I think the basic one--is the intensity and variety of my feelings, and my low threshold for handling other people's intense feelings, especially negative ones. I have quite often experienced a euphoric 'high' that is much like being in contact with some greater reality or meaning to life--accompanied by a kind of added brightness or extra dimension to everyday things around me. The other side of the coin, though, is a very intense anxiety from nowhere that typically hits me quite suddenly after a short period of time without medication. The two feelings are opposite, yet somehow connected.

"Feelings are 'the stuff life is made of,' and I do not regret a lot of what I have experienced, but the terrible feelings are bad enough to make me opt for the medication-- at least an adequate amount to give me control, even with some remaining discomfort. I have been taking one of the phenothiazines for almost 7 years, and I am concerned about the many potential problems with long-term use, particularly tardive dyskinesia. However, I feel there is no effective alternative to the drug, particularly if I am to maintain my normal lifestyle, with a husband and 9-year-old son.

"My son--our son--is a very healthy, active boy, with a 'take things in stride' disposition and an interest in many things, among them fossils, reading, the weather, swimming, soccer, and drawing. He is doing very well in school, too. He has a sensitive nature, yet is quite self-sufficient. My

233

husband is supportive of me, but in many ways I am supportive of him, too. We talk well together; he spends many
hours listening to me philosophize, or talk about my
problems.

"I am convinced that my normal `facade' arises mainly
when other people expect me to become emotionally involved
with them. I find emotions tremendously complex, and I am
quite acutely aware of the many over- and undertones of
things people say and the way they say them. Generally, I
like direct, honest, kind people, and I have difficulty
handling social situations that require me to be artificial
or too careful.

"Another problem I have to deal with to a greater or
lesser degree is my `runaway thinking.' I `free associate'
rather easily, and sometimes forget what I was saying
because other ideas are in my mind. If I concentrate, however, this can be an advantage, because I have a ready
supply of new ideas--I don't bore myself. Concentrating,
though, is sometimes easier said than done.

"Intimacy is an interesting problem in my life. In a
way, I am capable of the deepest spiritual intimacy with
people, yet I am less capable than most people of handling
the demands of relationships. I cannot share negative feelings other people have, because I am too sensitive to them;
yet I can give a great deal of love and concern when I am
protected against feelings like anger and cynicism.

"I used to think a great deal about unlikely, unreal
things, like being watched or filmed and events being
orchestrated around me by other people or outside forces, or
being literally an alien, since I felt so different and
basically unattached to the world. I still have similar
feelings and thoughts, but less so than before. In any
case, they come and go and don't affect me greatly. The
only pervading feeling that is a problem sometimes--on too
little medication--is a general one of unreality or being
unattached. The particular ideas that stem from the feeling
are not the problem for me.

"Overall, I feel I have a good life, and I am, in spite
of my frequent doubts, a success in many areas. I have good
people as friends, and a fine family, and I am not forced
into a position of taking on too much independence or of
being too dependent. I am a unique and interesting person;
I don't always quite fit in with the world, but I think I
add something to it."

More First Person Accounts

Many students enjoy reading first person accounts of the experience of mental illness, such as that quoted above. Each issue of Schizophrenia Bulletin contains a first person account from an individual with schizophrenia or a parent or other concerned layperson. The following poem, written by Lynne Morris, a woman with schizophrenia, appeared in a compilation of first person accounts in the 1988 issue of the journal.

I
am
the
rear tire
of a bicycle,
not trusted enough
to be a
front tire,
expected to go
round and round
in one narrow rut,
never going very far,
ignored
except
when I
break down.
Then
I get lots of
frightening,
angry
attention
and
I am put into
a
garage,
sometimes for months,
where
I forget my function
and
I become afraid
to function
and all functions seem useless.

Next time out
I think I will be
an off-ramp
from a
freeway.

Kraepelin and the Diagnosis of Schizophrenia: Then and Now

A demonstration of just how far the United States concept of schizophrenia has swung back toward Kraepelin's original definition of the disorder can be found in a recent study. James and May (1981, American Journal of Psychiatry, 138, 501-504) re-diagnosed the patients in 32 case histories that were presented in Kraepelin's textbooks. Material relevant to Kraepelin's original diagnosis was stricken from the case histories so that the modern day raters were blind to his diagnoses. DSM-III diagnostic criteria were then used to make new, independent diagnoses. (In addition, independent diagnoses were made according to Spitzer's Research Diagnostic Criteria.) The results? Of 15 cases diagnosed as dementia praecox by Kraepelin, 14 were diagnosed as schizophrenic according to modern criteria. Of 13 cases diagnosed as manic, depressed, or manic-depression by Kraepelin, 11 were similarly diagnosed according to DSM-III. Two cases of paranoia were identically diagnosed by Kraepelin and DSM-III as was one case of somatization disorder (hysteria in Kraepelin's terms). Finally, one case that Kraepelin diagnosed as senile dementia was classified as "atypical psychosis" according to DSM-III. Overall, the reliability of diagnosis was 91% between raters making judgments 75 years apart. Kraepelin, apparently, would be quite comfortable making diagnoses according to modern criteria.

High-Risk Studies of the Etiology of Schizophrenia

What are the precursors to schizophrenia? High-risk research has become an increasingly popular method of answering this question, and Asarnow (1988, Schizophrenia Bulletin, 14, 613-631) offers an excellent review of 24 high-risk studies initiated between 1952 and the present, summarizing their answers from a developmental perspective. The findings are organized by age periods (conception to infancy, early childhood, middle childhood, adolescence, early adulthood) and type of risk factor (neurointegrative functioning, social functioning, symptoms, general stressors, and family stressors). (See Table 2 on pages 619-621 for a clear and concise compilation of results.) Some findings:

Conception to infancy. Pregnancy and birth complications among children of schizophrenics are associated with enlarged brain ventricles in infancy and negative symptoms of schizophrenia 8 years later. Exposure to influenza virus during the second trimester of fetal development may increase risk for schizophrenia. Children of schizophrenics have been found to show disturbances in social functioning in infancy, including difficult temperament, lower thresholds to stimulation, more apathy and withdrawal, less response to verbal commands, and less spontaneity.

    <u>Early childhood</u> (ages 2-4). Young children of schizophrenic patients show lower reactivity, poorer gross and fine motor performance, more schizoid behavior (emotionally flat, withdrawn, passive, irritable). In one study, parental separation and resultant institutionalization during the first five years predicted breakdown in sons of schizophrenic mothers. Schizophrenic parents have been found to be relatively passive and lacking in warmth in interactions with their children.

    <u>Middle childhood</u>. Neuromotor impairments, including problems in motor coordination and sensory perceptual functioning are more common in children of schizophrenics, as are attentional difficulties and information processing deficits on complex tasks. Some studies have also found verbal IQ deficits in these high-risk children, particularly those who show behavioral problems in middle childhood. Social deficits in this age-group are comparable to those found in other groups of clinically disturbed children, and are not specific to children of schizophrenics. Problems specific to families with a schizophrenic parent include low rates of interaction, low warmth, and more sibling rivalry.

    <u>Adolescence</u>. Adolescent children of schizophrenics have been found to have deficits in motor coordination, balance, and sensory perception, difficulty with information processing, higher scores on the schizophrenic and psychopathic deviate scales of the MMPI, more social isolation, and more "micropsychotic" experiences. High-risk adolescents have IQ scores lower than they had in middle childhood, and lower than offspring of nonpsychotic parents. All studies reviewed found evidence of social dysfunction in adolescence among the high-risk group, including poor affective control and difficulty making friends. Adolescents who exhibited a failure to inhibit negative behavior during interaction with their parents were more likely to develop schizophrenia spectrum disorders five years later. Parental behaviors associated with increased risk for development of schizophrenia include communication deviance, negative affective climate, and high expressed emotion.

    <u>Early adulthood</u>. Studies of biological children of schizophrenics reared in adoptive homes point to a diathesis-stress model: children of schizophrenics, but not those of non-schizophrenics, were more likely to develop schizophrenia spectrum disorders if raised in disturbed adoptive homes than if raised in healthy adoptive homes. Further, children of schizophrenics raised by their biological parents were less likely to develop schizophrenia if they had satisfactory relationships with their parents.

Apparently, genetic vulnerability, attributes of the rearing environment, and attributes of the child interact in the development of schizophrenia; the direction of the effects is not yet clear.

Efficient Treatment of Schizophrenia

As is discussed in the text, several controlled studies have demonstrated that family therapy is highly effective in reducing the relapse rates of schizophrenics, particularly when this treatment succeeds in reducing the expressed emotion (EE) of High-EE relatives. Indeed, educational or behavioral family therapy in conjunction with neuroleptic medication is becoming the treatment of choice in the schizophrenia literature. More recently, efforts are being made to discover what components are necessary to improve the relapse rates of schizophrenics. Regular family therapy sessions, often held in the patient's home, require a great deal of professional time; is there a more efficient way of accomplishing the same result?

This question was addressed in a recent study by Leff, Berkowitz, Shavit, Strachan, Glass, and Vaughn (1989, British Journal of Psychiatry, 154, 58-66). Subjects in the study were schizophrenics with at least one relative rated as high in expressed emotion and having at least 35 hours per week of face-to-face contact with the patient. The 23 subjects who met these criteria were randomly assigned to two groups; one group received family therapy twice monthly, conducted in the patient's home, and families in the other group were invited to attend a twice monthly relatives group led by a professional, outside of the home. All subjects also received anti-psychotic medication, and all families received two sessions of education about schizophrenia, conducted in their homes, without the patient present. The primary aim of the study was to determine whether the relatives group, which required much less professional time, was as effective as family therapy in reducing relapse.

The results suggested that when families complied with the treatment offered, family therapy and the relatives group were equally effective in reducing relapse. Relapse rates were 8% for the family therapy group and 17% for those who complied with the relatives group (a non-significant difference). (A control group receiving standard individual supportive treatment and medication had a 50% relapse rate, consistent with findings from other studies.) However, the families assigned to the relatives group were much less likely to comply with the treatment; while 11 out of 12 families complied with family therapy, 5 out of 11 of the relatives group failed to attend a single session. Those subjects who did not comply with the treatment had a 60%

relapse rate, comparable to the control group.

The authors conclude that for those families who are willing and able to attend a relatives group, this form of treatment provides an effective and more efficient means of preventing relapse. Since many families do not comply with this treatment, however, alternative treatments should be available. Previous research by the same authors suggested that one or two sessions of family therapy in the home by the professional who leads the relatives group is sufficient to ensure that most families will subsequently attend the group. For those families who cannot or will not attend a group outside their home, family therapy remains an effective option.

NOTES

DISCUSSION STIMULATORS

Biographies of Mental Illness

It may be useful to assign a biography for the class to read in order to have them get a closer feel for the phenomenology and social reactions to serious mental disorders. Sylvia Plath's The Bell Jar and Mark Vonnegut's The Eden Express are two excellent accounts. You may also want students to render a diagnosis after reading the biography. It has been suggested that the cases of "schizophrenia" that are portrayed in such popular literature are really misdiagnoses, and that this leads to undue optimism about the possibility of recovery from schizophrenia. See North and Cadoret (1981, Archives of General Psychiatry, 38, 133-137) for a detailed discussion of the appropriate diagnoses for the characters portrayed in the two books mentioned above, as well as other biographies.

Genetic Counseling

What sort of genetic counseling would members of the class offer to an apparently healthy 25-year-old who wanted to have children but had a schizophrenic parent? Along the same lines, what sort of intervention programs (or childrearing experiences) would the class members want to provide to children at risk for developing schizophrenia? Encourage the students to try to apply research findings, not just speculate.

Mental Hospitals

Have any of the class members ever been in or worked in a mental hospital? What were their experiences like? What was the physical layout of the ward and how did this affect patient behavior? Was there much contact between the patients and the professional staff? What would it be like to be a patient there?

The Right to Refuse Treatment

While discussed in the text in Chapter 21, the issue of the right to refuse treatment, particularly antipsychotic medication, often arises in the treatment of schizophrenia. Appelbaum (1988, American Journal of Psychiatry, 145, 413-419) recently reviewed and discussed court decisions on the right to refuse antipsychotic medications. While the right of voluntarily committed inpatients to refuse medication has been accepted easily, the issue becomes more complicated with involuntary patients: why commit a patient because they are judged to need treatment, and then allow them to refuse that treatment? Changes in the commitment laws in the 1970s led to a criterion of dangerousness (to self or others), rather than need for treatment, as the rationale for involuntary commitment; this change made the right to refuse treatment less illogical (dangerous behavior could be controlled by hospitalization without medication).

Since the Supreme Court has never decided the issue, state laws vary, though all have established some degree of right to refuse treatment. Treatment-driven approaches to the issue limit patients' interests to the receipt of appropriate care; if a person is involuntarily committed, the physician's judgment determines what treatment is given, regardless of the patient's wishes. In some variations of this approach, an independent clinical review must support the physician's decision before a patient's refusal can be overridden. The treatment-driven model is generally favored by clinicians and administrators, and opposed by patients' rights advocates.

The rights-driven approach emphasizes the right of competent patients to control the treatment they receive. In different variations of the model, the determination of competence may be made by clinical review, or by a judge, either during the commitment hearing or after commitment. In general, the latter variation is most palatable to patients' rights groups, and raises concern among clinicians that patients will not receive needed treatment (and that clinicians' judgments of appropriate treatment are being distrusted).

After presenting these models for addressing the issue, (and possibly assigning the above article, plus a first person account by a parent upset by her daughter's successful refusal of treatment [Slater, 1986, Schizophrenia Bulletin, 12, 291-292]) you might set up a debate in class between four principals: (1) a patients' rights advocate, (2) a concerned clinician, (3) a parent of a schizophrenic young adult who has refused treatment, and (4) a schizophrenic patient who has refused to take antipsychotic medication. Students not participating in the debate could be asked to serve as high court judges and reach a decision on the issue.

INSTRUCTIONAL FILMS

1. <u>Schizophrenia: The Shattered Mirror</u>. (UCEMC-6799, 60 min., 1966) Discusses possible causes of schizophrenia and various somatic and psychological treatments. Somewhat dated in its description of treatment, but an excellent opportunity for students to see actual schizophrenic patients.

2. <u>Victorian Flower Paintings: Pictorial Record of a Schizophrenic Episode</u>. (UCEMC-7641, 7 min., 1968) "Rare, breathtaking clinical history of schizophrenia as manifested in a folio of floral watercolors painted by an unknown person between 1863 and 1868. The first serene paintings give way to grotesqueries; at the climax of the illness, the paintings are wild, chaotic; then the mood gradually subsides, violence disappears, and the last few paintings are as gentle and tranquil as the first. Modern commentary points out distortions and explains them."

3. <u>A True Madness</u>. (BBC-TV, Time-Life Films, 35 min., b&w, 1971) Researchers discuss possible causes of schizophrenia. Film also includes conversations with schizophrenics.

4. <u>Through a Glass Darkly</u>. (JF, b & w, 1961) Depicts the schizophrenic process, both before the onset of the disease and as the female character experiences hallucinations.

5. <u>Escape from Madness</u>. (Films, Inc., 52 min., color, 1978) "Examines treatment of the mentally ill in the 1970s. Discusses breakthroughs in drugs which eliminate bizarre behavior and tendencies toward madness. Shows the social treatment-management of the lives and minds of people unable to cope with everyday reality."

6. <u>R. D. Laing: A Dialog on Mental Illness and its Treatment</u>. (HAR, 22 min., color, 1976) An interview in which Laing discusses schizophrenia, hysteria, the semantics of psychiatry, therapy, and his criticisms of psychiatry.

CHAPTER 15

Emotional and Behavioral Disorders of Childhood and Adolescence

CHAPTER SYNOPSIS

Classification

While DSM-I and II treated childhood problems as downward extensions of adult disorders, the current diagnostic system reflects increased knowledge about childhood disorders and the influence of developmental psychopathology. Disorders of childhood are now viewed within the context of knowledge about normal life-span development. A useful classification, which organizes the present chapter, divides childhood disorders into those of undercontrol (behavior excesses) and those of overcontrol (behavior deficits). Other disorders discussed include anorexia nervosa and bulimia nervosa, and enuresis, which is discussed in a box.

Disorders of Undercontrolled Behavior

The undercontrolled child lacks control over behavior that is expected in a given setting for a child of that age. Behaviors are defined as problems depending on their topography--their type and form.

Attention-deficit Hyperactivity Disorder

Previously known as hyperactivity, minimal brain dysfunction, or hyperkinesis, the term attention-deficit hyperactivity disorder now focuses on the difficulty concentrating and non-goal-oriented motor movements which characterize this common behavior problem. The inattention and impulsiveness of these children are often associated with academic difficulties. Conduct problems and difficulty with peer relationships are other common associated problems. While the overactivity usually diminishes with age, attention problems and academic difficulties continue at least into adolescence.

Physiological theories of the causes of ADHD include heredity, food additives, underarousal, and brain damage; while each theory explains some cases of ADHD, none has been strongly confirmed by research. Psychological theories have focused on the childrearing environment. While mothers of hyperactive children have been found to be more critical and less affectionate than other mothers, the causal direction is not clear; it may be that rearing a difficult child causes such characteristics in parents.

Stimulant medication is a common treatment for hyperactivity, and has been shown to lead to dramatic short-term improvements. Unfortunately, such drugs have little effect over the long term. Treatments based on learning principles include operant reinforcement for classroom and home behavior. The optimal treatment seems to require the use of both stimulants and behavior therapy.

Conduct Disorders

The term conduct disorders covers many behaviors which violate societal norms and the basic rights of others. Two types are distinguished: conduct disorder-group type and conduct disorder-solitary aggressive type. In general, conduct problems are defined by the impact of the child's behavior on people and surroundings; moral judgments are inherent in our conception of the disorder. Research indicates that antisocial behavior, and particularly aggression, are remarkably stable; the long-term prognosis for children with conduct disorder is poor.

Genetics, family conflict, and childrearing have all been implicated in the etiology of conduct disorders. Research into the background of these children reveals a pattern of family life lacking in factors believed to be central to the development of a strong moral sense, such as affection, firm moral demands, and consistent, non-physical discipline. The family environment of conduct-disordered children has been hypothesized as failing to help them develop a superego, or leading to modeling and reinforcement of antisocial behavior. Patterson's coercion hypothesis suggests that conduct problems are rewarded inadvertently; parents give in to the child's demands in order to stop the unpleasant behavior in the short term. Finally, sociological factors such as poverty appear to contribute to delinquency and conduct problems.

Just as antisocial behavior in adulthood is notoriously difficult to treat, conduct problems in childhood and adolescence present a challenge to contemporary society. Some of the most promising approaches involve intervening with the parents of the antisocial child; they are taught social learning principles and learn to reward prosocial behavior and limit antisocial behavior consistently. Direct intervention with the children themselves is based on findings that children with aggressive behavior seem to have a cognitive bias toward interpreting ambiguous acts as being hostile. Anger-control training has been used to teach aggressive children self-control in anger-provoking situations. While these measures are preventive, children or adolescents who have already had contact with the juvenile justice system are more difficult to treat. In fact, studies of "diversion" suggest that avoiding contact with the court system may be essential to success in treating delinquents.

Disorders of Overcontrolled Behavior

Overcontrolled behavior usually creates more problems for the individual child than for others. Childhood fears, social withdrawal, and depression are the specific problems discussed in this section.

Childhood Fears

Most children have many fears that are outgrown in the normal course of development. Fearful children, not having the experience to know their fears are baseless, may suffer greatly; many have physical symptoms and chronic anxiety. One childhood fear, school phobia, can be quite disruptive and does not usually subside with the passing of time. The roots of this phobia include actual fear of school and, particularly, separation anxiety which may be exacerbated by a parent's dependence on the child.

Gradual exposure to the feared object or situation is the most common treatment for childhood fears. Modeling, desensitization, and skills training are other methods used. Research suggests that time-limited treatment of children's phobias can be very effective.

A box in this section describes the use of play therapy and family therapy for treating childhood problems.

Social Withdrawal

Children with social-withdrawal disorder often have warm and satisfying relationships with family members, but are extremely quiet and shy with strangers, sometimes even showing elective mutism. This withdrawal may be caused by anxiety, lack of social skills, or lack of experience interacting with other children. Treatment of this problem usually involves social learning programs using modeling, gradual exposure, and social skills training.

Affective Disorders in Childhood

In the DSM-IIIR, the criteria for childhood depression are included in the diagnosis for adult depression; age-specific features include somatic complaints in children, and in adolescents, drug use and sensitivity to rejection in love relationships. Controversy surrounds the application of this diagnosis to children; some researchers assert that symptoms of adult depression are very common in children and should not be called a disorder, while others note that the whole syndrome of depressive disorder is a useful guide for targeting children in need of intervention.

Theories of the etiology of childhood depression point to a genetic factor and interpersonal relationships. Differences have been found between the mother-child, peer, and sibling relationships of depressed children and those of both normal children and children with diagnoses other than depression. However, the causal relationship between poor social bonds and depression has not yet been clarified.

While depression in young people heightens suicide risk, personal conflicts (such as the breakup of a love affair) and child abuse and neglect are also important contributors to suicide.

Eating Disorders

Anorexia Nervosa

In anorexia nervosa, serious weight loss, an intense fear of becoming obese, and a refusal to eat lead to life-threatening physiological changes. The disorder is much more common in young women than in men, and usually begins during adolescence. Preoccupation with food, a distorted body image, and perfectionism are associated with anorexia.

Anorexia nervosa has been explained as a substitute for sexual expression, a weight phobia, the result of societal pressure for thinness, and caused by organic malfunctioning. Treatment of the disorder includes immediate weight gain (often accomplished through hospitalization) and long-term maintenance of the weight gains. The latter goal is not reliably achieved through medical, behavioral, or psychodynamic interventions. Family therapy is a promising treatment, although long-term effects have not been adequately studied.

Bulimia Nervosa

Often referred to as the binge-purge syndrome, <u>bulimia nervosa</u> consists of episodes of gross overeating followed by induced vomiting or overdoses of laxatives. The purge may serve to reduce the anxiety and guilt caused by overeating. Bulimics frequently suffer periods of depression (discussed further in a box) and experience difficulties with interpersonal relationships, family problems, and work impairment. Physiological problems are common, especially if the purging involves vomiting. Treatment approaches include changing the equation of thinness with success, assertion training, self-monitoring, prevention of vomiting following binges, and anti-depressant medication.

Behavioral Pediatrics

A box in this chapter discusses the field of <u>behavioral pediatrics</u>, which usually studies normal children in abnormal situations such as chronic illness. The combination of behavior therapy and pediatrics may be used to help children and parents cope with long-term diseases and their treatments; pain is a particular problem accompanying cancer, hemophilia, and other diseases and addressed by behavioral pediatric practitioners. Other areas focused on in this field include obesity and therapeutic compliance.

NOTES

STUDENTS SHOULD KNOW . . .

Key Points

1. While previously understudied relative to adult disorders, childhood problems are receiving increasing attention in recent years.

2. Overcontrol and undercontrol are two broad dimensions of childhood disorders that are consistently identified. Overcontrolled behavior (behavior deficits) are most problematic for the individual child, while undercontrolled behavior (behavior excesses) create problems for those around the child.

3. Attention-deficit hyperactivity disorder is a disorder of undercontrolled behavior characterized by difficulties paying attention and excessive non-goal-oriented motor movements. Academic difficulties, conduct problems, and problems with peer relationships frequently accompany the disorder. They are treated using a combination of stimulant medication and behavior therapy.

4. Conduct disorders are defined by the child's impact on the environment. They tend to be long-lasting, and are treated primarily through parent training in social learning principles.

5. Childhood fears are common and are usually outgrown. School phobia is a more serious fear rooted in separation anxiety.

6. Social withdrawal may be caused by anxiety, poor social skills, or lack of experience interacting with children. Treatment for fears and withdrawal involves gradual exposure, modeling, and skills training.

7. Childhood depression is a controversial disorder, associated with poor interpersonal relationships and increased suicide risk.

8. Anorexia nervosa is characterized by severe, often life-threatening loss of weight. Bulimia nervosa involves binge-purge cycles. Much more common among females, these disorders involve a distortion of body image and preoccupation with weight.

New Terms
(key terms underlined)

undercontrolled, overcontrolled, attention-deficit hyper-activity disorder, topography, enuresis, bell and pad, conduct disorders, conduct disorder-group type, conduct disorder-solitary aggressive type, coercion hypothesis, separation anxiety disorder, avoidant disorder, school phobia, elective mutism, social-withdrawal disorder, anorexia nervosa, bulimia nervosa, play therapy, behavioral pediatrics

New Names
(key figures underlined)

Bruno Bettelheim, Gerald Patterson, Salvador Minuchin

NOTES

LECTURE LAUNCHERS

One Child's View of Being Hyperactive

The following are quotes from taped therapy sessions with a nine-year-old hyperactive boy named David. The quotes are taken from the front matter of Ross and Ross' excellent book, Hyperactivity (1982, New York: Wiley).

" . . . The very first day Mrs. K. (teacher) says, 'Oh, you're David J.,' and right in front of everyone she says when do I take my pills."

" . . . then the new girl says, 'Is your brother MR?' and Sal (sister) says that I got minimal brain dysfunction and the other girl says, 'That's MR.'"

"Chrissie Wilson had her Reckless Robert Robot in science class and it got started and wouldn't stop and Randy said, 'Man that robot's hyper just like Davey! Give it a pill, Davey,' and everyone laughed."

"The doctor says I'll be OK when I'm 14. Well, I'm only nine. He acts like 14 is next week."

"Dad started telling the Rec Leader about me and he just laughed and says, 'No problem, Mr. J., I was too and so was Tom Edison and two of my buddies who are in think tanks now' . . . and when he told who were the new ones that day all he said was, 'Glad to have you, Dave, I know your brother' . . . just like I'm like the other kids."

" . . . when it's special like a party I have to go to the sitter's . . . I heard my Mom say, 'If only we could send him away to school.'"

" . . . and then she (mother) gives Dad one of those looks and he like reads it and then he says, 'Maybe just Sal and Peter (brother) should go this time.' They think I'm really stupid. I know I never get picked to go . . . Every time is this time."

" . . . Sal has to take me places like I'm a dog and when we go to the Safeway where all the boys are Sal goes like, 'Mom, do I have to take Davey?' and she's practically crying. So when we get to the park I say, 'Sal, can I swing?' and she gets me on the way back."

"I don't get them (pills) weekends so I can grow and it's scary because I'm one of the smallest in my class now and how can I catch up on only growing two days a week?"

" . . . medications is like in a big thick space suit with ear muffs and things get real fuzzy like far off."

"I got no friends coz I don't play good and when they call me Dope Freak and David Dopey I cry, I just can't help it."

" . . . in my best one (daydream) I pretend I'm Richard Dean and it's the city play-off the next day and Mr. Simpson (P.E. teacher) looks at me and say, `We really need you tomorrow, Rich.'"

Learned Helplessness in Children

Evidence suggests that the reformulated learned helplessness model of depression, described in Chapter 9 of the text, is applicable to children as well. A recent study by Nolen-Hoeksema, Girgus, and Seligman (1986, Journal of Personality and Social Psychology, 51, 435-442) explored the relationship between negative life events, explanatory cognitive styles, and depression in 168 elementary school children. The following measures were administered: the Children's Depression Inventory, a forced-choice measure of explanatory style developed by Seligman, a Life Events Questionnaire, a Student Behavior Checklist (filled out by teachers), and an academic achievement test. The first three were administered five times over a period of one year, to obtain longitudinal data.

As predicted, the authors found that children with a maladaptive explanatory style (those who viewed bad events as having internal, stable, global causes) were more likely to be depressed both concurrently and at subsequent testing periods over the year. In addition, the interaction of experiencing several bad life events and having a maladaptive explanatory style was associated with higher levels of depression, supporting a diathesis-stress model of depression. The maladaptive explanatory style was also associated with lower achievement and more helpless behaviors in the classroom.

While a maladaptive explanatory style may be seen as a symptom of depression rather than as causing depression, analyses of the data indicated that the explanatory style predicted future depression, after initial depression was partialled out. Interestingly, depression at time 1 also predicted a subsequent maladaptive explanatory style, suggesting that depression may play a role in the development of this cognitive style. The causal relationships between depression and cognition are not yet clear. However, it is interesting to note that the learned helplessness model may help us to understand and treat depression in children as well as adults.

Treating Depression in Adolescents

Cognitive-behavioral therapy has been found to be highly effective in alleviating depression in adults. What about with adolescents? Reynolds and Coats (1986, Journal of Consulting and Clinical Psychology, 54, 653-660) compared cognitive-behavioral therapy and relaxation training for treating adolescents reporting depressive symptoms on the Beck Depression Inventory and/or the Reynolds Adolescent Depression Scale (no formal diagnosis of depression was made). Thirty subjects (average age = 15 1/2 years) were randomly assigned to a cognitive-behavioral therapy group, a relaxation training group, or a wait-list control group. One therapist conducted both treatments, and tapes of sessions were used to monitor adherence to the treatment condition. Both treatments involved meeting in groups of two to three students for ten sessions over a five-week period. Reinforcement was given for attendance and participation. The authors predicted that both types of treatment would be superior to the wait-list control, and that cognitive-behavior therapy would be more effective than relaxation training.

The results? On all depression measures, both treatment groups were significantly improved relative to the wait-list group, and there was no difference between the two types of treatment. Following treatment, depression scores for the treated subjects were in the normal range. These results held after a five-week follow-up. The following results are from the Reynolds and Coats article (p. 657):

Beck Depression Inventory Scores

	Pre-	Post-	Follow-up
cognitive-behavioral:	21	6	2
relaxation:	17	6	4
wait-list:	17	18	16

Effectiveness of Psychotherapy with Children

Casey and Berman (1985, Psychological Bulletin, 98, 388-400) provide an excellent review and meta-analysis of the results of 75 therapy outcome studies with children. Overall, they found that the average outcome for treated children was over two thirds of a standard deviation better than that of untreated children. This result is comparable to that found in studies of the effectiveness of therapy with adults.

When results were divided into those for behavioral vs. nonbehavioral treatment approaches, behavioral therapy faired much better. However, differences in the types of outcome measures used in studies of the two kinds of treatment may account for the apparent superiority of behavior therapy; behavior therapies were more likely to use outcome measures which were very similar to activities used as part of treatment. When studies using therapy-like outcome measures were excluded from the analysis, the overall effect size was reduced to just less than one half of a standard deviation, and the difference between behavioral and nonbehavioral treatments largely disappeared.

Other characteristics of therapy were also examined for differential effectiveness. Outcomes did not differ depending on whether or not play techniques were used, nor for individual vs. group treatments. Treatment involving parents did not differ in effectiveness from treatment administered to the children alone. Finally, neither experience, education, nor sex of the therapists related to treatment outcome. While briefer therapies were found to be more effective, this finding may have been due to the tendency of shorter treatments to use therapy-like outcome measures.

Regarding characteristics of the children, the greatest improvements were demonstrated for reducing fear and anxiety in the treated children; self-esteem, global adjustment, and social adjustment improved less. The lack of diagnostic information provided in most studies precluded clear conclusions about the relative effectiveness of therapy for different childhood disorders.

Overall, the results reviewed by Casey and Berman indicate that children receiving treatment improve significantly more than untreated children, and little evidence demonstrates one form of treatment to be superior to others.

Children's Rights in Psychological Treatment

Because children do not typically seek psychological treatment at their own instigation, Koocher has proposed a bill of rights for children in treatment (1976, <u>Children's rights and the mental health professions</u>. New York: Wiley). According to Koocher, children are entitled to:

The right to be told the truth. Although children's verbal reasoning may be somewhat limited, it remains the therapist's obligation to convey the goals and methods of treatment to the child.

The right to be treated as a person. While children are subject to legal restrictions which limit their autonomy, they are still entitled to basic human rights of confidentiality, privacy, and honesty.

The right to be taken seriously. What the child has to say has intrinsic value and should be heard.

The right to participate in decision-making. Although the child is not the sole person who will make a decision regarding treatment, the child has a right to input in the decision-making process.

NOTES

DISCUSSION STIMULATORS

Bell and Pad Demonstration

The bell and pad is available from Sears (Wee Alert!) and other department stores. This simple but clever biofeedback device can be purchased and easily demonstrated to the class. The reactions you are likely to receive in purchasing the device may also add material for discussion about stigmatization.

Personal Experiences with Divorce

Divorce is a prevalent event in contemporary American family life. It is estimated that one-third of the current generation of children will experience a parental divorce by the time they are 18. It is certain that a number of students in your class will have experienced a parental divorce. What do they believe the effects of divorce are on children? Is it harmful for life? Is it an easy transition? Was it a relief for some? What about divorce makes it hard--not seeing one parent as much, getting caught in loyalty bonds, feeling different from others, losing economic resources, etc.? What role should a child play in deciding where he or she is to live following a divorce? What advice would students who have gone through this experience give to parents to help their children adjust to the change?

Adjustment in "Latchkey" Children

As more women become employed and more families are headed by single parents, "latchkey" children--elementary-school-aged children who are regularly unsupervised after school for some period of time--are becoming more common. You might first ask students to discuss their ideas about the effects of self-care on children: Did they supervise themselves after school when they were in elementary school? Do they know youngsters (brothers/sisters, nieces/nephews) who might be classified as latchkey children? How do they imagine that variables like age, sex, socioeconomic status, length of time in self-care, etc. might influence the adjustment of these children? As an exercise in research design, you might ask them to design a study to determine the effects of self-care on children, attending to issues such as control groups, sampling, determining how to measure adjustment, and deciding what variables to measure in addition to adjustment and latchkey status.

255

Then, present some research findings about the adjustment of latchkey children (from Lovko, A. M. & Ullman, D. G., 1989, Journal of Clinical Child Psychology, 18, 16-24), and see how closely your students' research design and hypotheses fit the findings of an actual study. Lovko and Ullman studied 97 "latchkey" children (mean age = 10 1/2 years) and 19 control children who did not spend any time in self-care. Parents filled out information about demographic variables, stressful life events for the family, and a behavior problem checklist. Children completed measures of their general anxiety and self-efficacy in peer inter- actions. The authors found that background/demographic variables and latchkey situation variables accounted for a significant portion of the variance in the latchkey children's adjustment. The most anxiety was found in girls, children who had experienced more life stress, and children staying with other children while in self-care. Lower income children and children spending fewer hours in self- care were rated as having more behavior problems. Inter- estingly, no significant differences were found between the adjustment of latchkey and non-latchkey children. In summary, being a latchkey child was shown to be much less important for children's adjustment than were background/ demographic variables.

In discussing these results, students might be asked to consider factors other than adjustment which might be important to examine. For example, variables such as health, number of accidents, and feelings of safety might be affected by self-care. (See more articles on "children on their own" in this special issue of Journal of Clinical Child Psychology.)

Resource for Research on Children

An excellent resource for current information about children and their development, useful for more lecture material or for students to tap for term papers, is the February, 1989 issue of American Psychologist (44). This volume includes sections on "frontiers of current research" (developmental perspectives; learning and teaching), health and development (mental health and behavior disorders; children at risk), children and social change: social and behavioral problems, culture and American children, and children and social policy.

Bulimia on Campus

Another problem that is likely quite common among students in your class is bulimia. Some estimates suggest that as many as 20% of college females engage in some forms of binging and purging. Among some, it is the "perfect diet" and almost has a faddish quality. I ask my students to tell me about bulimia, as they know more about its social qualities than I do. This often leads into a discussion of feminism and what aspects of ourselves we value.

NOTES

INSTRUCTIONAL FILMS

1. **The Hyperactive Child**. (AV Services Penn State University, 34 min., color, 1969) Portrays a hyperactive child at home and at school. Some causes of and treatments for hyperactivity are discussed.

2. **Catch 'em Being Good**. (Research Press, 30 min., color, 1983) A presentation on a behavioral program for treating hyperactive children in the classroom.

3. **Child Aggression: A Social Learning Approach to Family Therapy**. (Research Press, 31 min., color, 16mm) "As a basic introduction to the social learning viewpoint for lay or student audiences, the film is a very worthwhile tool." Gerald Patterson demonstrates his behavioral approach.

4. **Scared Straight**. (Pyramid Films, Santa Monica, CA, 35 min., color, 16mm, 1978) Peter Falk narrates an intriguing film about juvenile offenders who are "scared straight" by prison inmates. Interesting and entertaining, but the optimistic conclusions about effectiveness have not been supported by subsequent research.

5. **Violent Youth: The Unmet Challenge**. (HR, 23 min., 1976) Three incarcerated juveniles describe their feelings about themselves, society, and their crimes.

6. **Afraid of School**. (AV Center, Indiana University, 31 min., b & w, 1965) Case study of school phobia.

7. **Adolescent Suicide**. (AACD, 39 min., color) Commentary by Dr. Seymour Perlin on the reasons for suicide and the nature of stressors that affect teenagers.

8. **Diet Unto Death: Anorexia Nervosa**. (MIT, 17 min., color video) Originally a segment on the television show "20/20," this film focuses on anorexic patients in a hospital setting.

CHAPTER 16

Learning Disabilities, Mental Retardation, and Autistic Disorder

CHAPTER SYNOPSIS

The focus of this chapter is developmental disorders, which are characterized by a disturbance in the acquisition of cognitive, language, motor, or social skills. The course of these disorders tends to be chronic, usually persisting into adulthood.

Learning Disabilities

Classified as specific developmental disorders in DSM-IIIR, the learning disabilities refer to a child's failure to develop to the degree expected by his or her intellectual level in a specific academic, language, or motor skill area. These disorders are more common in males and are usually identified and treated within the school system. Several forms of the disorder are specified in DSM-IIIR: Academic skills disorders include developmental reading disorder (dyslexia), developmental arithmetic disorder, and developmental expressive writing disorder. Language disorders can be receptive or expressive. In developmental articulation disorder, the child's speech sounds like baby talk. Finally, developmental coordination disorder is a motor skills disorder new to DSM-IIIR.

Evidence suggests that some learning disabilities may be genetically influenced, and researchers continue to look for neurological differences between learning disabled children and normal learners. While psychological theories have in the past focused on perceptual deficits as underlying dyslexia, recent research points to language-processing problems and deficiencies in verbal memory. Structural or hormonal differences and differences in sensorimotor integration between boys and girls may account for the some of the variation in learning between the sexes.

Treatment of learning disabilities has included linguistic approaches using a logical, sequential, multisensory method, cognitive approaches which correct deficits in metacognitive strategies, and behavioral techniques which use a success-oriented approach.

Mental Retardation

The DSM-IIIR definition of mental retardation is based on standards set by the American Association of Mental Deficiency; the criteria include (1) significant subaverage general intellectual functioning, (2) deficits in adaptive behavior, and (3) onset in childhood or adolescence.

Classification of Mental Retardation

Mild mental retardation comprises 85% of the retarded, most of whom show no signs of brain pathology, come from families with low intelligence and socioeconomic status, and can usually work in unskilled jobs as adults.

Moderate mental retardation comprises 10% of the retarded, and is frequently accompanied by brain damage and physical defects. While most cannot live independently, some of these individuals can do useful work and most learn self-care skills.

Severe mental retardation comprises 3-4% of retarded individuals, and is commonly accompanied by congenital physical abnormalities and limited sensorimotor control; most are institutionalized.

Profound mental retardation constitutes 1-2% of the retarded, and requires total supervision and nursing care.

Mentally retarded children are usually placed in classrooms based on their individual strengths, weaknesses, and the amount of instruction needed.

Nature of Mental Retardation

Mentally retarded individuals have deficiencies in adaptive skills needed for daily living, in the areas of communication, social skills, academics, sensorimotor skills, self-help, and vocational skills. Two aspects of general cognitive abilities may underlie these deficits in adaptive behavior: structural features, which are fixed, and control processes, which may be improved through training. Specific cognitive problems associated with mental retardation include attention to different aspects of stimuli and deficits in short-term memory, processing speed, executive functioning, and the control function of language.

Etiology of Mental Retardation

No Identifiable Etiology. For most cases of mental retardation, particularly those of mild or moderate severity, the etiology is unknown. Zigler proposed the developmental theory of etiology; rather than a structural deficit, retardation is seen as a normal expression of the population gene pool and caused by motivational factors. An alternative view hypothesizes that brain damage, too slight to be detected, underlies mild retardation.

Known Organic Etiology. A number of factors are known to cause mental retardation. Genetic or chromosomal causes include Down's syndrome or trisomy 21, usually identifiable through amniocentesis, and fragile X syndrome. Phenylketonuria is a recessive-gene disease in which a deficiency of liver enzyme causes brain damage if not corrected through diet. Infectious diseases present during pregnancy or in infancy can cause brain damage, as can accidents, prematurity, noxious chemical substances such as thalidomide and alcohol (which causes fetal alcohol syndrome), and environmental hazards such as lead and the DPT vaccine.

Prevention of Mental Retardation

The eugenics movement in the early 1900s advocated segregation and sterilization as means of preventing mental retardation; forced sterilization continued until the 1960s. Current prevention efforts include early intervention for children at risk through impoverished circumstances; Project Head Start is the best-known example.

Treatment of Mental Retardation

"Deinstitutionalization" involves providing retarded individuals with educational and community services rather than institutional care. Community residences have enabled many individuals to live more independently, and the majority who remain in institutions are severely or profoundly retarded with physical handicaps.

Early intervention programs seek to improve the eventual functioning of retarded individuals through training in specific behavioral objectives. While improvements in some areas have been demonstrated, long-term changes in IQ and school performance have not been achieved.

Public Law 94-142, passed in 1975, requires the education of all handicapped children within the public school system and in the least restrictive environment, with annual review of individual education programs.

Teaching strategies for retarded children include applied behavior analysis for teaching adaptive skills, and cognitive therapy to improve the cognitive and social functioning of children with mild to moderate retardation. For those children with speech difficulties, nonvocal communication is taught.

Autistic Disorder

Autistic disorder is characterized by extreme autistic aloneness, failure to develop social relations and learn language, and ritualistic and compulsive activities. About 80% of autistic children are mentally retarded, though their pattern of cognitive deficits is different. The social development of autistic children is extremely deficient; they may never form an attachment to their caregiver or to other children, showing more interest in inanimate objects than people. About 50% of autistic children never learn to speak, and even when they do, peculiarities such as echolalia and pronoun reversal are evident. Ritualistic acts such as rocking and even self-injurious behavior are common; a box discusses the treatment of such behaviors. The prognosis for children with autistic disorder is very poor.

Boxes in the chapter discuss the idiot savant and classification of pervasive developmental disorders.

Etiology of Autistic Disorder

Both psychoanalytic and social-learning theorists have suggested that parents cause autism in their children; systematic investigations have failed to support this view. While genetic studies are difficult to conduct with such a rare disorder, evidence from family and twin studies does suggest a genetic basis to autism. Neurological dysfunction has been found in a large percentage of autistic children, including EEG abnormalities and underdevelopment of the cerebellum; still, many autistic children show no signs of brain damage, and most brain-damaged children are not autistic.

Treatment of Autistic Disorder

Several problems make treatment of autistic children difficult: they do not adjust well to changes in routines, behavior problems and stereotyped behavior interfere with learning, effective reinforcers are difficult to find, their attention is often limited to one aspect of a stimulus, and

they have extreme difficulty generalizing learning.
Behavior therapy techniques have had the most success;
Lovaas' intensive operant program enabled many young
autistic children to achieve normal functioning in school.
Bettelheim's psychodynamic milieu treatment has not been
studied in controlled investigations. Evidence of elevated
serotonin levels in autistic children led to treatment with
fenfluramine. While early reports of its effectiveness were
quite positive, some recent investigations have failed to
replicate these findings and raised concern about negative
side effects.

NOTES

STUDENTS SHOULD KNOW . . .

Key Points

1. Learning disabilities are specific developmental disorders, deficits in a particular academic area relative to the child's intellectual level.

2. Mental retardation is defined as (1) significant subaverage intellectual functioning, (2) deficits in adaptive behavior, and (3) onset during childhood.

3. Mentally retarded individuals have difficulty in a variety of areas, including adaptive and self-help skills, communication and social skills, academic and vocational skills, and sensorimotor skills. They also show deficits in general cognitive abilities.

4. The specific etiology for the majority of cases, those of mild retardation, is unknown. These cases have been attributed to normal variations in intelligence, cultural deprivation, or undetected brain impairment.

5. The known causes of mental retardation include genetic or chromosomal abnormalities, recessive-gene diseases, infectious diseases, accidents, prematurity, noxious chemical substances, and environmental hazards.

6. Current treatment of retardation includes deinstitutionalization and education in the least restrictive setting. Teaching strategies include applied behavior analysis, cognitive-behavior therapy, and nonvocal communication.

7. Autistic disorder is characterized by extreme autistic aloneness, failure to develop social relations and learn language, and ritualistic behaviors. Most autistic children are also mentally retarded. The prognosis for the disorder is very poor.

8. The specific etiology of autistic disorder remains unknown. However, some sort of physiological, rather than psychological, factor is almost certainly the cause.

9. Highly structured social-learning treatments have been successful in reducing self-injury, improving communication and self-care skills, and, in a recent study, improving social and academic functioning, in autistic children.

New Terms
(key terms underlined)

specific developmental disorders, learning disabilities, academic skills disorders, developmental reading disorder, dyslexia, developmental arithmetic disorder, developmental expressive writing disorder, developmental articulation disorder, developmental coordination disorder, mental retardation, adaptive behavior, visual recognition memory, mild, moderate, severe, and profound mental retardation, structural features, control processes, executive functioning, Down's syndrome or trisomy 21, fragile X syndrome, phenylketonuria (PKU), fetal alcohol syndrome, eugenics movement, deinstitutionalization, Public Law 94-142, individual educational programs, applied behavior analysis, autistic disorder, extreme autistic aloneness, echolalia, pronoun reversal, idiot savant, pervasive developmental disorders, childhood schizophrenia, time-out, fenfluramine

New Names
(key figures underlined)

American Association of Mental Deficiency, Edmund Zigler, Langdon Down, Project Head Start, Leo Kanner, Ivar Lovaas

NOTES

Chapter 16

LECTURE LAUNCHERS

The Genetics of Various Childhood Disorders

McGuffin and Gottesman have written a superb summary of the methods of behavioral genetics for studying psychopathology in which they present some interesting and provocative data regarding various psychological disorders of childhood (In Rutter and Hersov, 1985, Child and Adolescent Psychiatry. London: Blackwell Scientific). Among the conclusions that these investigators have reached are the following:

Infantile autism: While existing data can be used to support a polygenic model for the disorder (they did not include the Ritvo data discussed below in their review), the data are also consistent with the possibility that in utero insult is the cause of the disorder. They note that for congenital malformations which are caused by the in utero environment, concordance rates of 34% are found for MZ twins, while for DZ twins they are .7%. These rates are very similar to those reported by Folstein and Rutter, as mentioned below.

Delinquency: There is no evidence to support a genetic model of delinquency; rather, a familial model is supported. They do suggest that data support a genetic model of adult antisocial behavior, however, which creates a paradox. If there is considerable consistency between delinquency and antisocial behavior in adulthood, how can genetics explain one but not the other? No conclusive answer to the puzzle is offered.

Reading difficulties: Data clearly support a familial clustering of reading disorders, but genetic data are more equivocal. There are at least some data, however, to support a genetic model.

Hyperactivity: Some data support a genetic model, but the inadequacy of existing studies, particularly in regard to diagnosis, preclude any firm conclusions.

Enuresis: There are familial and twin data which suggest that genetics plays a role in the disorder.

Chapter 16

What is Intelligence?

While traditional IQ tests have demonstrated their validity for predicting success in school (at least in Western societies), critics have argued that such a criterion does not capture the full meaning of the word "intelligence." Howard Gardner, in particular, has proposed a theory of "multiple intelligences" to encompass a broader vision of the nature of the mind (1983, Frames of Mind, New York: Basic Books). His prerequisites for an area of skill to be called an intelligence include: (1) it must enable the individual to resolve genuine problems or difficulties and create (where appropriate) an effective product, and (2) it must include the potential for finding or creating problems. In other words, the skill must be useful in some way, although the value of particular abilities can vary across cultures and time frames: the navigational skills of an Indian sailor, the musical prowess of a Mozart, the language ability of a Dostoyevski, all may be seen as useful within the individual's culture (though perhaps not in another culture).

In addition, Gardner has outlined a number of criteria or "signs" which most often signal the presence of a separate intelligence: (1) potential isolation by brain damage, (2) the existence of idiots savants, prodigies, and other exceptional individuals within the domain of ability, (3) an identifiable core operation or set of operations, (4) a distinctive developmental history and definable set of "end-state" performances, (5) an evolutionary history and evolutionary plausibility, (6) support from experimental psychological tasks, (7) support from psychometric findings, and (8) susceptibility to encoding in a symbol system.

Finally, Gardner presents his provisional compilation of six domains which qualify as separate intelligences: linguistic, musical, logical-mathematical, spatial, bodily-kinesthetic, and personal intelligences (the latter includes the ability to access one's own feeling life, and the ability to notice and make distinctions among other individuals, particularly their moods, temperaments, motivations, etc.). Students might be encouraged to evaluate this set of candidates for intelligence, arguing for the exclusion of any of the domains, the inclusion of other domains not listed, and the value of considering multiple areas of intelligence vs. the traditional conception of intelligence favored in our society.

Chapter 16

The Scope of PL 94-142

While the text emphasizes the importance of Public Law 94-142 for mentally retarded children, it is worth informing students of the broader scope of the law and its influence on education in the 15 years since its implementation. Since the passage of PL 94-142, public schools are required to provide (or pay for a private school to provide) adequate education for all handicapped children, including those with severe emotional disturbance and specific learning disabilities, as well as those with severe developmental disabilities such as mental retardation and autism. This law greatly increased the responsibility of the public school system for educating all children, and has required school districts to develop programs for both assessing the needs of special-needs children and for providing specialized education when indicated, either within a normal classroom, through a separate classroom within the public school, or through providing funds for a specialized private classroom.

A Twin Study of Autism

Ritvo and colleagues recently reported data comparing the concordance for autism among MZ and DZ twins (1985, American Journal of Psychiatry, 142, 74-77). Before briefly summarizing the results of this investigation, it should be noted how rare it is to find an autistic child who is also a twin. If five out of every ten thousand children are autistic and one out of every seventy births is a twin, then, assuming the two events are independent, five out of every 700,000 births contain an autistic twin. This information may help the class to appreciate Ritvo's report on 40 twins pairs.

The findings? Of the 23 monozygotic twin pairs in the sample, 22 or 95.7% were concordant for autism. Of the 17 dizygotic pairs, 4 or 23.5% were concordant. This remarkable finding contrasts with earlier data obtained by Folstein and Rutter who found higher concordance among MZ than DZ twins, but the concordance rate for MZ twins was 34% while it was 0% for the DZ twins. Ritvo posits that these data support the notion that autism is a disorder caused by autosomal recessive inheritance, since one would expect a concordance rate of 100% for MZ twins and 25% for DZ twins if this were the case. It will be difficult to replicate these results for the reasons outlined above, but the data seem compelling enough that a search for a genetic marker should be vigorously pursued.

Controversy and the Lovaas Findings on Treatment of Autism

The landmark Lovaas (1987) study described in the text reports that nearly half of the autistic children given the intensive experimental treatment achieved "normal functioning" by the end of the program. Normal functioning in this study was defined as an IQ above 80 and successful participation in a mainstream public school classroom. These dramatic and unusual results have generated considerable controversy, as researchers challenge the methodology and conclusions of the study. Students may benefit from reading the comments in _Journal of Counseling and Clinical Psychology_ (1989, 57, 162-167) by Schopler, Short, and Mesibov, and the rejoinder by Lovaas and colleagues. But first, students could be asked to meet in groups and come up with a proposal for a treatment outcome study of autism, including how they would choose subjects, how subjects would be assigned to treatment groups, and what outcome measures they would use. This exercise will alert them to the issues which arise in designing treatment outcome research, and increase their appreciation of the points raised in the Lovaas controversy.

Schopler et al. challenge the Lovaas study on three points: (1) the usual outcome measures, such as standard assessments of social, behavioral, and communication functioning before and after treatment, were not used. The classroom placement criterion used by Lovaas may be influenced more by school policies regarding special-needs children and advocacy by parents and treatment staff than by actual changes in the children. IQ changes may reflect increased compliance rather than improvement in cognitive functioning. (2) Schopler et al. assert that the method of subject selection was biased, resulting in a relatively high functioning subject group. (3) The control group in the Lovaas study was criticized as being inadequate: control subjects were not assigned to the group randomly and may have been those whose parents were less involved, and the control treatment involved less time and energy, so that greater improvements in the experimental group may have been the result of greater attention rather than the specific (and costly) behavioral techniques employed.

In their reply, Lovaas, Smith, and McEachin address each of the points raised by Schopler et al., defending their choice of outcome measures as clinically relevant, challenging the assertion that their subjects were higher functioning than other groups of autistic children, and noting that an attention control group would not be expected to achieve a favorable outcome, based on the failure of dedicated and attentive parents and teachers to cure the disorder.

Chapter 16

The Idiot Savant

Most students are intrigued by the idiot savant syndrome, and the movie <u>Rain Man</u>, featuring Dustin Hoffman in the role of an "autistic savant," has probably piqued their interest. In a fascinating and comprehensive article, Treffert (1988, <u>American Journal of Psychiatry</u>, <u>145</u>, 563-572) reviews the world literature on the idiot savant syndrome, describes recent cases, catalogs idiot savant abilities, and outlines theories to explain the condition.

<u>Definition</u>. The term "idiot savant" was coined a century ago to describe individuals with very limited intellectual capacity who possess a remarkable island of ability, skill, or knowledge. The condition occurs in males more frequently than females in a ratio of approximately 6:1. (This ratio could be accounted for by the higher male to female ratio in autistic disorder.) The classic early work describing the syndrome is Tredgold's chapter in his textbook, <u>Mental Deficiency</u> (1914, New York: Williams Wood). Approximately 100 cases of savants have been described in the literature to date.

<u>Categories of Skills</u>. The following skills are found in case studies of savants: mechanical ability, lightening calculation and mathematical ability, exceptional mnemonic skills, calendar calculating, musical skills (in particular, a triad of blindness, musical genius, and mental retardation has been identified), map memorizing, visual measurement, extrasensory perception, unusual sensory discrimination, writing and composition based on memorization, and perfect appreciation of past or passing time without knowledge of a clock face. The abilities most commonly found in savants are music and memory, which are often linked in the same individual.

<u>Theories to Explain the Savant</u>. No single theory has been able to explain the savant syndrome; what follows is a brief description of the major theories advanced thus far. (1) Vivid eidetic imagery has been used to explain the skill of calendar calculation. (2) Savants may coincidentally inherit two sets of factors, one for mental retardation and one for special ability. (3) Sensory deprivation due to social isolation or defective sensory channels has been hypothesized to lead to boredom and thus sensitize the savant to minute changes in the environment and bizarre or trivial preoccupations, concentration, or rituals. (4) Unable to think abstractly, savants may come to rely on concrete thinking. (5) The savant's special abilities may be developed to compensate for limited general skills and be reinforced by praise. (6) A number of organic explanations have been proposed, including left brain damage (leading to retardation) accompanied by compensatory development of the right hemisphere, and idiosyncratic brain circuitry.

Recent Findings. Several recent cases of the savant syndrome have emerged in the literature: a 30-year-old sculptor with an IQ of 40 who creates life-size bronze works of animals (he was featured on a 60 Minutes television program), and several individuals with severe mental retardation who are highly skilled musically, able to understand the rules of musical structure and to improvise. One 35-year-old man has perfect pitch and exceptional musical memory (he can reproduce lengthy piano compositions after a single hearing) despite blindness, mental retardation, and extremely limited speech and language skills. Newly enhanced communication between researchers and through the media has enabled more sizable samples to be gathered than was previously possible, providing the opportunity for controlled studies to be carried out in the future.

Hormonal effects on brain structure have recently been proposed to explain the predominance of males with the savant syndrome and the predominance of right brain skills in savants. This hypothesis is supported by findings of left hemisphere damage in savants, their unusual frequency of left-handedness, and evidence of motor and language functions being "taken over" by the right hemisphere. An abnormally high incidence of prenatal or perinatal complications in these patients suggests an ischemic-hypoxic injury as a cause of the syndrome. Other researchers have distinguished the savant's noncognitive "habit" formation system from a truly cognitive "memory" system, suggesting that different neuronal circuits underlie the two types of memory. Support for this hypothesis comes from findings of idiosyncrasies in the hippocampus, selected areas of the amygdala, the cerebellum, and other forebrain areas in savant subjects.

NOTES

DISCUSSION STIMULATORS

Should Learning Disabilities be Classified as
Mental Disorders?

The DSM-IIIR manual itself questions the inclusion of specific developmental disorders within a classification of mental disorders, since many learning disabled children evidence no signs of emotional disturbance. Students might be asked to discuss the advantages, disadvantages, and implications of such a classification.

Mainstreaming

Mainstreaming and deinstitutionalization are two important and politically sensitive topics. What perspectives do the class members have on these issues? Would they be willing to live near a group home for the retarded? If they already lived in a neighborhood where it was proposed to build a group home, would they be concerned about the impact on property values? Did they attend classes that had been "mainstreamed"? Did/does mainstreaming help those who are different by teaching others that they are not that different, or did/does mainstreaming set up the child who is different for social rejection and stigmatization?

Treatment of Self-Injurious Behavior

As discussed in Box 16.3 in the text, there are times when psychologists and other mental health workers employ aversive means for controlling self-injurious behavior (SIB), particularly with retarded and autistic children. In a manner similar to the work of the Association for the Advancement of Behavior Therapy task force, students might be asked to debate the ethical issues surrounding the use of aversive procedures for reducing SIB and come up with guidelines to govern the use of such techniques. They should consider in their discussion the conditions under which aversive punishment might be appropriate, alternatives to the use of aversives, the cost of not employing an effective though controversial treatment, the concerns of parents and other advocates for the rights of retarded individuals, and ways to evaluate the effectiveness of the procedures.

Naturalistic Use of Behavioral Principles: Helen Keller's Teacher

Social-learning techniques are often portrayed in very mechanistic ways. But the naturalistic use of behavioral principles is a goal of behavior therapists even if it is not always presented as such. An excellent example of the naturalistic use of contingencies can be seen in the movie The Miracle Worker. Helen Keller's teacher, Anne Sullivan, understood behavioral principles, at least intuitively. As the movie demonstrates, she relied on these principles heavily in teaching Helen to speak.

NOTES

INSTRUCTIONAL FILMS

1. <u>Aphasia in Childhood</u>. (USC, 30 min., b & w) The film describes the communication difficulties of a 12-year-old girl, including her language comprehension and usage skills, arithmetic skills, and progress in speech therapy. The girl was normal until the age of 10, when she suffered a head injury resulting in expressive and receptive aphasia.

2. <u>One Child in a Hundred</u>. (BBC-TV, Time-Life film, 20 min) Discusses techniques of developing retarded children's capabilities, the question of whether to institutionalize, and the problems of adjusting to and living with a mentally retarded child.

3. <u>Debbie</u>. (SH, 15 min., b & w) Without narration or professional commentary, this film covers many areas of the life of a mentally retarded girl and her struggle to become self-sufficient.

4. <u>Mental Retardation: The Long Childhood of Timmy</u>. (McG, 53 min., b & w) The film is a warm depiction of a mongoloid child, making the transition from his family to a school for the retarded.

5. <u>Hewitt's Just Different</u>. (TLM, 47 min.) Portrays the friendship between a 16-year-old retarded boy and his 12-year-old neighbor.

6. <u>Harry</u>. (Research Press, 38 min., color) Popular documentary film about the behavioral treatment of self-injury.

7. <u>Education for All Children</u>. (Research Press, 28 min., color) Attitudes toward handicapped children are examined, and the Right to Education Movement is discussed.

8. <u>Autism's Lonely Children</u>. (PCR, 20 min., 1967) An excellent film which portrays many of the psychological disorders of childhood.

9. <u>A Broken Bridge</u>. (TLM, 35 min., color, 1980) A therapy session with autistic children focusing on establishing communication.

CHAPTER 17

Aging and Psychological Disorders

CHAPTER SYNOPSIS

Concepts and Methods in the Study of Older Adults

In order to describe the diversity of the elderly, gerontologists divide those over 65 into three groups: the young-old (aged 65 to 74), the old-old (aged 75 to 84), and the oldest-old (over 85 years old). Chronological age is a complicated variable in psychological research because of the need to tease out such factors as age effects, cohort effects, and time-of-measurement effects. A cohort is a group of people who have been born within a certain time period. In cross-sectional research, people of different ages (and different cohorts) are studied at the same time; age differences, but not age changes, can thus be studied. A longitudinal study periodically re-tests one selected cohort; while this allows age changes to be examined, conclusions are limited to one cohort, and selective mortality is a problem. Time-of-measurement effects also limit the conclusions drawn from longitudinal studies, as third variables may influence measurement.

In addition to the above factors, problems in the classification of psychopathology among the aged, as well as concurrent social and physical changes, make the study of psychological disorders among this group a difficult task.

Some Basic Facts about Older Adults

The proportion of older people in the population has increased greatly in the past century, and is continuing to grow. Women are overrepresented among the elderly.

Many physical functions decline with age, and over 80% of older persons have at least one chronic illness. Still, most people over 65 are able to function independently.

Research suggests that some intellectual abilities, particularly measures of fluid intelligence, decline with age, while crystallized intelligence may even improve with age. Older people generally do better on verbal than performance tests of intelligence. Cohort and health effects complicate these findings.

Age differences in learning generally disappear when the elderly are given more time to learn new material. While complex memory tasks are generally more difficult for older people, few older adults feel handicapped by forget-fulness. Medications and anxiety may account for the memory impairments found in the elderly.

A number of cross-sectional and longitudinal studies indicate that for personality, stability rather than change with age is the rule.

Health care for the elderly is expensive, though a recent extension in Medicare to cover catastrophic expenses may help. Medical care is often inadequate, as many maladies are chronic and physicians become discouraged.

Poverty, particularly among non-whites and women, is a serious problem for many of the elderly. The majority of older adults live independently in the community, though up to 30% are estimated to live in substandard housing. The percentage of older people living in institutions does increase dramatically with age. Finally, ageism is reported to be prevalent in our society.

Brain Disorders of Old Age

Dementia

Dementia is a gradual deterioration of intellectual abilities to the point that social and occupational functioning are impaired. About half of all dementia cases are in the form of Alzheimer's disease. A box discusses the aftermath of cerebrovascular diseases such as stroke, which often causes aphasia, and cerebral hemorrhage, which usually disrupts all functions of the brain.

While some cases of dementia are reversible, there is no effective treatment available for reversing Alzheimer's disease. The focus of psychological interventions is educa-tion and support for both the patient and family members.

Delirium

One of the most frequent organic mental disorders in older adults, delirium is defined as a clouded state of consciousness, involving trouble concentrating, restless-ness, disorientation, and swings in activity and mood. The causes of delirium include drug intoxication, nutritional imbalance, infection, and stress. Complete recovery is possible if the underlying cause is identified and treated. Untreated, brain damage and mortality can result. Family members need to be educated about the symptoms of delirium and its reversible nature, so it is not misinterpreted as dementia and left untreated.

Chapter 17

Psychological Disorders of Old Age

Most psychopathology found in the elderly is **not** directly linked to the physiological processes of aging. A box in this chapter discusses the prevalence of mental disorders in later life.

Depression

Depression is less common in older than in younger adults, but accounts for half the admissions of older adults for acute psychiatric care. Depression is often misdiagnosed as dementia. Also, physical illness is linked to depression, probably due to both the emotional impact of illness and to medication side-effects. While bereavement may cause depression, most older people adapt to such life stresses without developing a mental disorder. Behavioral, cognitive, and brief psychodynamic therapies have been found to be very effective in treating depression in the elderly. Antidepressant medications may be less effective with this group, and more serious side-effects of medication indicate that nonpharmacological approaches are particularly important with the elderly.

Delusional (Paranoid) Disorders

The exact prevalence of paranoid disorders in the elderly is not known. It may be the continuation of a disorder that began earlier in life, or may accompany an organic brain disorder. Paranoid ideation has been linked to sensory losses, and particularly hearing; a box discusses the idea that paranoia may fill in the gaps in input that result from hearing losses. Treatment involves empathic understanding of the person's distress, correction of any hearing or visual problems, and increase in social contacts. Medication may be effective, although toxicity needs to be considered, and paranoid patients may be suspicious of medication.

Schizophrenia

In the very few instances in which it appears for the first time in old age, schizophrenia is often called paraphrenia, and is milder in form than early-onset schizophrenia. The course of schizophrenia in old age has not been adequately studied, although some researchers suggest that the positive symptoms become muted.

Psychoactive Substance Use Disorders

Alcoholism is generally believed to be less prevalent in the elderly, partly because of early death of alcoholics, cohort effects, and physiological intolerance. Illicit drug use is quite rare in the elderly, but this may change as younger cohorts age. Misuse of prescription and over-the-counter medications is a more serious problem in the elderly; this may be deliberate or the result of misinformation.

Hypochondriasis

While it is a common impression that a high proportion of the elderly complain of nonexistent physical symptoms, recent evidence suggests that, in fact, the aged may under-report symptoms. Hypochondriacal complaints may represent in part a cohort effect; the present older generation may find it more acceptable to complain about physical than emotional ailments.

Insomnia

Serious sleep disturbance is present in 25% of those aged 65 to 79. Physiological changes occur normally in the sleep patterns of older adults, leading to more interruptions of sleep, less REM sleep, and much less stage 4 sleep. Other causes of sleep problems include medications, illness, pain, stress, depression, and lack of activity. Sleeping medications quickly lose their effectiveness and may create additional problems; information about sleep and relaxation training are more helpful.

Suicide

Suicide rates for people over 65 are three times greater than for younger individuals. Moreover, older persons communicate their intentions to commit suicide less often and their suicide attempts are more often lethal.

Sexuality and Aging

Surveys indicate that older people continue to have considerable sexual interest and capacity, particularly when recent cohorts are studied. Physiological changes in men with age include taking longer to reach an erection and a slower, less intense sexual response cycle. Like men, older women take longer to become aroused. Physical illness and some medications have an adverse effect on sexual functioning. Interventions to improve sexual functioning in old age include giving information and permission, as well as sex therapy techniques similar to those used with younger people.

General Issues in Treatment and Care

Older people apparently do not receive their share of mental health services, in part because of insurance reimbursement policies and bias of practitioners. Improving the quality of nursing home care is particularly important, as the nursing home environment itself has been shown to have adverse effects on mental and physical health. A box discusses the mindlessness and lack of control associated with living in a nursing home. Well coordinated community-based care should provide a continuum of aid to allow the frail elderly to remain in their homes. Services range from practical help such as providing hot meals to home visits by professionals and support for caretakers.

Several therapy issues are specific to working with older adults. Content issues include recognition that emotional distress may be a realistic reaction to problems in living, addressing feelings about death and practical concerns about planning for death, and philosophical or religious examination of one's life. Many clinicians suggest that therapy with the aged should be more active and directive, focusing more on the here and now, and helping more with practical issues.

NOTES

STUDENTS SHOULD KNOW . . .

Key Points

1. Students should understand the concepts of age effects, cohort effects, and time-of-measurement effects, and how these effects make interpretation of studies of aging difficult.

2. The prevalence of chronic physical illness is greatest among the aged, poverty rates are higher than for younger age groups, and many major life events (e.g., death of loved ones) are experienced. These factors, together with social prejudice, affect the psychological status of the aged.

3. Fluid intelligence declines with age, but crystallized intelligence stays the same or improves. Older people take longer to learn new material and have more difficulty with recall memory.

4. Dementia is a gradual deterioration of intellectual abilities to the point that social and occupational functioning are impaired.

5. Most cases of dementia are irreversible; treatment focuses on support and education of caretakers. Some cases are caused by medication or depression, and can be reversed.

6. Delirium is a clouded state of consciousness characterized by difficulty in concentrating, restlessness, and fluctuations in mood and functioning.

7. Delirium is usually caused by an underlying problem such as stress, medication, or drug intoxication, and complete recovery is possible if these problems are recognized and treated.

8. Despite assumptions to the contrary, psychological problems such as depression, paranoid disorder, substance abuse, and hypochondriasis are not more prevalent in older adults. Still, the unique situation of the older adult needs to be considered in understanding and treating each of these disorders. Sleep disorders, particularly insomnia, are more common among the elderly.

9. Individuals over age 65 are three times more likely to commit suicide than are younger adults.

10. Most older adults maintain sexual interest and enjoy sexual activity. A general slowing of the sexual response cycle does occur with age, and the intensity of sexual arousal may be less.

11. Older adults are underserved by the mental health system.

12. Nursing home placement can have a detrimental effect on the mental and physical health of older adults. Community care seeks to maintain continuity of care to allow the elderly to remain at home.

New Terms
(key terms underlined)

age effects, cohort effects, time-of-measurement effects, cross-sectional and longitudinal designs, fluid and crystallized intelligence, dementia, Alzheimer's disease, delirium, stroke, aphasia, insomnia

New Names
(key figures underlined)

Philip Lombardo, Ellen Langer

NOTES

LECTURE LAUNCHERS

Biological Theories of Aging

Why do people change as they age? People change with age in body, mind, and social roles, and it is not necessarily true that changes in these spheres are linked to each other in any simple correspondence. At present, it is generally accepted that aging is not a unitary process, but involves changes which can be described and understood at different levels of organization. Despite this general consensus, psychological and sociological theorizing on aging is poorly developed, as are integrative theories addressing the interplay of different change processes. Perhaps because aging is so manifestly, if not exclusively, a biological process, biological theories of aging abound.

Most generally, biologists argue that there appears to be a strong genetic component to aging. Each species has a rather distinct upper limit to its members' life spans, limits which vary markedly from species to species. For instance, mayflies live about one day, dogs about twelve years, horses about twenty-five years, and humans about seventy-two years. Normal cells in vitro can only divide so many times, and this number depends on the type of cell and the species to which it belongs. Longevity seems to be heritable. The clearest example of this is with purebred strains of mice; some strains have a life span of about 260 days while others average 800 days. While the evidence for a genetic component is substantial, the mechanisms through which the genetic influence would be expressed are not well articulated.

More specific biological theories of aging include cellular error theory, which explains aging as the result of diffuse cell death caused by intracellular failures of protein synthesis. A recent version of cellular error theory holds that cumulative errors in the protein synthesis process, perhaps stemming from damaged RNA, result in eventual malfunction or death of the non-dividing cells. It is in these cells, such as neurons and muscle cells, that most of the effects of aging are seen.

Another cell-death theory is the accumulated toxins theory. Here, the hypothesis is that certain toxins are incompletely metabolized by the cells, slowly accumulate, and eventually kill the cell. Empirical evidence for this theory is slight.

More substantial evidence exists for the cross linking hypothesis. It is observed that in certain very large molecules, elastin and collagen for instance, cross linkages, or abnormal bonds between two molecules or between two different sections of the same molecule, accumulate in the body over time. It is believed that declines in skin and connective tissue elasticity result from the changes in the physical and chemical properties of the collagen molecules induced by these cross linkages. Further, since 25 to 30% of the body protein is collagen and because collagen surrounds blood vessels and cells, changes in collagen could affect a wide variety of physical functions. It is also speculated that other proteins and enzymes may be damaged by cross linking.

Wear and tear theory is the popular idea that the body, like a machine, wears out with use. Evidence cited in its support includes reports that the rate of oxygen use per unit weight is inversely proportionate to life span in between-species comparisons, and that cold blooded animals die sooner in warm environments while warm blooded animals die sooner in cold environments. Proponents interpret these data as showing that the harder or faster the body works, the sooner the animal dies, but critics point out that this evidence is equally compatible with any theory based on chemical reactions (e.g., cellular error or cross linking). Wear and tear theory also ignores the substantial ability of the body to repair itself.

Another popular but unsubstantiated theory is stress theory, the idea that aging is the inevitable residual damage resulting from the body's response to any physically or psychologically noxious stimulus.

Recently, much attention has been devoted to the role of the immune system in aging. The general idea is that the immune system may become less good at identifying noxious bacteria and dead and mutated cells which it normally cleans from the body. Two types of errors could occur. First, the system could fail to identify harmful bodies, and second, the system could erroneously identify healthy cells as malignant. In the first case, the person would become more vulnerable to infection and cancer, and in the second case, the body would attack itself, a condition known as autoimmune disease. And in fact, all three of these diseases increase in frequency in advanced age. It has also been suggested that even if the immune system's identification functions are intact, the aged person lacks the capacity of younger persons to produce the needed antibodies. Immune system theories of aging are attractive in part because they hold promise for a modern fountain of youth. Rejuvenation of the immune system seems within the realm of possibility. Experiments have shown that certain timely alterations of the immune system of mice can extend their life span.

Finally, it has been proposed that failure in the two basic self-regulatory systems of the body--the endocrine and nervous systems--are responsible for aging. In support of this, it is pointed out that activities demanding coordinated performance decline faster than static muscle strength. Substantial changes occur in body systems with age, although the specific effect of those changes on their regulatory functions have not been demonstrated. (Summary based on Shock, N. W., 1977, Biological theories of aging. In J. E. Birren & K. W. Schaie, Eds., Handbook of the Psychology of Aging. New York: Van Nostrand Reinhold.)

Hearing Loss and Psychiatric Illness Among the Aged

The text reviews the interesting hypothesis that hearing loss may be associated with the development of delusions among older adults. Eastwood and colleagues recently offered some findings that would seem to be consistent with this theorizing (1985, British Journal of Psychiatry, 147, 552-556).

In a sample of 102 elderly residents of British nursing homes, these investigators assessed the association between hearing loss and "paraphrenia," dysphoric states, and cognitive impairments. In their sample, 66% of the nursing home residents had a clinically significant hearing loss, and this condition was found to be associated with some psychiatric disorders. Paraphrenia or paranoid disorder was found to be particularly strongly correlated with hearing disorder; no patients without hearing loss received the diagnosis, compared to 10% of the hearing impaired residents. In addition, 8% of the patients with hearing loss had a diagnosable affective disorder, while none of the patients without hearing loss were so diagnosed. No relationships was found between hearing loss and cognitive impairments, supporting a functional interpretation of the obtained findings. While these data are far from conclusive, they do provide some empirical support for an interesting speculation.

Memory Improvements Following Treatment of Depression

It has been suggested that one of the factors that needs to be considered in assessing cognitive impairments among older adults is depression. Clinical reports have suggested that memory impairments result from depressive episodes in some cases, and may, therefore, be partially reversible. While depression is clearly only one of several possible causes of memory difficulties among the aged, such clinical observations seem worth investigating. Plotkin, Mintz, and Jarvik have recently done just that (1985, American Journal of Psychiatry, 142, 1103-1105).

The focus of this investigation was to examine the subjective memory complaints of older (55 years and above) patients before and after outpatient treatment for depression. Some patients received psychotherapy, while others were given antidepressant medication. However, the treatment modality was not found to differentially affect outcome. Moreover, a decrease in memory complaints was found to accompany the lifting of depression in both treatments. A correlation of .42 was obtained between a decrease in depression and a decrease in memory complaints for the two combined treatment groups. Among the 16 patients who showed a good improvement in depression ratings, 12 also had fewer complaints about their memory, while only 4 of 13 patients who did not become less depressed reported improved memory. While the small sample size makes generalization tenuous, it does appear that memory difficulties, as subjectively experienced, are associated with depression among the aged, and that improvement in the depression can lead to improvement in memory.

The Challenge of Alzheimer's Disease

The November, 1985 issue of **American Psychologist** devoted several articles to the subject of Alzheimer's disease. One by Crook and Miller (pp. 1245-1250) uses an engaging format for answering common questions about the disease and describing the National Institute of Mental Health multidisciplinary effort now underway to enable us to better understand and cope with AD. Presenting a case of a 73-year-old woman with symptoms of mild to moderate memory loss, the authors point out the difficulty of definitively determining when Alzheimer's disease exists. Many of your students may have concerns about memory loss in grandparents or other relatives--when are memory problems simply "old age," and when are they signs of something more serious? Several research efforts funded by the NIMH are underway to develop a sophisticated cognitive battery with extensive normative data with elderly populations, in order to detect Alzheimer's disease in its earlier stages. The association between memory problems and depression makes the assessment more complicated. The only way at present to diagnose AD (short of a brain autopsy) is to systematically exclude alternative explanations (such as depression or delirium) for the symptoms.

A top priority of NIMH is to develop drugs that will have a clinically significant effect on the memory impairment of AD; none are available at this time. The discovery that acetylcholine is depleted in AD patients has led to various attempts to improve symptoms by using cholinergic drugs, but none have been successful thus far. While common psychotropic drugs may be helpful in treating concomitant problems such as depression and sleeplessness, care must be taken when administering medications to those suspected of having AD. For example, tricyclic antidepressants, quite effective in relieving depression in the elderly as in younger patients, have been found also to deplete brain acetylcholine, thereby exacerbating the cognitive impairment of AD.

The cause of Alzheimer's disease remains unknown. A slow-acting transmissible virus and toxins such as heavy trace metals have been proposed as possible causes, but neither hypothesis has yielded compelling results. There is evidence for a genetic link in AD, and early-onset cases appear to have the greatest genetic component.

Mortality and Bereavement

The expression "to die of a broken heart" is more popular among writers than scientists, but research shows that it may indeed hold a certain truth. One of the best studies of mortality subsequent to bereavement is that of Rees and Lutkins (1967, British Medical Journal, 4, 13-16). They studied a small Welsh town whose 2350 people were all served by the same doctor for many years. First, a list was compiled from county records of the names of all town residents who had died in a six year period, and each of the deceased was matched with a living resident of the same age, sex, and marital status. Then, using that register and a nurse's memory, lists of all close relatives (spouses, parents, children, siblings) of both groups were compiled. Mortality rates among the two groups of relatives after the date of the deceased's death constitute the data of the study.

In the five years following the date of death, two to three percent of the control families each year experienced the death of a close member, whereas among the bereaved families, almost 12% experienced another death in the first year, 5% in the second year, and 3%, 2%, and .1% in the third, fourth, and fifth years respectively. Statistical tests showed that the spouses, children, and siblings of the bereaved were all significantly more likely to die in the first year following bereavement than were control relatives. The increased risk was most clearly elevated for widows.

It has been suggested that relatives may die in quick succession for reasons other than the emotional impact of the loss. For instance, a husband and wife may be infected by the same disease or may have lived the same unhealthy lifestyle. Contrary to this prediction, Rees and Lutkins found that of families where the deceased died at home, 7.1% experienced another death within the year. In contrast, in families where the deceased died suddenly when away from home, 37.6% experienced another death that year. In this sample, all such deaths were unexpected, thus they likely were more traumatic for the survivors.

Finally, it should be noted that death following bereavement was largely confined to the elderly. The youngest relative to die within a year of bereavement was 44; most were over 70.

NOTES

Chapter 17

DISCUSSION STIMULATORS

Ageism

Consider the following scenes:

- A 60-year-old man is asked his age as he registers at a hotel, so that he may receive the proper deference by hotel staff.

- A dress shop has clothing arranged according to age groups, with clothing appropriate for older people grouped together.

- A 55-year-old employee of a large company is asked to retire.

- The eldest son and his wife are expected to care for the elderly father, while the youngest son bears no responsibility.

These situations describe typical treatment of the elderly in Japan, a country we associate with respectful and positive views of old age. Do they represent ageism? Kimmel (1988, American Psychologist, 43, 175-178) says yes. But what is wrong with treating people differently based on their age? Kimmel asserts that both positive and negative stereotypes about the elderly have powerful effects on older persons' views of themselves, and on public policy. One study found that elderly nursing home residents had ageist beliefs themselves; when given plausible alternative explanations for their behavior and symptoms (floors are slippery because they must be kept clean, and even young people slip on them) instead of attributions about aging or personal failure, the residents improved in their participation and sociability. In public policy, ageism is evident in mandatory retirement at a specific age, and in entitlement programs based solely on age. You might ask students to debate whether "ageism," defined as discrimination of individuals based on age, is always wrong. What do they think of mandatory retirement? Of senior citizen discounts? Of special deference for the aged in Japan?

288

Differential Diagnosis: Dementia vs. Delirium

The successful differentiation of dementia and delirium is an extremely important task for those working with the elderly. Since delirium is very often reversible, while dementia is often not, it is essential to recognize the difference between the two. For example, it is not uncommon for factors such as malnutrition, unintentional overmedication, or surgery involving general anesthesia to create a state of delirium in an older person which may be misinterpreted as dementia by family members who then believe there is nothing they can do to correct the symptoms. Present the following cases to your class for practice in distinguishing the two problems:

Chapter 17

CASE A: Fred White is a 72-year-old man who was brought to
the clinic accompanied by his wife and children. While Fred
denied having any memory problems, his wife reported that he
had been forgetting where he put things around the house,
and then would accuse the housekeeper of taking them. He
also could not remember social engagements, and recently at
a party failed to recognize a couple of friends. His wife
Lilly reported that these problems had been occurring for
some time, perhaps as long as two years. At that time she
noticed he was having trouble finding his keys, but she did
not think anything was wrong since he had always misplaced a
few things around the house. When he started accusing the
housekeeper of stealing items, which happened about one year
ago, she started to think something was wrong, especially
since he had always liked the housekeeper.

   Fred made five errors on the Kahn mental status test.
He did not know the name of the clinic or its address. He
did not know the date or month, and could not remember the
President before Reagan. Fred denied feeling depressed and
was not overly concerned when he made errors on the mental
status test.

CASE B: June West is a 79-year-old woman who was brought to
the clinic by her neighbor, who noted a sudden change in
June's behavior. According to the neighbor, Sam Spade, June
had always dressed immaculately and had been fairly reserved
and polite.   In the last week, however, she had begun
appearing somewhat disheveled, and also made some overt
sexual overtures to Sam (e.g., "Hey big boy, looking for
some action?").   While she had previously walked her dog
only during the daytime, Sam now observed that June went out
walking with the dog at random hours, including late at
night. June's apartment, which had always been immaculate,
was now in disarray, and Sam had noted that there was no
food in the refrigerator.

   When asked how she was doing, June denied having any
problems or having made any overtures to Sam. June made 4
errors on the mental status test. She incorrectly identified the clinic as a hotel, and giggled when she said it.
She did not know the date or month or the President before
Reagan (she said "Kennedy"). She also thought she knew the
interviewer from a night club and thought he might be the
maitre d'. She denied feeling depressed and appeared to be
in good spirits.

The following factors are among those that should be considered in distinguishing dementia from delirium:

- Onset: The onset of dementia is usually gradual and insidious, whereas that of delirium is usually abrupt and obvious.

- Symptoms: Early symptoms of dementia include failing attention, memory loss, and declining mathematical ability; the person may also make errors of judgment, show irritability, personality changes, or loss of a sense of humor. Symptoms of delirium include restlessness, fluctuating alertness, confusion, decrease in amount of sleep with day-night reversal, and sexual acting-out. Both dementia and delirium patients may deny their symptoms.

- Responses to test questions: While both patients with dementia and those with delirium may make the same errors on a mental status exam, the quality of their responses is likely to be different: those with dementia commonly make denotative errors, whereas delirium patients often give connotative, symbolic responses.

After presenting this information, it should be easy for students to identify Case A as dementia, and Case B as delirium.

Aging in Literature

There are at least two well-written and absorbing novels that provide excellent windows into the life of the elderly. You might refer your students to these books as a means of helping them understand and consider the issues involved in growing older. May Sarton's <u>As We Are Now</u> tells the story of a 76-year-old woman who has suffered a heart attack and been committed to an old people's home. The first-person account offers a searing insight into the hope, despair, anger, and compassion of her experiences there. <u>The Diary of a Good Neighbour</u>, by Doris Lessing, depicts the developing relationship between a fashionable, successful middle-aged woman and a fierce, vulnerable 80-year-old woman after they meet by chance in the local pharmacy.

Chapter 17

INSTRUCTIONAL FILMS

1. <u>Nobody Ever Died of Old Age</u>. (Films Inc., 55 min., color, 1976) A series of interviews with older people on the subject of what it is like to age in America. "Beautifully acted, well-written, and expertly crafted" (Mental Health Materials Center review).

2. <u>Aging</u>. (McGraw-Hill films, 22 min., color, 1975) "A diversified, up-beat film essay on aging that effectively flouts stereotypes . . . lots of excellent discussion material" (Mental Health Materials Center review).

3. <u>Make a Wish</u>. (PSU, 5 min., color, 1973) Attempts to give some insight into the problems sensory impairments create for the aged by using audio and visual techniques to simulate a 75-year-old's view of her 5-year-old granddaughter's birthday party.

4. <u>The Last of Life</u>. (Filmakers Library, 27 min., color, 1978) " . . . this nicely produced documentary turns out to be an excellent review of the process of aging and its effects upon humans." Considers both biological and emotional aspects of aging. (Mental Health Materials Center review.)

5. <u>See No Evil</u>. (Filmakers Library, 15 min., b & w, 1977) A compressed tale of an elderly romance. "This sensitive and moving documentary gives us a remarkably intimate and detailed picture of what older people need and what they actually get . . . especially useful for opening up discussion on the sexual and emotional needs of the aging" (Mental Health Materials Center review).

6. <u>Never Trust Anyone Under 60</u>. (USNAC, 60 min., color, 1971) "Describes graphically problems of aging, such as isolation, housing, and other problems."

7. <u>Learning About Stroke</u>. (EBEC, 19 min., color) The film explores the three kinds of stroke, cerebral hemorrhage, cerebral embolism, and cerebral thrombosis, and their effects. Risk factors involved with stroke are discussed, including hypertension, obesity, heart disease, stress, and high blood cholesterol.

8. <u>Old Age</u>. (TL, 45 min., color) This film from the <u>Family of Man</u> series explores aging as it occurs in five cultures.

CHAPTER 18

Insight Therapy

CHAPTER SYNOPSIS

While all psychotherapies attempt to prevent, lessen, and eliminate mental and emotional suffering, there is little general agreement about what really constitutes psychotherapy. It is important to note that the people who seek professional help have usually tried but not obtained relief from other means such as support from family and friends.

Insight therapy assumes that behavior, emotions, and thoughts become disordered because people do not adequately understand what motivates them; the therapy focuses more on uncovering the causes of their distress than on directly changing them.

The placebo effect refers to an improvement in physical or psychological condition that is attributable to a patient's expectations of help rather than to any specific active ingredient in a treatment. All psychotherapies derive some of their healing power from faith in the healer and hope for improvement, and researchers have argued that the term "placebo factors" should be replaced with the concept "common factors," since the expectation of being helped can be an active ingredient in therapy.

Psychoanalytic Therapy

Basic Techniques and Concepts in Psychoanalysis

The focus of psychoanalytic therapy is not on the presenting problem, but on lifting repression of unconscious conflicts existing in the psyche from childhood.

Perhaps the most important technique for lifting repression is free association, in which the client is encouraged to report thoughts without screening. Resistances are blocks to free association, and are important in providing the analyst with information about what areas are sensitive. Dream analysis is used to tap into unconscious processes which emerge during sleep when defenses are lowered.

Carefully timed _interpretations_ of the underlying meaning of dreams, resistances, or free associations, are used to help bring unconscious material into the conscious mind. The core of psychoanalytic therapy is the _transference neurosis_, illustrated in a box, in which patients respond to the therapist as if he were one of the important people in their childhood. _Countertransference_ refers to the feelings of the analyst toward the patient; therapists undergo a training analysis to help reduce the frequency and intensity of countertransference reactions. Analysts remain detached intentionally, avoiding direct suggestions and advice.

Ego Analysis

The ego analysts assert that the individual is as much ego as id, and place more emphasis on a person's ability to control the environment. While still exploring historical causes of behavior, they focus more on current living conditions than do traditional Freudian analysts.

Evaluation of Analytic Therapy

Psychoanalysis is difficult to evaluate scientifically, and basic tenets such as the unconscious and the nature of insight have been questioned. Outcome research on Freudian psychoanalysis has shown that patients with severe psychopathology (e.g. schizophrenia) do less well than those with anxiety disorders and patients with more education improve more in analysis. Evidence is conflicting about whether its outcome is better than what would occur with the passage of time. A study by Sloane (1975) compared the effectiveness of behavior therapy and psychoanalytic _brief therapy_; the results can be interpreted in a number of ways and raise methodological issues important in therapy outcome research. In other studies, brief therapy has been found to be as effective as time-unlimited treatment.

Process research examines features of analytic therapy; thus far, little light has been shed on how psychoanalytic therapies work.

Humanistic and Existential Therapies

Humanistic and existential therapies are also insight-oriented, but they place a greater emphasis on free will.

Carl Rogers' Client-Centered Therapy

Carl Rogers made the following assumptions about human nature: (1) we must adopt a phenomenological view to understand people; (2) healthy people are aware of their behavior; (3) people are innately good and effective; (4) behavior is purposive and goal-directed; and (5) therapists should not attempt to manipulate events for clients. The client takes the lead while the therapist focuses on demonstrating the core qualities of genuineness, unconditional positive regard, and empathic understanding, rather than on using specific procedures. Accurate empathic reflections help the client to acquire a new phenomenology.

Rogers pioneered the whole field of psychotherapy research, focusing on relating outcome to personal qualities of the therapist. Such research has not demonstrated that qualities of warmth, genuineness, and empathy are sufficient to help clients change. Rogerian therapy has been criticized for its reliance on subjective reports in treatment outcome research, questions about how a therapist can truly understand a client's phenomenology, the lack of specification about self-actualization, and doubts about the basic assumption that humans are innately good.

Existential Therapy

The existential view also emphasizes human growth but is more pessimistic, stressing the anxiety that stems from a finite existence, our helplessness to change chance circumstances, our responsibility for our actions, the necessity of creating our own meaning, and the knowledge that we are ultimately alone.

Existential therapy includes support and empathy, but also emphasizes confrontation of past and particularly present choices. Authenticity in relationships, including the therapeutic one, is highlighted, with the principal goal of making the patient more aware of his or her own potential for choice and growth. Research on the effectiveness of existential therapy is nonexistent; indeed, scientific study of individuals is seen as dehumanizing.

Gestalt Therapy

Like Rogers, Perls held that people's innate goodness should be allowed to express itself. Gestalt therapists focus on the here and now and on the individual as an actor responsible for his or her role. "Why" questions are discouraged. Gestalt therapy is noted for its emphasis on techniques, including talking in the present tense, using "I" language instead of "it" language, the empty-chair technique, behaving the opposite of what one feels, focusing on nonverbal cues, and interpreting dreams. Research on Gestalt therapy is just beginning, and some positive effects have been demonstrated. However, questions have been raised about the problem of discouraging responsibility for others, and the consequences of relatively new, inexperienced therapists arousing strong emotions in their clients.

NOTES

STUDENTS SHOULD KNOW . . .

Key Points

1. There is little general agreement as to what constitutes psychotherapy and differentiates it from help offered by a friend; however, most people who seek professional help have not found relief in the support of friends and family.

2. The placebo effect, a part of all therapies, refers to improvement that is attributable to expectations of help, rather than to a specific active ingredient.

3. Insight is the major goal of psychoanalytic, humanistic, existential, and Gestalt therapies.

4. In traditional psychoanalysis, free association, resistance, dream analysis, interpretation, and transference are the major tools used to lift repression and achieve insight.

5. Ego analysts share many of Freud's views but place a greater emphasis on the ego or the conscious mind. They are more likely to deal with current problems in living.

6. Many of the concepts in analytic therapy make it particularly difficult to evaluate; evidence is conflicting over whether it results in more improvement than the mere passage of time.

7. Psychotherapy outcome research evaluates the effectiveness of a treatment in comparison to an alternative. Psychotherapy process research links therapeutic interaction with therapy outcome.

8. The concept of free will is emphasized by humanistic, existential, and Gestalt therapists.

9. Carl Rogers argued that therapy should be directed by the client, and that the therapist's major goal is to demonstrate genuineness, unconditional positive regard, and empathy. While research does not support the idea that these therapist attitudes are sufficient for change to occur, Rogers was the pioneer of psychotherapy research.

10. Existential therapists are less optimistic about the human condition, noting that free will carries with it the confrontation of some painful realities. Existential therapists emphasize authenticity, awareness, and the exercise of choice.

11. Perls' Gestalt therapy highlights the here and now and uses various techniques to help people become aware of their present desires.

New Terms
(key terms underlined)

insight and action therapies, placebo effect, free association, resistance, manifest and latent content of dreams, interpretation, transference neurosis, countertransference, ego analysis, outcome and process studies, brief therapy, client-centered therapy, unconditional positive regard, empathy, existential therapy, Gestalt therapy

New Names
(key figures underlined)

Karen Horney, Anna Freud, Erik Erikson, David Rappaport, Heinz Hartmann, Carl Rogers, Rollo May, Victor Frankl, Frederich Perls

NOTES

LECTURE LAUNCHERS

Can Positive Regard Be Unconditional?

Rogers argues that the task of therapy is to create conditions under which the client's natural tendency to self-actualize will flourish. Since self-actualization is inhibited when the client is overly concerned with pleasing others, the therapist should let the client take the lead in directing therapy, should avoid imposing his or her values on the client, and the esteem and caring of the therapist for the client should not depend on anything the client does; positive regard should be given unconditionally.

Does this actually happen in client-centered therapy? In a frequently cited study, Truax tested whether empathy and acceptance were, in fact, dispensed unconditionally by the therapist (1966, Journal of Abnormal Psychology, 71, 1-9). Truax randomly selected 40 therapist-client exchanges from tape recorded sessions of therapy conducted by Carl Rogers and had five experienced clinical psychologists, blind to the study's hypotheses, rate the segments to describe what the client said and how Rogers had responded. Therapist responses were rated for empathy, acceptance of the client, and directiveness.

When these ratings were correlated with those describing client behavior, it was found that the therapist's behaviors were not unconditional; the extent to which the client expressed new discriminations among old feelings and behaviors correlated .47 with empathy and .37 with acceptance. Therapist empathy and acceptance were also found to be more common after the client expressed insight and when he expressed himself in the therapist's style. When the client's statement was ambiguous, the therapist tended to be directive and not empathic or accepting. Other client behaviors, including catharsis, blocking, anxiety, and expressing negative feelings, were not significantly correlated with any of the rated therapist behaviors.

The pattern of empathic and accepting responses by the therapist was clearly non-random, and appeared to depend on the type of statement by the client. This raised the possibility that these therapist responses served to selectively reinforce certain types of client behavior. If so, one would expect client behaviors more often followed by empathy and acceptance to become more frequent as therapy progressed, and those less often reinforced to decrease in frequency. Truax tested this hypothesis by comparing the frequency of the different types of client statements in early and later sessions. For 7 of the 9 statement types the prediction was borne out; the frequency of those statements which correlated with therapist responses changed appropriately whereas the others did not change.

This is not to say that therapist empathy and acceptance are important only as reinforcers, nor that verbal reinforcement is the "active ingredient" of Rogerian therapy. It does show, however, that even when intending not to, therapists may directly change clients' behavior. If influence in inevitable, it may be best that therapists recognize it as such and use it deliberately.

Meta-Analysis of Psychotherapy Outcome Studies

Smith and Glass have published a number of very influential reviews concerning the effectiveness of psychotherapy (1977, American Psychologist, 32, 752-760). Using meta-analysis, they combine the results of different research reports. These results are standardized by subtracting the mean difference between the treated and untreated groups and dividing this by the standard deviation of the untreated group. The resulting statistic is termed the effect size. While the pooling of results across studies is very useful, a problem with meta-analysis is that the methodological adequacy of various studies is not weighted differentially once they have been included in the sample.

One reason the Smith and Glass meta-analyses have been so influential is that they report favorable results regarding the outcome of therapy. In the report cited above, which included almost 400 different research reports, they found an average therapy effect size of .68 standard deviation units. Another way to interpret this finding is that the average patient in psychotherapy was better off than 75% of the untreated controls. (The studies included in the sample represented the treatment of 25,000 experimental and control subjects. On the average, clients received 17 hours of therapy from therapists with three and one half years experience.)

Effect sizes differed depending on the type of outcome measure that was employed. Measures of fear or anxiety reduction showed an average effect size of .97, and self-esteem measures had an effect size of .90. Measures of "adjustment"--including such indices as hospitalization or incarceration--had a smaller effect size of .56. Finally, indices of school or work achievement changed the least for treatment groups, with an average effect size of .31.

Different effect sizes were also found for different types of therapy, although the small number of studies for certain types of therapy precluded firm conclusions about their effectiveness. The various average effect sizes and the number of studies included in determining them are presented below:

Therapy Type	Effect Size	N of Effect Size
Psychodynamic	.59	96
Adlerian	.71	16
Eclectic	.48	70
Transactional analysis	.58	25
Rational-emotive therapy	.77	35
Gestalt therapy	.26	8
Client-centered therapy	.63	94
Systematic desensitization	.91	223
Implosion therapy	.64	45
Behavior modification	.76	132

Smith and Glass went further in comparing the effect sizes of different therapies. They divided therapies into groups according to the results of multidimensional scaling. Two large groups were formed: behavioral therapies (implosion, systematic desensitization, and behavior modification) and nonbehavioral therapies (psychodynamic, Adlerian, Rogerian, rational-emotive, eclectic therapy, and transactional analysis). On the average an effect size of .8 was found for the behavioral therapies, while an effect size of .6 was found for the nonbehavioral ones. Since the nonbehavioral studies, as a whole, employed longer-term follow-ups and more objective outcome measures, Smith and Glass suggested that the small difference between the two groups is even smaller than it appeared. Moreover, they found only a .07 difference in effect size for 50 studies that directly compared behavioral and nonbehavioral therapies.

Smith and Glass concluded that psychotherapy is effective, but that evidence does not support the differential effectiveness of behavioral and nonbehavioral therapies.

More on Placebo Effects

The term "placebo" has many negative connotations--ineffective, fake, and deceptive are a few that come immediately to mind. But are these connotations deserved? Not according to Arthur Shapiro and Louis Norris, who suggest that "the placebo effect may have greater implications for psychotherapy than any other form of treatment because both psychotherapy and the placebo effect function primarily through psychological mechanisms" (p. 369, in S. L. Garfield and A. E. Bergin (Eds.), 1977, Handbook of psychotherapy and behavior change. New York: Wiley). Part of the issue has to do with the definition of placebo, which is, according to Shapiro and Morris,

301

any therapy or component of therapy that is
deliberately used for its nonspecific, psychological, or psychophysiological effect, or that is used
for its presumed specific effect, but is without
specific activity for the condition being treated.
A placebo, when used as a control in experimental
studies, is defined as a substance or procedure that
is without specific activity for the condition being
evaluated. (p. 371).

In their excellent and intriguing review of the placebo
and placebo effect, Shapiro and Morris reach the following
conclusions: (1) the history of medicine and of psychology
is largely a history of the placebo effect, since the
specific action of various treatments has been discovered
only recently; (2) data do not support the notion that there
are particular patients who are "placebo reactors;" (3)
situational factors, such as the setting's "milieu,"
therapist interest, and an element of mysticism about the
treatment procedure do seem to strongly influence placebo
response; and (4) the therapist's belief in the effectiveness of a treatment is also important to the placebo
response. In discussing the various factors related to a
positive placebo response, they note the well-worn
admonition: Treat as many patients as possible with the new
remedies while they still have the power to heal.
Rather than dismiss the placebo effect, Shapiro and
Morris suggest that it provides excellent material for
psychotherapists to study in attempting to improve the
effectiveness of psychotherapy. If such psychological
factors as persuasion, role demands, guilt reduction,
expectancy, hope, and misattribution are explanations for
the placebo response, it is worth investigating means for
maximizing the therapeutic action of these psychological
factors. Moreover, according to the definition of a
placebo, once we begin to systematically study specific
psychological factors and predict their specific effect in
the therapeutic process, we are not longer using a placebo!
A recent trend is to abandon the term "placebo" in
describing control groups in treatment studies, and instead
call such controls nonspecific treatments (Critelli and
Neumann, 1984, American Psychologist, 39, 32-39); they
contain ingredients common to all therapies, but not assumed
to be inert (as the term placebo implies).

Common Factors in Effective Therapy

In assessing the relative efficacy of various types of therapy, researchers have found themselves referring to the "Dodo verdict" from Alice in Wonderland: after arranging a race in which all participants run around randomly within a circle, the Dodo announces, "All have won, and all must have prizes" (Luborsky et al., 1985). Given that dramatic and consistent differences in effectiveness between different types of therapy have not been demonstrated, and given that "placebo" effects appear to be important (perhaps the most important) ingredients in all therapies, some researchers have begun to focus on the common factors which predict success in treatment.

In order to examine what factors influence treatment effectiveness, Luborsky et al. (1985) assigned male drug addicts to three treatment groups: (1) supportive-expressive + drug counseling; (2) cognitive-behavioral + drug counseling; or (3) drug counseling alone. Outcome measures included assessments of depression and other psychiatric symptoms, drug use, and criminal activity. The authors examined the different success rates of individual therapists, and found great variability. The study then focused on determining what factors made some therapists more successful than others. Factors they considered included patient qualities (some therapists might have easier patients), therapist qualities (such as skillfulness, personal adjustment, desire to help others), aspects of the patient-therapist relationship, and qualities of the particular type of therapy used.

First, the authors found that the patient qualities did not differ across therapists; all therapists could be considered to have equally difficult cases to work with. As a measure of therapist qualities, colleagues of each therapist were asked to provide ratings on the therapist's interest in helping patients, psychological health and adjustment, and skill as a therapist. A composite score encompassing these therapist factors correlated moderately with the improvement of the patients under that therapist's care. The Helping Alliance Questionnaire, filled out by patients in the early sessions, was used to assess the quality of the patient-therapist relationship: this measure correlated highly with effectiveness. Finally, the study revealed that the two types of therapy (supportive-expressive and cognitive-behavioral) were more effective than drug counseling alone, and did not differ from each other. Interestingly, a measure of how closely the therapists adhered to the treatment manual (assessed through supervision and ratings of tape recorded sessions) was correlated with effectiveness: those therapists who stuck to the treatment, regardless of which treatment they used, were more effective than those who used techniques from other therapy schools (a blow for eclecticism, perhaps?).

Some Views on Effective Psychotherapy

Reprinted in Marvin Goldfried's excellent book <u>Converging Themes in Psychotherapy</u> (1982, New York: Springer) is a discussion in which some of today's prominent therapists air their views on the "active ingredients" in all forms of psychotherapy. The comments are particularly interesting in that factors that are not part of many or any therapeutic paradigm were frequently mentioned. Moreover, the therapists frequently mentioned the influence of factors that are "outside" of the paradigm that they are most strongly associated with. Among the comments found in this intriguing discussion are the following:

John Paul Brady: "Development of a therapist-patient relationship, characterized by trust, mutual respect, and positive emotional feelings."

Gerald Davison: "It is my abiding belief that therapy overall is a moral enterprise, that we are society's secular priests, that we basically offer clients a philosophy of life, a set of biases not amenable to empirical test."

Jerome Frank: "Inspiring the patient's hopes, which may be healing in itself and also encourages the patient to explore him- or herself and enter situations he or she has previously avoided out of fear, and to try out new ways of dealing with problems."

William Rotter: "There are few things that seem to be true of successful therapy regardless of the method employed. One of these is that increasing the patient's belief that he or she will get better, that he or she will be able to achieve a more satisfying adjustment by doing what is required in the therapy, is related to successful outcome."

Hans Strupp: "I view all forms of psychotherapy as varieties of interpersonal experiences that promote learning (structural change)."

The Evolution of Psychotherapy Conference

The Evolution of Psychotherapy Conference, held December 11-15, 1985 in Pheonix, Arizona and attended by 7,000 clinicians and graduate students from around the world, drew together the leading practitioners and theorists in the field of psychotherapy to present their ideas and comment on one another's work. The book which compiles many of their presentations is an excellent source for the original words of these speakers (J. K. Zeig, Ed., 1987, The Evolution of Psychotherapy, New York: Brunner/Mazel).

Sections relevant to Chapter 18 of this text include those on humanistic/existential therapies (pp. 179-222), with contributions by Carl Rogers, Ruth Sanford, R. D. Laing, and Rollo May (and commentary by Miriam Polster, Thomas Szasz, and Bruno Bettelheim) and on psychoanalytic therapists (pp. 223-284), including presentations by Bruno Bettelheim (discussion by R. D. Laing), James Masterson (comments by Jay Haley), Lewis Wolberg (comments from Arnold Lazarus), and Judd Marmor (with discussion by Aaron Beck).

NOTES

DISCUSSION STIMULATORS

How Does a Therapist Differ From a Friend?

A good way to begin a discussion about psychotherapy is to ask students to consider how a therapist differs from a friend. You could write their suggestions on the board and add some of your own; this usually encourages students to air their views on the worth of therapy. A possible list of differences:

1) Advantages of getting help from a therapist rather than from a friend:

Expert opinion (a therapist presumably has expertise and training in helping people)

Knowledge of resources (a therapist will be able to refer you to appropriate resources which you may need)

Understanding of serious problems (a therapist is trained to recognize and handle more serious problems)

Confidentiality (a friend might disclose what you say, whereas a therapist is bound not to)

Objectivity (a friend may be too intimately involved with you to have an objective perspective on your problem)

Separation from personal life (you can disclose personal material to a therapist knowing that you will not be facing that person later at a social occasion)

2) Advantages of getting help from a friend rather than a therapist:

Cost (a friend will not charge you!)

Less stigma (sharing your problem with a friend does not expose you to the stigma of having "mental problems")

Convenience (your friend may be more available, particularly on short notice)

Intimate knowledge (your friend may know you better, over a longer period of time and in more varied situations, and may also know the significant others in your life)

Pre-Test on Views Related to Psychotherapy

The following survey could be passed out before beginning the classes on intervention, to give students an opportunity to consider their views related to psychotherapy. (You may want to have students fill out the same survey again at the end of the course, to see how their opinions have changed.)

Survey of Views Related to Psychotherapy

1. What is the purpose of therapy?

2. Who should select the goals of therapy: the client, the therapist, or both? Explain your answer.

3. Should therapists give specific advice to clients?

4. What is the most important feature of effective therapy?

5. Is therapy generally helpful? Why or why not?

Insurance Reimbursement and Psychotherapy

There has been a push to conduct more psychotherapy outcome research for a very practical reason: insurance companies that reimburse certain mental health professionals for conducting psychotherapy want to know that they are getting something for their money. As potential consumers of psychotherapy services (or as nonconsumers concerned about the high cost of insurance), what do students think about the provision of third party payment for psychotherapy? Should only therapies that have been demonstrated to be effective be paid for by insurance companies? Should reimbursement cover lengthy psychoanalysis which may involve several appointments a week over a number of years? Should only certain mental health professionals be reimbursed? What is the empirical justification for such a policy? Putting this discussion in the context of licensing laws and reimbursement policies in your own state will make it more relevant.

Issues in the Use of Control Groups in
Therapy Outcome Studies

One area of considerable debate in psychotherapy outcome research concerns what percentage of patients improve over time without treatment. Eysenck suggests that the figure is about two out of three, the same as the number who improve in psychotherapy. Bergin agrees that two out of three people improve in psychotherapy, but he argues that only one out of three improve over time. Some of the problems that come up in attempting to address this question include: Is it ethical to put someone on a "waiting list" when they request treatment in order to study the natural process of change? Will someone on a waiting list in fact wait or will they seek help from relatives, friends, or other professionals? If we were to find that therapy does not help more people than does the mere passage of time, but that therapy hastens the process of recovery, is this justification for the treatment? Should the appropriate control group be people who ask for therapy and are given a sham treatment designed to maximize their expectations of being helped ("placebo" control)? What are the ethics of this alternative? Exactly what is "improvement" in psychotherapy and how is it to be measured?

Exercise in Types of Therapeutic Communication

To help students get a flavor for the actual interchange of therapy, it is helpful to give them a chance to talk with each other in purposeful ways and observe the different effects. One method is to conduct the following exercise using different "response modes" which are commonly used in therapy.

1) Questions. For the first exercise, have students sit in a circle (or several smaller circles if you have a large class).

A. Closed-ended questions. Have students go around the circle, asking the person next to them a closed-ended question (can be yes-no, specific, or multiple-choice). That person replies, and then asks the next person a closed question. Continue this for a few minutes, or until everyone has had a turn.

B. Open-ended questions. Go around the circle again, but this time, only open-ended questions may be asked. (Spend some time explaining what an open-ended question is and give a few examples yourself.)

Discuss students' experiences with this exercise, including the following questions:

What differences did you observe in the types of responses generated to the two types of questions? (Closed-ended questions usually yield briefer answers and a narrower range of responses; open-ended questions allow for a broader range of responses, longer answers, and usually have a longer latency, as the responder needs more time to think.)

From the point of view of the answerer, how did it feel to be asked the two types of questions? (Most people find answering closed-ended questions more frustrating, as they are constricted in how they are allowed to answer.)

From the point of view of the questioner, how did it feel to be asked the two types of questions? (Most people find open-ended questions more difficult to think of.)

In the context of therapy, which type of question would be used for what purpose? (Closed-ended questions might be useful in assessment, where a large amount of information needs to be collected; open-ended are usually preferable for building rapport, encouraging the client to give his or her own perspective, etc.)

2) <u>Silence</u>.

    A. "Silence is poison." For this exercise, the group has to keep talking for 5 minutes and avoid any silence at all costs. They should be encouraged to interrupt and overtalk. Briefly discuss their reactions afterward.
    B. "Silence is golden." Now, have another 5 minute discussion, but this time there must be at least 5 seconds silence between speakers (advise them not to count out the seconds, though).

In discussing their reactions to this exercise, consider again what happens in the group and how the individuals feel about the different types of talking. "Poison" leads to talking faster, listening less, thinking less, and quieter students usually feel frustrated. "Golden" allows the talker more time and thought, and also provokes more anxiety. You might spend some time talking about how silence is used in psychotherapy.

3) <u>Reflection</u>. While empathic reflection is one of the hallmarks of Rogerian therapy, all therapists use reflections to some extent in order to build rapport and help the client to feel understood. For this exercise, first review what a reflection is and demonstrate some reflective statements. Then have students pair up. One person talks about a topic of their choice, and the other person responds using only reflections (no questions!). After five minutes, the partners switch roles. Alternatively, you might have the students remain in a group; you make statements that a client might make, and ask the students to take turns reflecting.
    Students might be encouraged to try using reflections when talking to friends outside of class; first warn them to pick a time when they are prepared to listen, since this way of responding encourages people to continue talking! You could then discuss their experiences in a later class.

4) <u>Interpretation</u>. When giving an interpretation, the therapist speaks from another frame of reference, pulls in related pieces of information, makes connections for the client. You might pass out a case description and have the class come up with interpretations of the behavior or personality described.

5) <u>Advisement</u>. Advice giving is a controversial aspect of therapy, and interesting to discuss with students. In some forms of therapy, such as behavioral, "advice" might be common in the form of specific suggestions for behavior change. In other forms of therapy, such as client-centered, advice would never be given. You might try an exercise

similar to that used for reflections, but this time only advice can be given. Discuss with students what it feels like to be on the receiving end of advice, when advisement might be appropriate, etc.

Using Therapy Tapes in Class

The films listed below, Three Approaches to Psychotherapy, include interviews by Rogers and Perls of the same client, a woman named "Gloria." The material described above on different modes of therapeutic communication can be applied quite fruitfully to the showing of these films in class. Before showing the film, write on the board the five types of responses (questions, silence, reflections, interpretations, and advisement), and ask each student to make headings for each type of response mode on a piece of paper. During the showing of the film, have the class keep a record of the number of times each response mode is used. For example, whenever Rogers responds with a reflection, students should make a mark under the Reflections column. You might limit this exercise to the first five minutes of the interview. Discussion of the film can then focus on observing the predominant response modes used by the therapist, theoretical reasons for his choice of response mode, and the impact of the therapist's responses on the client. Differences between Rogers and Perls will become quite dramatic as their "scores" are compared.

NOTES

INSTRUCTIONAL FILMS

1. **Three Approaches to Psychotherapy**, No. 1--Carl Rogers, No. 2--Fritz Perls. (PSYCHF, No. 1 - 48 min., No. 2 - 32 min., color or b & w, 1965) Two of three films in which the same patient, "Gloria," is interviewed by three different therapists. Rogers demonstrates the client-centered approach and Perls the Gestalt. (Albert Ellis is shown in film 3.)

2. **Otto**. (AVC, color, 1976) This is a series of five 30 minute films. The first presents Otto, a middle-aged editor who is becoming increasingly withdrawn, anxious, and ineffectual at home and work, and the remaining films discuss his case from different perspectives: No. 2--behavioral (John Gottman); No. 3--phenomenological (Gary Stollak); No. 4--psychoanalytic (Bruce Denner); and No. 5--social role theory (Richard Price). "We thought the first film to be an accurate presentation of the onset of a mental illness . . . acting is natural, dialogue believable . . . the perspective films are absorbing, informative, and provocative" (Mental Health Materials Center review).

3. **Psychological Defenses: Series A**. (HRM, 3 parts, 1982) Part I (The Unconscious Mind/Repression): Discusses the unconscious and defense mechanisms. Part II (Identification/Displacement): Illustrates these defense mechanisms through case studies. Part III (Reaction Formation/Sublimation): Discusses the use of these defense mechanisms for the secondary gain of social approval.

4. **Carl Rogers Conducts an Encounter Group**. (APGA, 70 min., color, 1975) Carl Rogers presents his ideas about how groups should operate, the importance of honest expression, and physical contact in the group. The film also reveals the quality of Rogers' personal interaction with people in a group.

5. **Frankl and the Search for Meaning**. (Psychological Films, 30 min., color) Victor Frankl discusses his approach.

6. **Gestalt--A Series**. (Films Inc., 25 min. each, color, 1969) This series of 8 films attempts to present "an up-to-date and comprehensive portrayal of the Gestalt therapy method." Of special interest may be "What is Gestalt," which features Perls working with a group, "Everything is Aware Process," in which Perls works with a vivid dream of a middle-aged woman, and "Memory and Pride," which shows the Gestalt approach to working with anxiety.

7. <u>Miracle Healers</u>. (ITVFP, 50 min., color, 1978) An investigation of alternative forms of healing including psychic surgery, magnetism, and faith healing. Could be used to prompt discussion of the placebo effect.

NOTES

A wide range of childhood problems have been treated with success using operant conditioning, including bed-wetting, hyperactivity, social withdrawal, aggression, and self-mutilation. The techniques are effective in training retarded and autistic children as well.

Modeling

Providing models of successful coping with a troublesome task has been demonstrated to be helpful for a number of problems ranging from sexual dysfunctions to fear of the dentist. Behavior rehearsal, similar to role-playing, is used by many behavior therapists. It is still unclear how the observation of a model is translated into changes in overt behavior; originally explained as a simple social learning process, cognitive factors are now considered important for understanding modeling. A box discusses assertion training, which often involves behavior rehearsal.

Cognitive Restructuring

Cognitive restructuring refers to changing a pattern of thought that is presumed to be causing a disturbed emotion or behavior. Ellis' rational-emotive therapy asserts that sustained emotional reactions are caused by internal sentences, called "irrational beliefs," that people repeat to themselves; therapy aims to change these cognitions by rationally evaluating them. One variation of RET, systematic rational restructuring, is modeled after system-atic desensitization; a different pattern of self-talk is paired with each step in the anxiety-hierarchy. Rational-emotive therapy has been found to be most effective in reducing self-reports of anxiety. It may also be useful in treating anger, depression, and antisocial behavior and in combination with behavioral techniques for treating sexual dysfunction. Questions have been raised about the ethics of RET, as some see the therapist as imposing his or her definition of rationality. A box discusses the use of RET with children.

Beck's cognitive therapy seeks to provide clients, particularly depressed individuals, with experiences that will disconfirm their negative schemata. Both behavioral and cognitive levels are addressed, and techniques include homework assignments such as monitoring mood or accomplish-ing seemingly insurmountable tasks, and exploration of automatic thoughts or dysfunctional assumptions which are aggravating the client's condition. Beck's therapy has been demonstrated to be effective in treating depression, and has been found to be superior to medication in some studies. A box discusses the NIMH Treatment of Depression Collaborative Research Program currently underway, including its preliminary findings.

While Beck's and Ellis' approaches share many similarities, an important difference between them is that Beck's is inductive whereas Ellis' is deductive. In addition, Beck is more likely to work to promote rapport with clients and acknowledge their frame of reference, whereas Ellis' approach is more didactic and forceful.

Social problem solving trains clients in a series of steps used for solving problems, including identifying the problem, brainstorming solutions, and evaluating the effectiveness of solutions. The procedure has been shown to be effective in the treatment of depression in adults and teaching children a general approach to handling social problems.

Some Reflections on Cognitive Behavior Therapy

Viewed from historical context, cognitive therapy represents a return to the earliest period of experimental psychology and the beginnings of behavior therapy. However, contemporary researchers believe behavioral procedures are more effective than strictly cognitive ones in changing cognitive processes; while cognitive therapists view cognition as the mechanism of change, they use behavioral techniques to bring about this change. Bandura's triadic reciprocality highlights the interrelatedness of thinking, behavior, and the environment.

The attention cognitive behavior therapists pay to their clients' perceptions of the world also brings them closer to the philosophy of the humanistic approach.

Behavioral Medicine

Behavioral medicine integrates the work of psychiatrists and physicians in psychosomatic medicine and that of psychologists in behavior therapy in order to improve a person's physical condition. One application of the field is in the area of chronic pain. Behavioral programs have effectively increased the activity level and decreased pain in these patients. Behavioral medicine also focuses on helping people develop and maintain healthy life-styles. Finally, biofeedback is used to control a variety of health problems, and has been shown to be particularly effective with neuromuscular disorders.

Generalization and Maintenance of Treatment Effects

Behavior therapists have developed a number of procedures for improving generalization and maintenance of treatment gains. These include intermittent reinforcement, moving from artificial to naturally occurring reinforcers, environmental modification, self-reinforcement, eliminating secondary gain, relapse prevention, and encouraging attribution of improvement to one's own efforts, not to the therapist.

Some Basic Issues in Behavior Therapy

Behavior therapy has become increasingly concerned with internal events as well as external events. While behavior therapists focus on symptoms rather than so-called unconscious underlying causes, they do concern themselves with controlling variables which may not be immediately obvious. In clinical practice, behavior therapists employ several procedures, using a broad-spectrum approach rather than attending to only one aspect of the problem. Like humanistic therapists, behaviorists consider a good relationship between client and therapist to be important.

In clinical practice, moving from the general theory to the specific client involves decision-making processes not conveyed in discussions of techniques. A rapprochement is increasingly developing between behavior therapy and other techniques, particularly psychoanalysis, as outlined by Paul Wachtel. Analysts become more active and directive as behavior therapists become more sensitive to early childhood experiences and the subtle, symbolic meaning of various life difficulties. A box provides a further look at rapprochement and eclecticism.

A box in this chapter describes and critiques the technique of meta-analysis and its use in determining the effectiveness of psychotherapy.

Key Points

1. Behavior therapy draws on the methods and discoveries of experimental psychologists in an attempt to change abnormal behavior.

2. In counterconditioning, a response to a given stimulus is eliminated by eliciting different behavior in the presence of that stimulus.

3. Systematic desensitization reduces anxiety by pairing imagined anxiety-provoking scenes with relaxation.

4. Aversion therapy pairs an aversive stimulus with an unwanted thought, emotion, or behavior. Questions about its efficacy and ethics have been raised.

5. Operant conditioning techniques such as the token economy involve establishing rules for expected behavior and systematically reinforcing behavior which meets those rules.

6. Modeling techniques have been used effectively to treat a variety of problems. The mechanism of change seems to involve cognitive factors rather than a simple social learning process.

7. Cognitive restructuring involves changing a pattern of thought presumed to underly maladaptive feelings and behaviors. Examples of this approach include rational-emotive therapy, Beck's cognitive therapy, and social problem solving.

8. Behavioral medicine involves the integration of psychosomatic medicine and behavior therapy to aid in the prevention, diagnosis, treatment, and rehabilitation of medical diseases.

9. Behavior therapists have developed a number of procedures for promoting the generalization and maintenance of treatment effects.

10. While cognitive behavior therapists view cognitive processes as the root of problematic behavior, they retain the importance of behavioral techniques for bringing about cognitive changes.

11. Behavior therapy in practice is more complex than it may appear from the description of techniques. It involves searching for controlling variables that may not be immediately obvious, developing a therapeutic relationship, and combining several techniques in broad-spectrum interventions.

12. A rapprochement may be developing between behavior therapy and psychoanalysis, as analysts become more active and directive and the behavior therapist grows more sensitive to childhood experiences.

New Terms
(key terms underlined)

behavior therapy, behavior modification, counterconditioning, systematic desensitization, aversion therapy, operant conditioning, Premack principle, time out, overcorrection, token economy, modeling, behavior rehearsal, cognitive restructuring, rational-emotive therapy, systematic rational restructuring, rational-emotive education, cognitive therapy, social problem solving, metacognition, assertion training, triadic reciprocality, behavioral medicine, biofeedback, meta-analysis, intermittent reinforcement, environmental modification, self-reinforcement, secondary gain, relapse prevention, broad-spectrum treatment

New Names
(key figures underlined)

Mary Cover Jones, Joseph Wolpe, Gordon Paul, Robert Lentz, Arnold Lazarus, Albert Ellis, Aaron Beck, Paul Wachtel

LECTURE LAUNCHERS

Bonuses or Bribes?

The use of tangible reinforcers, such as candy or prizes, has been criticized on both moral and practical grounds. A defense of tangible reinforcers has been mounted, however, by O'Leary, Poulos, and Devine (1972). They object to the description of reinforcers as "bribes." First of all, the primary meaning of the word is: a gift or favor offered to someone, particularly someone in a position of trust, to pervert a judgement or corrupt some conduct. The way tangible reinforcers are customarily used in behavior therapy, to facilitate learning or behaving, clearly differs from this definition of bribes. The secondary meaning of the word bribe is: something given to influence behavior. In this case, tangible reinforcers may indeed be considered to be bribes. However, because of the negative connotations of the word, it is hardly justifiable to use it in reference to tangible reinforcers. O'Leary et al. enumerate 11 common objections to the use of tangible reinforcers and answer these objections in turn.

1. "One should not be reinforced for something which is a requirement of one's general daily living." The fact that individuals are referred for help indicates that they have not yet learned to do their "moral duty." In these instances where moral exhortation has proven ineffective, tangible rewards can aid in teaching appropriate behaviors.
2. "One should engage in an activity because of intrinsic, not extrinsic, rewards." Some tasks may not be intrinsically reinforcing. Tangible reinforcers can help build intrinsic enjoyment.
3. "A reinforcement program will teach greed and avarice." This is a distinct possibility, especially with older children. The wisest course of action is to employ natural reinforcers such as privileges, recess, and free time.
4. "The recipients of tangible reinforcers will learn to use tangibles to control others." Ideally, programs move from concrete reinforcers to social reinforcers such as praise. They thus can serve as a positive model for children to use to change behavior--far superior to the typical model of aversive control.
5. "Rewarding a child for being good will teach him to be bad." This is the case only when programs are misused, for example, telling a child, "Stop crying and I'll buy you some ice cream."

6. "The dispenser comes to rely almost exclusively on concrete reinforcers, thereby losing or failing to develop more desirable means to control behavior." Tangible reinforcers should be paired with and eventually replaced by praise and approval.

7. "The token program will have adverse effects on other individuals such as siblings, fellow patients, or classmates." The program can be designed so that the subject's peers share in his reinforcement, or the contract with the subject can be kept private.

8. "The behavior change will be limited to the situation in which the token and backup reinforcers are given or to the duration of such reinforcers." It is probably necessary to specifically program generalization by fading out tangible reinforcers and fading in natural and social reinforcers.

9. "Behaviors in situations not supported by tangible reinforcers will be adversely influenced." Participation in the token program can be made contingent on appropriate behaviors during nontoken periods.

10. "The use of tangible reinforcers combined with a system of if-then statements is essentially self-defeating because our very words convey to him that we doubt his ability to change for the better." In fact, token programs can shape up the skills necessary to perform particular behaviors that were, perhaps, unreachable prior to the program. If-then statements, however, should be minimized because continually prompting subjects can become highly aversive.

11. "The use of token and backup reinforcers interferes with learning." While the short-term use of tokens may distract the individual (particularly children), over the long term the novelty wears off, while interest is sustained.

Operant Therapy with Children: Repression or Rehabilitation?

The application of behavior modification programs in classrooms has been the subject of some debate; students in your class may raise objections to the use of such programs. In a severe criticism of behavior modification in classrooms, Winett and Winkler (1972) accused behavioral psychologists of aiding the perpetuation of authoritarian practices in schools. In their review of the literature, they found that the behavior generally considered appropriate and therefore deserving of reinforcement included: attending to the teacher, raising of the hand and waiting for the teacher to respond, working on a workbook in seat or following in a reading text. Inappropriate behaviors included: getting out of seat (standing, walking, running, jumping, moving chairs), rocking, tapping feet, talking with other children, singing, whistling, turning towards another child, looking at another child, or showing things to him. Winett and Winkler claim that these values force children to spend their days acting like docile "young adults" rather than like the children they are. Speaking of the public school's conception of the "model child," they write that the studies they reviewed:

> described this pupil as one who stays glued to his seat and desk all day, continually looks at his teacher or his text, does not talk to or in fact look at other children, does not talk unless asked to by the teacher, hopefully does not laugh or sing (or at the wrong time) and assuredly passes silently in the halls. Unfortunately this description seems to fit perfectly with Silberman's (1970, <u>Crisis in the classroom</u>. New York: Random House) cogent observations of just what is wrong with our schools. We are forced to, thus, conclude that as currently practiced, behavior modification has done very little to change the deplorable state of our schools. If anything, it appears that behavior modifiers have been instruments of the status-quo, unquestioning servants of a system which thrives on a petty reign of 'law and order' to the apparent detriment of the educational process itself. What is, perhaps, most disheartening is that our procedures seem to work, and thus, make the system operate that much more effectively (p. 501).

In a well-argued rejoinder to Winett and Winkler, O'Leary (1972) criticizes them for their selective review of the literature. He takes them to task for ignoring studies which showed how behavior modification with children having special problems was able to increase academic response rates, talking, instruction-following and prosocial interactions. Studies have concentrated on improving academic behavior and reducing regressed crawling, crying and withdrawal in nursery school children. Disadvantaged children have been helped to develop language and reading skills. O'Leary writes: "Casual observation of children in these follow-through classrooms reveals children who beam with pride about their educational accomplishments and who show little if any of the docility which Winett and Winkler describe." Students have even been taught to use behavior modification principles to modify <u>teacher</u> behavior.

O'Leary also criticizes the setting up of a straw-man model child. He says that in most cases, if not all instances, the aim of studies has not been to reduce children's activity to zero, but to reduce disruptive behavior sufficiently to make academic progress more likely. Second, the skills acquired in the traditional classroom, such as attending and sitting still, may prove valuable to the child in the future.

> First of all, there are some skills which are probably most efficiently taught in a lecture class where being able to sit and attend are helpful--particularly where there is a very large student body and where introductory material is being presented. There are probably many courses one has as a college or professional student that are not very palatable yet which students clearly choose to take because mastery of the material is seen a useful . . . Similarly, there are jobs involving typing, key punching, and accounting which require one to sit and attend for lengthy periods. It is doubtful that such attending skills would be acquired in an open classroom if a child is always allowed to work on material of his own choice and for the amount of time he wishes (p. 508).

In closing, O'Leary readily concedes that one major point made by Winett and Winkler is very well taken.

> While one may disagree with some of the points made by Silberman and amplified by Winett and Winkler with particular relevance to current behavior modification, their general message should be taken very seriously, viz., if the behavior modifier is to have maximal impact in institutional settings such as schools and hospitals, he must seriously question whether the behavior he is being asked to help change should really be changed (p. 509).

Social Problem-Solving Training vs. Client-Centered Therapy in the Treatment of Antisocial Behavior in Children

In a well-designed test of the relative effectiveness of social problem-solving training and client-centered, relationship therapy for treating the intractable problem of antisocial behavior, Kazdin, Bass, Siegel and Thomas (1989, Journal of Consulting and Clinical Psychology, 57, 522-535) recently conducted a treatment outcome study with 112 7-13-year-old children referred for severe antisocial behavior. Children were randomly assigned to one of three treatment groups. The first, problem-solving skills training (PSST), provided training in the skills of generating alternative solutions, means-ends and consequential thinking, and taking the perspective of others, using modeling, role-play, corrective feedback, and social and token reinforcement of skills. The second group, problem-solving skills training with in vivo practice (PSST-P), was identical to PSST, but added therapeutically planned homework activities which required the children to apply problem-solving skills to situations involving parents, teachers, peers, and siblings outside of the therapy sessions. The aim of the in vivo practice was to increase the generalization of skills, as previous research has indicated that cognitive skills learned in treatment sessions are not reliably applied to problems in everyday life. The third treatment, relationship therapy (RT), was a client-centered therapy focusing on developing a close relationship with the child, providing empathy, unconditional positive regard, and warmth, and helping the child to express his or her feelings. All three treatments were administered individually for 25 sessions.

The results? While all three treatments resulted in significant improvements in children's behavior (as rated by parents and teachers using standardized measures), both forms of problem-solving training were superior to relationship therapy in effectiveness. These effects were evident both immediately post-treatment and at a one-year follow-up. In addition, PSST-P proved to be superior to PSST in its effects on school functioning post-treatment; however, the two treatments' effects were not significantly different at follow-up. To examine the clinical significance of the improvements, the authors compared the children's scores to normative data for the measures. Unfortunately, the mean scores for all three treatment groups remained in the clinical range for behavior problems at home and school, indicating that despite significant improvement, the majority of the children still exhibited considerable antisocial behavior.

The Integration of Psychotherapies

The text devotes a box in this chapter to the growing trend to integrate the various forms of psychotherapy, attempting to identify common ground between them and encourage dialogue between clinicians from heretofore competing paradigms. A recent article by Beitman, Goldfried, and Norcross (1989, _American Journal of Psychiatry_, _146_, 138-147) nicely summarizes this movement toward integration.

As discussed in Chapter 2, most contemporary psychotherapists describe themselves as eclectic, despite the negative connotations this term has acquired. The one factor that has been found to distinguish eclectic and noneclectic therapists is experience: interestingly, clinicians calling themselves eclectic tend to be older and more experienced, whereas inexperienced clinicians are more likely to adhere to exclusive theoretical orientations.

Why has the movement to integrate the psychotherapies become so popular in the last decade? The authors identify six factors which have fostered psychotherapy integration: (1) Proliferation of therapies (Over 400 different "schools" of therapy have been counted; how can students, teachers, supervisors, clinicians choose from this staggering array?); (2) Inadequacy of single theories (The growing consensus is that no one theory is adequate to explain all patients, problems, and situations.); (3) Equality of outcomes among therapies (As discussed in the lecture material for Chapter 18, research findings have suggested that "Everybody has won, and all must have prizes."); (4) Resultant search for common components (The most important contemporary psychotherapy trend may be the identification of change processes common to all therapies.); (5) Emphasis on patient characteristics and the therapeutic relationship (It may be most productive for therapists to modify their approach based on the patient's presenting problem, interpersonal style, personality, etc.); and (6) Sociopolitical contingencies (Pressures from insurance companies and others for accountability have made intertheoretical cooperation necessary.).

Having identified some of the themes which encourage integration between therapies, including the growing interaction of cognition, affect, and behavior, the need for a common language, and the search for common therapeutic principles, Beitman et al. outline some points of contention that remain between different schools of therapy. First, psychodynamic and behavior therapists may be seen as having differing world views: the behavior therapist's is "comic," holding that happiness can be obtained by removing environmental barriers, while the psychoanalyst's is "tragic," noting the limitations inherent in the human condition. Second, the role of the unconscious remains a hotly debated bone of contention. While radical behavior therapy and classical psychoanalysis have little common ground on this issue, today's psychodynamic therapists recognize the importance of conscious action, and behavior therapists sensitive to cognitive factors are more likely to recognize "implicit" thoughts. Transference remains a third area of conflict; still, modern psychodynamic clinicians are less likely to attempt to approach clients as a "blank screen," and cognitive-behavior therapists have become attentive to the importance or the client-therapist relationship. Finally, the goals of therapists from different paradigms may be at odds, as behavior therapists seek to change specific behaviors while psychodynamic therapists focus on helping the patient to understand and work through the historical influences on his or her present behavior.

Perhaps the most important development is that the above points of contention are being hotly debated by adherents to the different paradigms; therapists no longer surround themselves with those of their own kind, avoiding a true dialogue with dissenters.

Evolution of Psychotherapy Conference

The Evolution of Psychotherapy (Zeig, J. K., Ed., 1985, New York: Brunner/Mazel), a compilation of presentations from the Evolution of Psychotherapy conference, includes a section on cognitive/behavioral therapies featuring experts in the field. Selections by Albert Ellis, Joseph Wolpe, Aaron Beck, and Arnold Lazarus offer an inside look at these prominent theorists' views on theory, therapy, and future directions.

DISCUSSION STIMULATORS

Relaxation Exercise

You may wish to introduce the class to the technique of deep muscle relaxation by actually relaxing your students in class. Instructions for the procedure can be found in Lazarus, A., 1971, Behavior therapy and beyond. New York: McGraw-Hill, pp. 273-275 or in Goldfried, M. R. & Davison, G. C., 1976, Clinical behavior therapy, New York: Holt, Rinehart, & Winston, pp. 87-93. If you decide to do this exercise, be sure to preface the relaxation procedure by telling students who do not want to engage in the procedure to simply sit quietly. Also, you may want to warn the class that some people actually become more anxious rather than more relaxed the first time they try the technique. While the procedure is likely to seem straightforward to you, you can never be certain what ideas a student might have about it. These instructions will give apprehensive students permission to be a bit fearful.

Identifying Irrational Beliefs

Ellis presents the following list of irrational beliefs which are thought to underlie emotional distress (Ellis, 1962, Reason and emotion in psychotherapy. New York: Lyle Stuart; compiled by Goldfried and Davison, 1976, Clinical behavior therapy, New York: Holt, Reinhart, & Winston, pp. 160-161). You might photocopy this list for your students:

1. The idea that it is a dire necessity for an adult human being to be loved or approved by virtually every significant other person in his community (p. 61).
2. The idea that one should be thoroughly competent, adequate, and achieving in all possible respects if one is to consider oneself worthwhile (p. 63).
3. The idea that certain people are bad, wicked, or villainous and that they should be severely blamed and punished for their villainy (p. 65).
4. The idea that it is awful and catastrophic when things are not the way one would very much like them to be (p. 69).
5. The idea that human unhappiness is externally caused and that people have little or no ability to control their sorrows and disturbances (p. 72).
6. The idea that if something is or may be dangerous or fearsome one should be terribly concerned about it and should keep dwelling on the possibility of its occurring (p. 75).

7. The idea that is easier to avoid than to face certain life difficulties and self-responsibilities (p. 78).
8. The idea that one should be dependent on others and needs someone stronger than oneself on whom to rely (p. 80).
9. The idea that one's past history is an all-important determinant of one's present behavior and that because something once strongly affected one's life, it should indefinitely have a similar effect (p. 82).
10. The idea that one should become quite upset over other people's problems and disturbances (p. 85).
11. The idea that there is invariably a right, precise, and perfect solution to human problems and that it is catastrophic if this correct solution is not found (p. 87).

After discussing students' views on these beliefs--whether they are in fact irrational, what other beliefs might be added, etc.--present them with some case material and have them identify the irrational beliefs underlying a person's statements, behavior, or feelings.

For example, consider the following individuals: A college student insists that her boyfriend call her whenever he is leaving his room for any reason, so that in case she tries to call and he is not in, she will know where he is. She becomes angry and jealous when her boyfriend does not answer the phone and had not called to tell her he was going out; it turned out that he was in the shower and did not hear the phone ring. What irrational belief(s) does this woman hold? (# 1: I must be loved?) What irrational belief(s) does her boyfriend hold that keep him in the relationship and make him follow her restrictions? (# 8: I must be dependent on others? # 1: I must be loved?)

Another college student found it very upsetting to get a B rather than an A in any course. He was so afraid of "failing" (which to him meant getting a B), that he continually dropped out of his classes before the term was finished. What irrational belief(s) does this student hold? (# 2: I must be perfect?)

Rational Humorous Songs

Albert Ellis has written a collection of songs that encompass his ideas in humorous form. They are available in a songbook and a cassette tape called A Garland of Rational Songs (1977-1985, Institute for Rational-Emotive Therapy, New York). As an example of a "shame-attacking" exercise, try having your class sing a few of these:

I LOVE YOU UNDULY
(sung to the tune of I Love You Truly,
by Carrie Jacobs Bond)

I love you unduly, unduly, dear!
Just like a coolie, I persevere!
When you are lazy and act like a bore,
I am so crazy, I love you more!
I love you truly, truly, dear!
Very unduly and with no cheer!
Though you're unruly and rip up my gut,
I love you truly--for I'm a nut!

WHEN I AM SO BLUE
(sung to the tune of The Beautiful Blue Danube,
by Johann Strauss, Jr.)

When I am so blue, so blue, so blue,
I sit and I stew, I stew, I stew!
I deem it so awfully horrible
That my life is rough and scarable!
Whenever my blues are verified,
I make myself doubly terrified.
For I never choose to refuse
To be blue about my blues!

BEAUTIFUL HANGUP
(sung to the tune of Beautiful Dreamer,
by Stephen Foster)

Beautiful hangup, why should we part
When we have shared our whole lives from
    the start?
We are so used to taking one course.
Oh, what a crime it would be to divorce!
Beautiful hangup, don't go away!
Who will befriend me if you do not stay?
Though you still make me look like a jerk,
Living without you would be so much work!--
Living without you would be too much work!

I'M DEPRESSED, DEPRESSED!
(sung to the tune of The Band Played On,
by Charlie B. Ward)

When anything slightly goes wrong with my life,
I'm depressed, depressed!
Whenever I'm stricken with chickenshit strife,
I feel most distressed!
When life isn't fated to be consecrated
I can't tolerate it at all!
When anything slightly goes wrong with my life,
I just bawl, bawl, bawl!

LOVE ME, LOVE ME, ONLY ME!
(sung to the tune of Yankee Doodle)

Love me, love me, only me
Or I'll die without you!
Make your love a guarantee,
So I can never doubt you!
Love me, love me totally--really, really
  try, dear.
But if you demand love, too,
I'll hate you 'til I die, dear!

Love me, love me, all the time,
Thoroughly and wholly!
Life turns into slushy slime,
'Less you love me solely!
Love me with great tenderness,
With no ifs or buts, dear.
If you love me somewhat less,
I'll hate your goddamned guts, dear!

Self-Monitoring Exercise

The self-monitoring exercise described in the Discussion material for Chapter 4 of the Instructors Manual would also be appropriate for this point in the course. Alternatively (or in addition), you might have students monitor and challenge their dysfunctional thoughts, making a daily entry in the following categories:

1. Date.
2. Situation. Describe: 1) Actual event leading to unpleasant emotion or 2) stream of thoughts, daydream, or recollection leading to unpleasant emotions.
3. Emotion(s). 1) Specify sad, anxious, angry, etc.; 2) Rate degree of emotion, 1-100
4. Automatic thoughts. Write automatic thought(s) that preceded emotion(s).
5. Rational response. Write rational response to automatic thought(s).
6. Outcome. Specify and rate subsequent emotions, 1-100.

Observing Ellis in Action

As described in the discussion material for Chapter 18 of the Instructors Manual, the films Three Approaches to Psychotherapy may be used productively to help students appreciate the actual practice of psychotherapy. The third film features Ellis conducting a therapeutic interview with the same patient seen by Rogers and Perls in the earlier films. In addition to recording Ellis' use of the response modes of silence, questions, advice, and reflections (see Discussion material, chapter 18 of IM, for explanation), students might be asked to identify irrational beliefs exhibited by the patient, as well as Ellis' attempts to dispute her beliefs and encourage cognitive restructuring.

Students' Choice

After reading chapters 18 and 19, the students have been exposed to a number of different approaches to therapy. If they were seeking therapy for themselves or for a friend, what type of therapist would they choose? What are their reasons for that choice?

INSTRUCTIONAL FILMS

1. <u>Operation Behavior Modification</u>. (AVC, Indiana University, ES-1175, 40 min.) "Describes the program of the Parsons State Hospital and Training School in Kansas for trainable, educable handicapped which is based on a thorough program of behavior modification through operant conditioning. Follows the program from its initial collection of data and setting of goals, though the training of the girls, to their eventual placement as working members of the local community."

2. <u>Token Economy: Behaviorism Applied</u>. (CRM, 20 min., color, 1972) B. F. Skinner is interviewed in this film, and discusses historically mistreated groups, including psychotics, prisoners, old people, retarded people, and orphans. He explains how his theory can be applied to treating and educating such groups, particularly through token economy systems. The film includes a demonstration of a token economy in an institutional setting with retarded and delinquent adolescents.

3. <u>Parents and Children: A Positive Approach to Child Management</u>. (Research Press, 24 min., color) This film provides an overview of how to use behavior management procedures, including realistic examples of parent-child interaction and clear, nontechnical commentary by Dr. Richard Foxx.

4. <u>Behavioral Principles for Parents: A Discrimination Program</u>. (Research Press, 13 min., color) "This unique video training program consists of 31 short vignettes of parent-child interaction." Principles covered include positive reinforcement, punishment, extinction, and time-out. Some scenes are left incomplete to allow viewers to discuss possible conclusions, and a leaders guide accompanies the film, providing discussion questions for each scene.

5. <u>Behavior Modification in the Classroom</u>. (UCEMC-7697, 24 min., color, 1970) Use of operant conditioning and modeling procedures to increase task-oriented behavior in early, intermediate, and older primary school grades. Describes need to choose appropriate reinforcements and fade out tangible reinforcements.

6. <u>One Step at a Time: An Introduction to Behavior Modification</u>. (CRM, 30 min., color, 1972) Demonstrates the use of behavior modification in a variety of settings, including a normal classroom, a classroom for mentally retarded children, and a mental hospital.

7. <u>To Alter Human Behavior . . . Without Mind Control</u>. (IDEAL, 21 min., color, 1975) "Investigates new behavior modification techniques. Use of incentives to get students to learn; conditioning of monkeys to regain usefulness of damaged limbs; human regulation of autonomic nervous system. Hints at the ethical uses of behavior modification."

8. <u>Responsible Assertion</u>. (Research Press, 28 min., color) Drs. Arthur Lange and Patricia Jakubowski demonstrate their assertion training program.

9. <u>Rational Emotive Therapy</u>. (Research Press, 30 min., color) This film features Albert Ellis describing the RET approach, scenes with clients from the Institute for Rational Emotive Therapy in New York, and a shame-attacking exercise carried out by an RET student.

10. <u>Three Approaches to Psychotherapy</u>: Film No. 3--Albert Ellis. (PCR-40123, 37 min., 1968) One of three films in which the same client ("Gloria") is interviewed sequentially by three different therapists. Here Ellis presents the rational-emotive approach. The other two therapists are Fritz Perls and Carl Rogers.

11. <u>Stress and Behavioral Medicine</u>. (BMA Audio Cassettes, NY, NY, 60 min. each, 1978) Ten videotape cassettes of various leading researchers discussing their approach to behavioral medicine. Originally was a conference presentation.

12. <u>Pain as a Social Event: Behavioral Treatment Alternatives</u>. (BMA Audio Cassettes, NY, NY, 60 min., 1976) "Fordyce has evolved a theoretical rationale and set of practical strategies which are introduced extremely well in this tape cassette."

CHAPTER 20

Group, Family, and Marital Therapy, and Community Psychology

<u>**CHAPTER SYNOPSIS**</u>

<u>Group Therapy</u>

Group therapy has unique advantages in that it enables members to learn vicariously, utilizes social pressures, and offers the support of knowing one is not alone. A few of the many forms of group therapy are discussed in this chapter.

<u>Insight-Oriented Group Therapy</u>

Sensitivity training, or T-groups, and encounter groups were originally developed with the goal of increasing business efficiency by making executives more aware of their impact on others. Over the years, the focus has shifted to goals of individual growth and awareness of relationships with other people. These groups are educational, and not designed for seriously disturbed individuals. Various levels of communication are examined, with participants encouraged to focus on the here-and-now and to talk and listen openly. A number of variations of encounter groups have been developed, including Rogers' client-centered groups and <u>marathons</u>.

<u>Behavior Therapy Groups</u>

Some behavior therapy groups are more like individual therapy conducted in groups for reasons of efficiency; examples are group desensitization, weight loss, and stop smoking groups. <u>Social-skills training groups</u> and <u>assertion training groups</u> use group members in helping each individual master the skills being taught. These groups are different from sensitivity training groups in that between-session activities are assigned and attention is paid to generalization of changes made.

Evaluation of Group Therapy

T-groups have been criticized for teaching skills that are not generalized or are not appropriate in the real world. Research on these groups is difficult to conduct, but evidence does suggest that members view themselves more positively after the experience, feel more in control, and are more willing to disclose personal information. However, they do not appear to become more open-minded or empathic or less prejudiced. Conclusions about groups in general indicate they have beneficial effects on a wide variety of clients, although adequate research has not yet been conducted. Dependent people do better in highly structured groups, whereas better-functioning people benefit more from less structured groups. Cohesive groups promote change more than less cohesive ones, marathon groups are not particularly effective, and group feedback is helpful. Few casualties have been found to result from group therapy, although concern has been raised about <u>deterioration effects</u> (discussed in a box).

Couples and Family Therapy

Couples therapists and researchers agree that conflict is inevitable in a long-term relationship; it is the way these conflicts are dealt with that determines the relationship's quality and duration.

The approaches to individual therapy discussed in earlier chapters have been applied to couples and family therapy as well. A case study illustrates how a symptom (sexual dysfunction, in this case) may serve a function in a family system. Approaches used in marital and family therapy include applying the exchange theory of interaction by encouraging partners to reward each other, enhancing communication skills such as problem solving and empathic listening, and helping parents alter the reinforcement of a child with behavior problems.

In marital therapy, different approaches are appropriate depending on what stage of distress the couple is in. In some cases conjoint therapy may not be best, for example if one partner has a psychological problem caused by outside issues. In divorce counseling, partners are helped to cope with the loss of the spouse, regain self-esteem, and foster independence. <u>Divorce mediation</u> is an alternative to the usual adversarial process and has been found to increase satisfaction with the divorce agreements, result in more joint custody agreements, and reduce litigation.

Outcome research on marital and family therapies has demonstrated them to be effective for many family problems. Reviews have concluded that conjoint therapy is more effective for marital problems than individual therapy, family therapy is effective for reducing relapse rates in schizophrenics (see box), and involvement of the spouse improves treatment of agoraphobia. One study of a Gestalt approach to marital therapy demonstrated that focusing on affective issues was more effective than a behavioral problem-solving approach.

Community Psychology

Community psychology's focus on prevention sets it apart from other approaches. <u>Tertiary prevention</u> is similar to treatment, although it also emphasizes reducing the long-term consequences of a disorder. <u>Secondary prevention</u> consists of efforts to detect problems early and prevent their development into chronic disabilities. <u>Primary prevention</u> seeks to reduce the incidence of new cases of social and emotional problems. Overall, community psychologists emphasize the <u>seeking mode</u>--actively finding people in need--in contrast to the <u>waiting mode</u> of most forms of intervention. While most therapists intervene at the individual or small group level to help the client adjust to society, community psychologists attempt to intervene at the organizational or institutional level.

The greatest single impetus to community psychology was the Community Mental Health Centers Act of 1963, which mandated the creation of mental health centers to serve each community at low cost. The use of paraprofessionals in treatment settings, the development of suicide prevention centers, and the use of media to try to change life styles are some of the outgrowths of this movement. Half-way houses and aftercare centers for former residents of mental hospitals were also developed. The self-help movement has involved over 15 million Americans in programs such as Alcoholics Anonymous and support groups for parents, divorcees, and caretakers. Approaches to preventing child abuse, such as "competency enhancement" and hot-lines for parents under stress have been developed by community psychologists.

Primary prevention efforts have shown limited effectiveness, perhaps because some of the problems being addressed are caused by biological factors and not amenable to social change. Some evidence suggests that minority clients prefer therapists of their own race and are more open with them, although race differences have not been found to be insurmountable barriers. Problems with commun-

ity mental health centers have included control by
traditional mental health professionals who do not adhere to
principles of community psychology and establishment of far
fewer centers than are needed to reach underserved
populations. The goals of community psychology are large-
scale, and success is limited by social realities. In
addition, some have raised concern that the "seeking mode"
leads to the imposition of values and goals on clients.

NOTES

STUDENTS SHOULD KNOW . . .

Key Points

1. Unique benefits of group therapy include vicarious learning, group pressure to change, and social support, in addition to economic efficiency.

2. T-groups and encounter groups are used as growth experiences for well-functioning individuals. Learning to become more honest and open with others and obtaining feedback on interpersonal relationships are primary goals.

3. Some behavior therapy groups involve treatment similar to individual therapy but conducted in a group for efficiency, but other behavior therapy groups use the format to train social skills that are best learned in a group setting.

4. Research on group therapy is difficult to conduct, but available findings are positive.

5. Marital and family therapists see family members conjointly, and focus on helping partners reward each other, enhancing communication, and teaching parents to reinforce their children more appropriately.

6. Divorce counseling helps people cope with separation, while divorce mediation is an effective alternative to the usual adversarial process.

7. Outcome research suggests that marital and family therapy are effective for a variety of family problems.

8. Community psychologists focus on the prevention of emotional disturbance. Students should know the difference between primary, secondary, and tertiary prevention.

9. Community psychologists often operate in the seeking mode rather than the waiting mode, and target their interventions at the organizational and institutional level rather than the individual or small group level.

10. Community mental health centers, suicide prevention centers, the use of media to change life styles, half-way houses and aftercare, the self-help movement, and competency enhancement are all examples of community psychology efforts.

11. In many ways community psychology has not lived up to its promise, probably because of the nature of the problems tackled.

New Terms
(key terms underlined)

group therapy, sensitivity training group, T-group, encounter group, marathons, social-skills training groups, assertion training groups, couples therapy, family therapy, conjoint therapy, divorce mediation, community psychology, primary, secondary, and tertiary prevention, seeking mode, waiting mode, community mental health center, suicide prevention center, halfway houses, aftercare, self-help movement, competency enhancement, paraprofessional

New Names
(key figures underlined)

Arnold Lazarus, John Bell, Virginia Satir, Donald Jackson, Gerald Caplan

NOTES

Moreno's Psychodrama

Jacob L. Moreno, a Viennese psychiatrist, is said to have coined the term "group psychotherapy" in 1933. He was unquestionably one of the most influential and colorful figures in the field. The essence of the form of group therapy he introduced--psychodrama--is to have participants take parts and act out their feelings as though they were in a play, with the therapist assuming the role of director of the psychic drama. A male patient might be asked to converse with another group member playing the role of his father. By this spontaneous, unrehearsed playacting, the patient is apparently helped to express his feelings and perceptions about his father more effectively than were he to try to verbalize them. Like other forms of group therapy, psychodrama makes unique use of the group as a vehicle for changing people. Group members provide a company of potential actors with whom to stage the dramatic presentations.

To facilitate role taking and to give the proceedings that aspect of a true drama, Moreno advised using an actual stage. The presence of an audience also contributes to the theatrical atmosphere. Moreno suggested many kinds of role taking to promote the expression and confrontation of true feelings. For example, the mirroring technique is designed for patients who have difficulty expressing themselves in action or in words: another person, an "auxiliary ego," portrays the patient as best he can, thereby furnishing him concrete information on how others view him. In role reversal actors exchange roles; in magic shop the protagonist may "buy" a desired personal quality by temporarily giving up one already possessed. At all times the aim of the players is to express in dramatic form true feelings about certain situations. The therapist sometimes actively directs the "play" to ensure that therapeutic gain will be maximized.

Should psychodrama be classified as insight or action-oriented therapy? Clearly, the therapist assumes responsibility for what happens during the session; furthermore, he or she goads the patients into specific behavior during treatment. On the other hand, the ultimate goal of the treatment was seen by Moreno as insight into motivation. Thus psychodrama appears to be an insight therapy that goes beyond reliance on the verbal interpretive methods of psychoanalysis but still tries to help patients achieve an understanding of their true motivations and needs.

Unfortunately, there is no body of controlled research on psychodrama, so it is not possible to assess the efficacy of Moreno's ideas.

Chapter 20

Behavioral vs. Insight-Oriented Marital Therapy

In their summary of research findings about the
effectiveness of marital and family therapy in this chapter,
the authors note that little controlled research has been
conducted with nonbehavioral approaches, with the notable
exception of Johnson and Greenberg's (1985) comparison of
Gestalt-based marital therapy and problem-solving behavioral
therapy. A more recent exception is found in a study by
Snyder and Wills (1989, Journal of Consulting and Clinical
Psychology, 57, 39-46), who made a careful analysis of the
relative effectiveness of behavioral and insight-oriented
marital therapy approaches.

Seventy-nine distressed married couples were randomly
assigned to one of three treatment groups: (1) Behavioral
marital therapy (BMT) consisted of training in communication
skills, problem-solving skills, relationship enhancement,
and contingency contracting. (2) Insight-oriented marital
therapy (IOMT) emphasized the "resolution of conflictual
emotional processes that exist either within or between both
spouses separately, between spouses interactively, or within
the broader family system." This treatment focused on uncovering feelings, beliefs, and expectations, addressing
developmental issues, etc. (3) The treatment-on-demand
(TOD) control condition was a wait-list control in which
couples could request up to one session biweekly for
immediate crises which would jeopardize their remaining on a
waiting list for three months. Both BMT and IOMT treatments
were conducted for 25 sessions. Therapists were trained in
both modalities and were assigned couples in each treatment
group. Careful monitoring and scoring of tape-recorded
sessions enabled the researchers to ensure that the
therapists adhered to the assigned treatment for each
couple.

As is the case in many therapy outcome studies, the
results revealed that both treatment groups were superior to
the control group, and were essentially equivalent to each
other. Subjects improved in both interpersonal functioning
(less marital distress, improvement in the Areas of Change
Questionnaire) and in intrapersonal functioning (self-
concept and MMPI scores). The improvement in marital
functioning was clinically significant and was sustained at
a 6-month follow-up; about half of the couples showed both a
statistically significant improvement and a change from
dysfunctional to functional status from pre-treatment to
follow-up.

The authors discuss the implications of finding equivalent effectiveness in two technically and theoretically differing treatments. In line with previous theorizing on the importance of core common therapeutic processes, they speculate that both therapies may share the factors of reducing spouse's blaming behaviors, modifying maladaptive cognitions, and encouraging each spouse to examine his or her own contribution to relationship distress. These common factors may be more impactful than the specific techniques used by each treatment modality.

Family Systems Theory

Chapter 2 of the Instructors Manual contains material on the family systems approach, particularly that of Jay Haley, which is relevant here as well. In addition, instructors may wish to pass out copies of case material, as there are numerous sources presenting family cases and describing the therapeutic approaches used. Good resources for this purpose include Minuchin's Family Kaleidoscope (1984, Cambridge, MA: Harvard Univ. Press), with sections on families in transition and family violence, and Minuchin and Fishman's Family Therapy Techniques (1981, Cambridge, MA: Harvard Univ. Press). In addition, Jay Haley's Problem-Solving Therapy (1987, San Francisco, CA: Jossey-Bass Inc.) contains an excellent case description, "A Modern Little Hans," (pp. 244-261) which illustrates how a child problem (a dog phobia) can be treated within a family context.

Evolution of Psychotherapy Conference

The Evolution of Psychotherapy (Zeig, J. K., Ed., 1985, New York: Brunner/Mazel) offers a lengthy section on family therapy, including presentations from the following eminent participants in the Evolution of Psychotherapy Conference: Salvador Minuchin, Jay Haley, Murray Bowen, Cloe Madanes, Virginia Satir, Carl Whitaker, and Paul Watzlawick. In addition, a section on group approaches includes contributions by Mary McClure and Robert Goulding, Miriam and Erving Polster, and Zerka Moreno.

Chapter 20

A Tale of Two Cities

Considerable concern has been raised about the poor provision of aftercare that is available to discharged mental patients. While a great deal of progress has been made in deinstitutionalizing mental patients in the United States, the community resources that were supposed to be created to provide support outside of the hospital have been slow in coming. There is no doubt that the lack of aftercare has forced many former mental hospital residents to live in deplorable conditions in the community, but is the lack of follow-up also to blame for the "revolving door" phenomenon whereby many patients go in and out of the hospital repeatedly? Beiser and colleagues have recently provided data to suggest that this is the case (1985, American Journal of Psychiatry, 142, 1047-1052).

In this investigation, 200 carefully diagnosed schizophrenic inpatients were compared in regard to hospital readmission. 100 patients were residents of Portland, Oregon, and 100 were residents of Vancouver, British Columbia. Patients in these two Northwest cities were matched in terms of symptomatology and demographics, and each group was followed over a one year period. Both groups of patients were initially treated in mental hospitals which have university affiliations and which served as the primary triage unit in their respective cities. While the inpatient services were quite comparable, aftercare services differed markedly in the two locations. In Vancouver, patients can receive unlimited inpatient or outpatient care with little or no charge, and multidisciplinary community care is provided through a central government office. Patient advocates assist with such practicalities as housing, recreation, and employment, and emergency services are readily available. In Portland, in contrast, community services were severely limited because of financial problems. While care was available in community mental health centers, the staff-to-patient ratio was twice that of the Canadian city. Treatment was not centralized, and follow-up could not be guaranteed because of staff shortages.

While there was considerable attrition from the sample at the one-year follow-up, a number of differences were observed between the two cities. For the Vancouver patients, most had received some form of community follow-up care. For the Portland patients, most had their last contact with a mental health professional when they were discharged from the inpatient unit. Medication usage was similar among both groups of patient, however. Symptom levels, as measured by objective self-report ratings, were also very similar for the two groups, but the Vancouver group was functioning much better in terms of social adjustment. The Vancouver patients were twice as likely to be employed, and they reported greater satisfaction with their life adjustment. Most importantly, the two groups differed significantly in terms of their mean levels of rehospitalization. The Portland group averaged 2.0 hospitalization episodes during the year period, compared with a mean of .8 hospitalizations for the Vancouver group. Based on these data and similar reports cited by Beiser et al., it would seem that provision of adequate aftercare can have some very positive, and practical, consequences.

Footnote to the Paul and Lentz (1977) Study

The text aptly describes the study by Paul and Lentz (1977) as a model of what aftercare can be. Unfortunately, effective programs are not always compatible with and appreciated by the social systems they must work within. Shadish (1984, American Psychologist, 39, 725-738), in his examination of the public policy influences on deinstitutionalization, notes several problems Paul and Lentz's project had to confront. Not only was their use of time-out to control dangerous behavior dramatically curtailed by state policy, but their token economy (even within an inpatient setting) was "in conflict with legal opinion that patients could not be forced to perform labor for privileges, or without minimum wage compensation" (p. 727).

Treatment of the Homeless Mentally Ill:
The Seeking Mode

The authors raise an important issue in evaluating community psychology efforts to reach those in need of care: will the seeking mode result in the imposition of goals and values on unwilling clients? Two programs designed to improve the lot of the homeless mentally ill are presented here as differing examples of the seeking mode.

Bennett and colleagues (1988, American Journal of Psychiatry, 145, 1273-1276) describe their pilot program designed to improve access to inpatient psychiatric services for the homeless, a chronically underserved group. They managed to open 12 beds at Massachusetts Mental Health Center, a state hospital and community mental health center affiliated with Harvard Medical School, and sought referrals from shelters for the homeless. Thirty-three patients were referred and accepted into the program; the authors note that "as expected, many patients were unwilling to accept treatment and were committed involuntarily" (p. 1274). The authors cite as benefits of the program the positive response of the clinicians, who felt most of the patients benefitted from the services provided (more objective data on improvement were not available), the fact that most patients were able to establish eligibility for Supplemental Security Income, and that patients who had previously "fallen between the cracks," including those with disruptive behavior but no diagnosable mental illness, were reached. While this study is not best described as a community intervention (its developers were psychiatrists working within the hospital system, and treatment was provided apart from the community), its attempts to reach an underserved segment of the population using an outreach method make it relevant to a discussion of the seeking mode, its value and pitfalls.

The Los Angeles Men's Place (LAMP), noting that 20-33% of the homeless are estimated to be mentally ill, also recognizes that these people "'choose' freedom, independence, mobility, and their own symptoms to the mental health system, which they experience as punitive and confining and the drug treatment, which they maintain only causes worse physical and mental symptoms and 'results in no tangible cure." (LAMP brochure). Taking a vastly different approach to the problem than that described above, LAMP provides a drop-in day center and an overnight shelter on Skid Row in Los Angeles, designed to provide a secure haven in a dangerous neighborhood, food and other basic needs, on-site health and mental health care, crisis intervention, family re-connection, assistance in obtaining economic and social services, and an address for mail and messages. While progress is often slow and tenuous, Mollie Lowery, director of the center, maintains that a carefully paced approach, sensitive to the distrust and ambivalence these individuals feel toward the mental health system, is essential for lasting and meaningful contact to be made (1988, personal communication). Interestingly, while it began in the seeking mode, with staff walking the streets to find potential clients, the center has succeeded in reaching this population to the extent that its facility is always filled, voluntarily, as it has become a true community resource.

Chapter 20

DISCUSSION STIMULATORS

Reframing

Reframing--changing the frame in which a person perceives events in order to change the meaning--is a widely used technique in family therapy. While in its definition similar to the cognitive approach of rational restructuring, reframing differs in that its approach is less direct, less confrontational, more symbolic and metaphorical. Consider the following examples, which you may wish to present to the class (from Bandler, R. & Grinder, J., 1982, Reframing, Moab, Utah: Real People Press):

A family came to therapy concerned about the mother, who was obsessed with cleanliness and particularly harassed her family by insisting that they not walk on the carpet. She could not stand to see footprints in the rug--not mud or dirt, just the dents in the pile from her family's feet. The therapist used the following reframe:
"I want you to close your eyes and see your carpet, and see that there is not a single footprint on it anywhere. It's clean and fluffy--not a mark anywhere." This woman closed her eyes, and she was in seventh heaven, just smiling away. Then [the therapist] said **"And realize fully that that means you are totally alone, and that the people you care for and love are nowhere around."** The woman's expression changed radically, and she felt terrible! Then [the therapist] said "Now, put a few footprints there and look at those footprints and know that the people you care most about in the world are nearby." And then, of course, she felt good again (p. 6).

Man: My wife takes forever to decide on things. She has to look at every dress in the store and compare them all before she selects one.
Therapist: So she's very careful about decisions. Isn't it a tremendous compliment that out of all the men in the world, she chose you! (p. 13)

Woman: My children yell and run around too much.
Therapist: When they are playing outdoors or at sporting events, it must give you great satisfaction to see how uninhibited your children are, and how well you and your husband have preserved their natural exuberance (p. 14).

Try this exercise with your class: Have them pair up and take turns complaining and reframing. One person comes up with a complaint, either about someone else or about some quality in themselves, and the other gives it a reframe. Two types of complaints can be made: (1) "I feel X when Y happens," or (2) "I'm too Z," or "He's too Q." The reframer responds with the following type of reframe, depending on the type of complaint. For the first type, come up with a meaning reframe--considering a larger or different frame in which this behavior would have a positive value. (The first two examples above are meaning reframes.) For the second type, come up with a context reframe--considering in what context this behavior would have positive value. (The third example above is a context reframe.)

Practice in Applying the Family Systems Approach

If you have spent some time discussing the basic tenets of family therapy and the family systems view, your class might enjoy applying their knowledge to an actual case. It is common in family therapy to use a team approach, in which several therapists debate the value of various possible interventions before deciding on one to try, so this approach lends itself well to the classroom. You could present a case of your own, one from a family therapy book (see sources above in lecture material; the "Modern Little Hans" case is a particularly good one), or use the case that follows:

Roger D., an only child, was brought in for therapy by his parents. He is 8 years old, in third grade, and is having a terrible time doing his homework. Although he has no learning problems and understands the material, he spends up to 4 hours a night doing homework that his teacher says should take at most 1 hour. The parents are at their wits end, having tried everything they can think of to get him to do his homework. The usual routine at present is for Roger to begin his homework as soon as he gets home from school and continue until bedtime, with a break for dinner. Roger's mother stays on him to get his homework done for most of the afternoon; if he is still not done when his father gets home, his father takes over this task to give the mother a rest.

In interviewing the family, you find out the following information: the father is a "workaholic"--a physician who works long hours and is seldom home for dinner. While he is usually home on the weekends, he is tired then and spends most of his time watching sports on T.V. and relaxing. The mother is a housewife and spends much of her time trying to devise ways to get Roger to do his homework. While the parents do not report this as a problem, you find out during the interview that Roger has no friends his age. From their interaction in the session, you observe that Roger appears quite attached to his father and works hard to get his attention, and tends to avoid responding to his mother. While the mother feels that Roger's problem is quite serious, the father appears less concerned. There is little warmth or connection evident between the parents.

First, have the class approach the case as behavior therapists. Discuss the case from an operant conditioning standpoint, noting that Roger may be getting rewards (attention) for <u>not</u> doing his homework, there may be no adequate reinforcers for doing his homework promptly, etc. The students should use operant conditioning principles to develop a plan for intervention that will get Roger to do his homework.

Next, discuss the case from a family systems point of view. You might discuss the boundaries in the family (enmeshed relationship between mother and son, disengaged father, marital conflict) and the function the symptom appears to be serving (Roger gets attention from his father if he has not finished with homework when father gets home; focusing on their son's problem enables the parents to avoid focusing on their marital issues; Roger may be avoiding the fact that he has no friends by filling his time with homework; etc.). Then have the class break up into small groups ("therapy teams") and devise an intervention based on the family systems view of the problem. Bring the class back together to discuss the different interventions suggested, and the difference between this approach and the behavioral therapy approach developed earlier. Which do the students feel is more likely to work? Why? Which would they try first? What might cause the behavioral intervention to fail? What problems might arise with using the family systems intervention?

NOTES

INSTRUCTIONAL FILMS

1. <u>Behavioral Interviewing with Couples</u>. (Research Press, 14 min., color) Dr. John Gottman demonstrates how he conducts the six stages of his behavioral interview with couples who are experiencing marital distress.

2. <u>Three Styles of Marital Conflict</u>. (Research Press, 14 min., color) Dr. John Gottman illustrates common patterns of problematic conflict in a marriage.

3. <u>Family Issues Series, Part I: Patterns of Family Interaction</u>. (HSC, 25 min.) This film presents forms of family interaction, including the "disengaged" family, the "enmeshed" family, parent-child coalition based on gender activities, a mixed-sex parent-child coalition, parents competing with each other for the children's support, the detached father, generation gap, and the communicating family. No narration or explanation by professionals is included.

4. <u>Anyplace But Here</u>. (AV Center, Indiana Univ., 29 min., color, 1978) Discusses the dilemmas of institutionalization and deinstitutionalization as it follows two patients who are seeking release from a state institution.

5. <u>I'm O.K.</u> (UCEMC-8601, 33 min., color, 1973) Unusual therapeutic experience for delinquent boys run by the Stockton Community Parole Center in California. Chronicles a 26-day, 100-mile wilderness survival hike, including a final three day solo survival test. Unedited street language used.

CHAPTER 21

Legal and Ethical Issues

CHAPTER SYNOPSIS

The legal and mental health systems collaborate continually, though often subtly, to deny a substantial proportion of our population their basic civil rights. The mentally ill who have broken the law can be committed to a prison hospital through criminal commitment proceedings. Civil commitment is a set of procedures by which a person who has not broken a law can be incarcerated in a mental hospital.

Criminal Commitment

The mental condition of a person committing a crime has been taken into account in judging culpability for hundreds of years, and in modern times mental health professionals assist judges in their decisions about how mentally ill criminals will be handled.

The Insanity Defense

Historically, three rulings bear on the problems of legal responsibility and mental illness. The "irresistible impulse" concept suggests that the insanity defense is legitimate if a pathological impulse or drive compelled the person to commit a criminal act. The M'Naghten rule refers to the inability to distinguish right from wrong. Finally, the Durham test suggests that the insanity defense may apply if the act was a product of a mental disease or defect; it is no longer used because it is felt to allow too much leeway to expert witnesses. The American Law Institute has combined and somewhat broadened the irresistible impulse and M'Naghten rules in its proposed guidelines, and it excluded from consideration those individuals whose abnormality was manifested primarily in criminal activity. The most recent clarification of the insanity defense, resulting from the controversial not guilty by reason of insanity verdict in John Hinckley, Jr.'s trial, is discussed in a box. A compromise verdict, "guilty but mentally ill," has been adopted in some states.

The application of these abstract principles poses difficult challenges, especially since the jury only need consider the defendant's state of mind at the time the act was committed. The case of Jones v. United States is presented as an illustration of this difficulty.

Szasz' Case Against Forensic Psychiatry and Psychology

Descriptive responsibility refers to whether or not an act was committed by an individual, while ascriptive responsibility refers to whether or not society should inflict consequences upon someone who is descriptively responsible. Szasz has argued that the notion of limited ascriptive responsibility--as exemplified by the insanity defense--serves the function of masking social problems by attributing acts of social violence to a diseased mind. Murders of influential public figures are given as examples in support of this argument, as is the use of psychiatry in the Soviet Union. Szasz argues that the way out of this dilemma is to view all people as being responsible for their actions, that is, to eliminate the insanity defense.

Recent reforms of the insanity defense laws are consistent with Szasz' arguments. Critics of Szasz' position assert that some criminal acts are attributable to a mental illness; the question remains as to the best approach to handling such individuals.

Competency to Stand Trial

The insanity defense concerns the accused's mental state at the time of the crime. A second issue, whether the person is competent to stand trial, concerns the defendant's mental condition at the time of his or her trial. The courts do not want to try people in absentia, that is when the accused is not present; a mentally ill person may be physically present but mentally unable to participate meaningfully. Far greater numbers of people are committed to prison hospitals after being judged incompetent to stand trial than are found not guilty by reason of insanity.

When judged incompetent, bail is denied, a commitment for a pretrial evaluation is invoked, and, in some cases, very long periods can elapse before the individual is judged competent. Some have argued that even dramatically psychotic people should be allowed to stand trial, since the disadvantage of the confusion may be less than the disadvantage of a lengthy period of commitment without trial. The Supreme Court has moved in this direction by limiting the amount of time of pretrial commitment; if competence is found unlikely to be achieved, the accused must either be released or civil commitment proceedings must be instituted.

Civil Commitment

Civil commitment affects far greater numbers of people than criminal commitment. In almost all states individuals can be committed to a mental hospital against their will if they are judged to be mentally ill and a danger to self or others. Formal commitment proceedings involve a hearing before a judge, whereas informal or emergency commitment is a time-limited hospitalization which can be ordered without judicial participation.

Problems in the Prediction of Dangerousness

Civil commitment is a form of preventive detention, something our legal system carefully guards against in most areas. While some research suggests that dangerousness cannot be accurately predicted, Monahan has pointed out flaws in those studies' methodology and asserts that prediction of dangerousness in emergency situations is fairly accurate. More recent studies have begun to identify situations in which violence prediction is best. The question remains as to how good a prediction must be for someone's civil rights to be denied. The recent case of "Billie Boggs" in New York is described in a box.

Recent Trends for Greater Protection

Recent trends have established more safeguards in commitment proceedings--the trial must be timely, evidence must be "clear and convincing," and the danger posed must be "imminent." Court rulings have established that the "least restrictive alternative" to freedom is to be provided when treating disturbed people. A right to treatment has also been established to insure that people cannot be committed involuntarily without providing minimal standards of care. Further, the patient's status must be reviewed periodically to determine if the grounds for commitment still exist.

Involuntary patients have the right to refuse certain treatments, but physicians can override this refusal in emergency situations. Subtle pressures influence even voluntary patients to accept the treatment recommendations of professional staff, and value judgments necessarily arise in treatment decisions. Paul and Lentz have proposed that patients should not be allowed to refuse treatments that have minimal goals, such as self-care, but should be able to refuse treatments with optimal goals designed to enhance adequate functioning.

Deinstitutionalization, Civil Liberties, and Mental Health

Policies of deinstitutionalization, fueled by the goal of treating mentally ill patients in the community rather than in hospitals, has led to a great reduction in the number of individuals institutionalized in psychiatric hospitals. Unfortunately, community facilities have proven to be unprepared to handle the patients' needs. Many of these discharged patients are homeless and may not receive any social services or financial assistance.

Ethical Dilemmas in Therapy and Research

Ethical Restraints on Research

It is basic to science that what can be done is likely to be attempted. Unfortunately, this sometimes includes experimentation that is inhumane or does not adequately inform subjects of their rights. Guidelines for conducting research have been drawn up by several organizations, and "human subjects committees" have been formed to monitor research in institutions.

Rules regarding informed consent require the investigator to provide enough information to enable subjects to judge whether they want to take the risks inherent in a being a participant in research. Subjects must be legally capable of giving consent, there must be no deceit or coercion in obtaining it, and they must be free to withdraw from the study. The level of risk, potential benefit, knowledge about the consequences of the experimental technique, and freedom of subjects to give consent are all factors to be considered in determining the ethics of an experiment.

Confidentiality and Privileged Communication

The ethical codes of the helping professions dictate rules regarding confidentiality--protecting communications with a client. A privileged communication is one between parties in a confidential relationships that is protected by statute; the recipient of the information cannot be compelled to disclose it as a witness. Limits to the client's right of privileged communication exist; in California, for example, the right is eliminated in sanity determinations, malpractice suits, child abuse cases, evasion of the law, or if the client is a danger to self or others. The Tarasoff case, discussed in a box, led to a law requiring therapists to warn potential victims of a client's violence.

Who is the Client, What are the Goals of Treatment, and What Techniques Should be Used?

In some circumstances, therapists serve more than one client, such as the client's family or an institution, and must inform the client of their allegiances. When there are several clients--as in school consultation or marital therapy--therapeutic goals may run counter to the client's goals. Further, therapists cannot help influencing their client's choice of goals in subtle ways; a box discusses the ethics of therapy with homosexuals as an example. Finally, the issue of choice of therapeutic techniques arises. Particularly when the techniques are aversive, it becomes an ethical question as to whether or not their use can be justified.

NOTES

Key Points

1. Criminal commitment is the process by which mentally ill individuals who have broken the law can be committed to a prison psychiatric hospital.

2. Civil commitment is a set of procedures by which a person who has not broken the law can be incarcerated in a mental hospital.

3. The insanity defense can be based on one of three grounds: the M'Naghten rule refers to the inability to distinguish right from wrong; the "irresistible impulse" concept suggests that a pathological impulse or drive caused the crime; and the Durham test suggests that the crime was a product of mental disease or defect.

4. A mentally disturbed individual can be committed to a prison mental hospital if they are judged incompetent to stand trial.

5. A person can be committed involuntarily to a mental hospital if he is mentally ill and judged to be a danger to himself or others.

6. There is debate as to how accurate mental health professionals are at predicting the future dangerousness of a mentally ill individual.

7. A number of recent legal developments have increased protections for those people committed through criminal and civil proceedings. These include care in the least restrictive setting, the right to treatment, and the right to refuse certain treatments.

8. Deinstitutionalization has reduced the number of mental patients in hospitals, but community resources have proven inadequate to meet their needs.

9. Regulations have been formulated to protect the rights of subjects in psychological research. Subjects must be informed of the risks involved in the research and be free to withdraw at any time.

10. The ethical codes of various mental health professions dictate that, with certain exceptions, the communication between patient and therapist must be kept confidential. A privileged communication refers to a confidential communication protected by statutory law.

11. Therapists face additional ethical dilemmas in determining with what client their allegiances lie, what the goals for treatment should be, and what techniques should be used to achieve those goals.

New Terms
(key terms underlined)

criminal commitment, civil commitment, mens rea, insanity defense, irresistible impulse, M'Naghten rule, Durham test, competency to stand trial, descriptive responsibility, ascriptive responsibility, parens patriae power, formal commitment, informal or emergency commitment, "dangerousness," least restrictive alternative, right to treatment, right to refuse treatment, deinstitutionalization, informed consent, confidentiality, privileged communication

New Names
(key figures underlined)

Daniel M'Naghten, Judge David Bazelon, Thomas Szasz, Jones v. United States, Wyatt v. Stickney, Kenneth Donaldson, "Billie Boggs," Tarasoff case

NOTES

Diminished Responsibility

When the insanity defense is used, the facts of the crime are generally not in dispute. It is acknowledged that the defendant committed an act against the law, so what is at issue is whether the defendant should be held responsible for his or her behavior. The insanity plea pits two extreme views of the defendant in opposition: either he is sane, hence blameworthy and guilty, or insane, and innocent. Some scholars and lawyers have tried to chart a middle course by allowing that certain circumstances may mitigate blameworthiness without altogether eliminating guilt. What this means operationally is that the charge and sentence for a given act would vary according to circumstances. What circumstances is a matter of debate.

The least radical and best known version of what is known as the doctrine of diminished responsibility takes into account the context of the crime. Common examples of such mitigating circumstances are those where the person acted in self-defense, in response to provocation, in the heat of passion, or while intoxicated. As formulated in the model penal code, the issue is whether the act was "committed under the influence of an extreme mental or emotional disturbance for which there is reasonable excuse." Whether there is reasonable excuse for the disturbance is to be judged by how a normal person "in the [defendant's] situation under the circumstances as he believed them to be" would have felt. In essence, the relevant factors are situation, as opposed to person variables; what matters is not how the defendant actually felt, but how the situation would have made most people feel. It is common in most states for such factors to influence both the charge and the sentence for an illegal act.

A second, more radical version of diminished responsibility takes into account person variables which related to the "capacity of the accused to form the specific intent essential to constitute a crime" (People v. Wells, cited in Stone, 1975). For instance, first degree murder may be defined as a deliberate, premeditated killing; if it could be shown that the defendant lacked the intellectual capacity to plan the murder, or was so lacking in impulse control that premeditation was very unlikely, how others would respond to the circumstances of the crime is less important than how the defendant, by virtue of his or her capacities, could respond to it.

The third version of diminished responsibility proposes that the crime be judged in the complete context of the defendant's life, person, and circumstances. Responsibility would be reduced if the person was predisposed by upbringing in a deviant family or subculture to commit criminal acts, or if the person was generally unable to control his behavior or recognize the wrongfulness of his acts, or if the situation was a provocative one, etc. This highly flexible standard is not currently in use. If pursued to its logical extreme it seems to present the dilemma of why, given a determinist position, should anyone be held blameworthy for their acts? This may be why the courts shied away from the notion of diminished responsibility in the first place. As Stone notes, the free will premise of the legal system is most viable if the exceptions to the rule are sharply defined.

Joint Statement of the American Medical Association and the American Psychiatric Association Regarding the Insanity Defense

Below are excerpts from a joint statement on the insanity defense adopted by the American Medical Association and the American Psychiatric Association in April, 1985. As is made clear in the first paragraph, the two organizations adopted differing policies in regard to the defense, thus necessitating the statement. The complete statement and a commentary on it can be found in American Journal of Psychiatry, 1985, 142, 1135-1136.

"In the past two years the American Medical Association and the American Psychiatric Association have adopted position statements on the insanity defense. The APA took the position that the defense should be maintained but restricted to cognitive (as distinguished from volitional) matters that affect a defendant's behavior. The AMA, by contrast, urged that the defense be abolished and that the issue of a defendant's mental status be relevant only to the issue of criminal intent, which is that element of all major crimes referred to in legal terms of mens rea, and to the questions of appropriate disposition following trial. This difference in approach has led to considerable discussion and constructive debate within and outside of both associations. . .
". . . It is the firm belief of the representatives of both the AMA and the APA who met to discuss these matters that further information is likely to lead to a consensus on whether there should be an insanity defense and, if so, how it should be structured.
"This belief is buttressed by the fact that the motivating concern and basic judgments of both associations in this area essentially are the same. Both start from the proposition that, as a matter of sound public policy, the

criminal justice system must seek to assure a reasonable balance between the public's legitimate interest in protection from potentially violent offenders, and the mentally disordered defendant's entitlement to fair and humane treatment. Thus, both associations agree that mental impairment should exonerate criminal behavior in only a narrow class of cases, and that defendants so exculpated should not suffer punishment or hardship as a result. Beyond that paramount concern, there are two other matters directly affected by the insanity defense that are of special importance to the medical profession: 1) assurance of proper medical and psychiatric treatment to disordered criminal offenders; and 2) establishment of an appropriate role for physicians who testify in legal proceedings.

"The first concern has been an active one for both the AMA and the APA. There are many criminal offenders who, whether or not they successfully plead the insanity defense, are simply not receiving adequate psychiatric treatment. . . While there is no established correlation between mental illness and crime, the persistence of mental illness in a convicted offender can only impede the effective reduction of future criminal behavior by that offender.

"There is also a shared concern on the part of the AMA and the APA over the role of medical testimony in the legal system. While this concern is by no means limited to the use of psychiatric testimony in criminal trials, that use is nevertheless one of high public visibility. In general, the adversary system does not facilitate lay comprehension of reasoned medical judgment. To the contrary, the adversary system, by its nature, tends to polarize expressions of medical opinion and to highlight the differences even when a large degree of agreement is present . . . It is especially important that the law not seek to mask basic policy decisions in the guise of medical expertise. To be sure, medical knowledge is often critical to effective policy analysis, but the need for clear lines as to where medical expertise ends and value judgments begin is essential.

"This admonition is equally applicable to physicians who are called upon or choose to testify. While it is perhaps understandable that some physicians may become caught up in the combat of litigation, it is necessary that they not stretch their medical opinions beyond legitimate, estab-lished scientific and clinical knowledge. When physicians do overreach, they may make it easier for the side that they support in a case, but they bring disrepute on themselves and their profession. Society will not, and in our view should not, tolerate the misuse of medical expertise to serve unrelated legal ends . . ."

Psychologists in the Courtroom

There seem to be three basic roles which psychologists and psychiatrists play in the legal system: expert witness, consultant, and observer. As expert witnesses, one major type of testimony they are asked for is psychological information about a person involved in the case. Two familiar examples are cases involving the insanity defense, in which the court wants information about the person's psychological state at the time of the crime, and competency to stand trial hearings, where it wants information about the present capacities of the accused. Similar information may be requested in child custody hearings where the psychologist is asked to provide information about the future best interests of the child; evaluations of the child's and the parents' mental health may well be included in such reports. In many states, a marriage can be annulled if it can be shown that one of the partners entered the contract unaware that the other had intentionally concealed a severe mental disability, a determination which might well require expert opinion. The propriety of special class placements of school children depends on the intellectual, emotional, and behavioral functioning of the child and these matters, too, can come to court. A family or social agency may ask a court to declare a person incompetent to manage his or her own affairs; this usually requires a psychiatrist's statement. Finally, disability and compensation judgements can rest on experts' opinions of the extent of emotional and intellectual impairment brought on by accident or disease.

A second capacity in which the psychologist or psychiatrist can be called on to testify is as an expert in some aspect of human behavior. For instance, the question may be, are reports obtained through hypnosis reliable? Can polygraphs detect lies? What are the odds that an eye witness to a crime has a mistaken recollection of particular details? Is it possible for a person to be led into criminal behavior through watching television? These questions involve not the expert's opinion of the person accused, but of the scientific evidence bearing on a point of importance to the court.

A second role is that of consultant to a party in a dispute. Here the behavioral expert advises the lawyer on how psychology may serve his ends. For instance, the consultant may advise the lawyer on how to attack an opposing psychologist's testimony. A very controversial practice is that of aiding attorneys in the jury selection process. Each side can challenge, or block, the seating of a certain number of candidates for the jury and can therefore influence to some extent the composition of the jury. The claim of some psychologists is that they can shift the odds of acquittal by eliminating particular jurors on the basis of demographic and attitudinal variables (see Saks, M. J. & Hastie, R., 1978, Social psychology in court. New York: Van Nostrand Reinhold).

The third role is that of observer. Here, behavioral scientists study the psychology of the legal process. For instance, a great deal of work has been done using mock trials to determine the legally irrelevant determinants of conviction and innocence. For example, does the physical appearance of a witness influence the credibility of his or her testimony? The hope, at least, is that such studies will eventually help produce a more just judicial system.

Criminalizing Mental Disorder

Are mentally ill persons being shunted into the criminal justice system in the wake of deinstitutionalization? Is jail to become the poor person's mental health facility? As inpatient services are used less and community services are inadequate, many mentally disordered individuals live in the community without treatment and become a more visible presence. Some have hypothesized that the bureacratic and legal impediments to initiating mental health referrals make criminal arrests a less cumbersome means of removing a disordered person from the community; research by Teplin (1984, American Psychologist, 39, 794-803) indicates that this "criminalization of mental disorder" is indeed occurring.

Teplin conducted a large-scale observational study of the ongoing police activity of 283 police officers (randomly selected) over a 14 month period. Quantitative data collected included coding of concrete behaviors relevant to the police officer's handling of all police-citizen encounters. Qualitative data included more impressionistic data about the officer's behavior and the reasoning underlying his or her judgments in handling situations.

Results indicated that overall, 5.9% of suspects encountered were rated as being severely mentally disordered by the field workers. The probability of being arrested was 20% greater for suspects exhibiting signs of mental disorder than for those who apparently were not mentally ill: 14 of the 30 mentally disordered suspects were arrested (46.7%), as opposed to only 27.9% (133 of 476) of the suspects without signs of mental disorder. This difference was statistically significant. In addition, the findings indicated that the difference in arrest rates was not due to the mentally ill persons committing more serious offenses; in almost every category of offense, those with signs of mental illness were more likely to be arrested than those without:

Arrest Rates

	No Signs of Mental Disorder	Signs of Mental Disorder
Violent personal crimes	58.8%	100.0%
Interpersonal conflict	14.9%	11.1%
Major property crimes	83.3%	100.0%
Minor property crimes	61.2%	100.0%
Public health, safety, or decency violations	60.9%	100.0%
Violations of public order	20.7%	46.7%
Total	27.9%	46.7%

The propensity to arrest mentally disordered persons may be due in part to officers' lack of knowledge of the symptoms of severe mental disorder, as there was no significant difference in the arrest rates in terms of police officer's perception of their mental status. It may be that symptoms of mental disorder which are not violations of the law (verbal abuse, belligerence, disrespect) provoke a harsher response from police officers.

In addition, qualitative data indicated that police officers commonly obtained signed complaints in instances where they were going to seek psychiatric hospitalization for the suspect; in this way, arrest could be used as a back-up if hospital admission could not be arranged. Ironically, many hospitals refuse to accept patients they view as dangerous, although this is one of the few criteria by which involuntary admission can be made, and persons with mixed symptomatology, particularly a combination of drug or alcohol abuse and other mental disorder, are especially difficult to place; the only alternative to the police may be arrest.

Teplin makes the following recommendations based on the results she found: (1) police officers should receive training in recognizing and handling the mentally ill, and no-decline agreements should be established with hospitals; (2) the least restrictive alternative should be utilized where possible; (3) treatment systems must be designed to accommodate those individuals not fitting into a neat category of mental illness; (4) modes of care other than hospitalization must be available as alternatives for police referral of mentally disordered persons.

Chapter 21

Psychologists' Beliefs and Behaviors Regarding
Ethical Principles

A recent survey was conducted by Pope, Tabachnick, and Keith-Spiegel (1987, American Psychologist, 42, 993-1005) to assess the beliefs and practices of clinical psychologists regarding ethical guidelines for practice. One thousand psychologists were surveyed (of whom 456 responded) as follows: (1) A list of 83 behaviors were presented, and participants were asked to indicate to what extent they had engaged in the behavior, and to what extent they considered the behavior ethical. (2) Fourteen resources for guiding or regulating practice were listed (such as graduate program, state and federal laws, APA Ethical Principles, colleagues, etc.), and respondents were asked to rate each resource in terms of its effectiveness for promoting ethical practice. (3) Information was requested on the age, sex, work setting, and theoretical orientation of the participants.

The following results are of particular interest:

1) Relationship between behavior and beliefs. The psychologists' behavior was generally in accord with their ethical beliefs, as for almost all items, the frequency of reported behavior was less than the frequency of instances in which the behavior was judged to be ethical.

2) Behaviors that are almost universal. The following behaviors included in the survey were reported to be engaged in by at least 90% of respondents (indicating that "blank screens" are apparently rare): Use of self disclosure as a therapy technique, telling a client you are angry with him or her, allowing a client to address you by your first name, addressing your client by his or her first name, accepting a gift worth less than $5 from a client, and offering or accepting a handshake from a client. Less than 10% of respondents reported they had never been sexually attracted to a client.

3) Behaviors that are rare. All questions involving sexual activity with clients had extremely low rates; less than 3% of respondents reported engaging in sexual contact or erotic activity with a client. (This figure is lower than that found in previous studies.) Other rare practices included dishonesty in helping candidates become degreed or licensed, financial or business practices with clients, directly soliciting a person to be a client, blatantly breaching confidentiality, doing therapy under the influence of alcohol, and failing to interview the child when making a custody evaluation.

4) Difficult judgments. Behaviors to which at least 20% of respondents indicated "don't know/not sure" included financial and sexual issues, such as accepting goods as payment, and engaging in sexual fantasy about a client.

The following guidelines for ethical practice, the first five of which are contained in the Hippocratic Oath, might be presented to students. They could be asked to consider which of the 83 items in the survey (reproduced in the article) they would consider to be unethical, based on these guidelines.

1) Above all, do no harm.
2) Practice only with competence.
3) Do not exploit.
4) Treat people with respect for their dignity as human beings.
5) Protect confidentiality.
6) Act, except in the most extreme instances, only after obtaining informed consent.
7) Practice, insofar as possible, within the framework of social equity and justice (p. 999).

Ethical Issues in Psychotherapy Research

Conducting research on psychotherapy raises difficult ethical issues which differ from those issues common to all research with human subjects. In a thought-provoking article, Imber and colleagues (1986, American Psychologist, 41, 137-146) discuss these issues in the context of the NIMH Treatment of Depression Collaborative Research Program's handling of ethical dilemmas. The NIMH depression study is described in Chapter 19 of the text. Since students will be familiar with the project, they might be asked first to identify ethical issues which may arise in the project and ways to resolve those issues, before the following material from the Imber et al. article is presented.

In determining whether a patient was admitted to or withdrawn from the study, the research investigator, rather than the patient's therapist, had ultimate authority in this study. Does this policy provide the best care to the patient? The study addressed this issue by basing guidelines for eligibility and withdrawal on clinical care considerations as well as research purposes, weighing the patient's preference and therapist's recommendations heavily, and preserving patients' right to drop out unilaterally.

In a controlled trial such as this one, treatment regimens were standardized rather than based on the flexible clinical judgment that is used more often in non-research psychotherapy settings. This issue was addressed by standardizing broad guidelines and suggestions for treatment rather than rigid directives.

Treatment assignments were made randomly, rather than being based on patient preferences or evaluation findings about the patient. Do patients adequately understand the random nature of treatment assignment, and feel they would have access to alternative treatment if they refused the research protocol? To address this issue, the NIMH project instructed researchers not to exert pressure on potential candidates, to provide adequate referrals if the research protocol was refused, and to allow patients to drop out if they preferred an alternative treatment to the one they were assigned (which 10% of patients did).

One of the treatment conditions in this study was a pill-placebo control. Should patients be assigned to an inactive treatment when effective interventions are available? Safeguards implemented to address this problem included screening out subjects who were imminently suicidal, providing regular contact with a pharmacotherapist, periodic independent evaluations, and a clear mechanism for patient withdrawal and referral to appropriate treatment.

Long delays may occur (in this study about 3 weeks) between the time a potential subject requests treatment, and the time treatment actually begins, due to screening procedures and scheduling problems. Are patients in acute distress put at unnecessary risk by this waiting period? In this study, the waiting period was used for several clinically relevant tasks, such as evaluating the patient condition and "washing-out" drugs which would interact adversely with imipramine. When immediate treatment was deemed compelling, patients were withdrawn from the study and treatment was arranged elsewhere.

Following treatment, informing patients of the treatment condition they were in and referring for further care where indicated, while good ethical practice, may confound the results of the follow-up assessments. To balance research purposes with patient care, this study referred patients who had not improved for further treatment, but asked those who had improved to put off further treatment; the latter were seen later for an appointment to re-evaluate their request for a referral. For ethical reasons, patients on pill-placebo were told of their treatment status at termination, despite the fact that this might contaminate their follow-up evaluations.

In any psychotherapy study, some patients will withdraw from treatment, despite considerable energy having been expended in their care. Will the resulting frustration for researchers preclude their following up these patients who may remain at risk? In the NIMH study, careful efforts were made to maintain contact with drop-outs for the duration of the study and refer them for appropriate treatment.

DISCUSSION STIMULATORS

Commitment Decisions

Draw the following matrix on the board:

The patient is really:

	sick	well
commit	A (correct)	B (wrong)
don't commit	C (wrong)	D (correct)

The matrix represents the possibilities open to the diagnostician faced with an individual who is either "sick" or well. He can commit him to a hospital or not commit him. In the case of physical illness, decision A represents proper medical procedure (treating someone who is sick); decision B, conservative medicine (better to err on the side of caution); decision D illustrates diagnostic acumen; and decision C is what physicians try to avoid (not treating someone who really needs treatment). Thus physicians would prefer to err in making decision B than in making decision C. In cases of uncertainty, the rule is to diagnose illness, unless the treatment itself is quite dangerous.

In the case of psychiatric disorder, the outcome of decisional errors is vastly different. Committing someone who is really well (B) deprives him of constitutionally guaranteed civil liberties, and unlike a diagnosis of physical illness, stigmatizes the individual for life. Not committing someone who is really "sick" (C) rarely results in death and, in fact, may not even result in further deterioration (cf. R. B. Stuart, 1970, Trick or treatment. Champaign, IL: Research Press). Diagnosis is further complicated by the apparent tendency of many clinicians to see mental disorder whenever an individual is labelled by himself or others.

The Insanity Defense

The not guilty by reason of insanity defense has created considerable controversy. Some, like Alan Stone, argue that it reinforces our notion that the majority of people _are_ responsible for their actions. Others, like Thomas Szasz, argue that the insanity defense is a political maneuver which is used as a way of ignoring social unrest. Maybe most people simply feel that it is a trick used to help a clever attorney to get a guilty client off with a lighter punishment. Frustration with the insanity defense comes and goes, but it was particularly high following its successful use in the defense of John Hinckley, who attempted to assassinate then-President Reagan. What do students in the class think about the insanity defense? What broader purposes do they think it serves? What do they think of one alternative that has been proposed--guilty but insane? According to this view, a person who is descriptively responsible for an act is also held to be ascriptively responsible, but the insanity is viewed as a mitigating factor which may influence the judge's disposition of the case.

Ethics in Research

Students likely have participated in various psychological experiments in your psychology department. What were they told about the experiments, and what sort of informed consent procedure did they go through? Did they feel free to withdraw at any time? Perhaps you could review your department's human subjects guidelines with the class.

Milgram's Research

Milgram's famous obedience to authority studies created considerable controversy regarding the protection of human subjects in psychological experimentation. The film of these studies, _Obedience_, is certain to provoke reactions from the students regarding this issue.

Ethics in Marital Therapy

The text raises the important question: Who is the client in marital therapy? What if one partner's goals are at odds with those of the other? Margolin (1982, _American Psychologist_, _37_, 788-801) raises several other ethical issues related to marital therapy which might be discussed in class. One of particular interest involves confidentiality. Imagine that Mr. and Mrs. Crack are being seen in marital therapy, and Mr. Crack requests an individual appointment with the therapist. During this session, he discloses that he is having an affair, and asks the therapist to keep this information confidential. What should the therapist do? Should the information be disclosed? Should the therapist have granted an individual interview? Should the therapist have implied that she would keep information from the spouse? These questions are hotly debated by marital therapists, who reach very different conclusions. Some therapists will not see the spouses individually. Others will consent to individual appointments, but inform the couple in advance that information disclosed there might not be kept confidential (thus giving the client the chance to decide whether to share the information or not). Other therapists agree to keep disclosures confidential, and may even encourage the sharing of "secrets." To make the issue even more complicated, what if marital therapy is initiated after a client has been seen in individual therapy? Information obtained during the earlier individual sessions cannot ethically be disclosed to the spouse without the client's permission. If the client gives permission for confidentiality to be broken, does she actually remember all that she has disclosed individually? Would she have responded differently if she knew before the fact that the information might be disclosed to her spouse? While a consensus has not been reached on these issues, an overriding ethical principle is to inform clients of the limits of confidentiality, so that they know before disclosing information whether the therapist has promised to keep it private or not.

Ethics Role-Play: Confidentiality

This role-play exercise will help students grapple with ethical issues involved in providing mental health services. There are four roles to be assigned; the rest of the class can observe the debate and give their opinions about the issues afterward. The following information might be photocopied and distributed to the class before asking for volunteers for the parts.

A walk-in clinic for teenagers within a large
children's hospital in Hollywood has been providing
counseling for adolescents who walk in on their own asking
from help with various medical and psychological problems.
Some of these adolescents are "street children" who do not
have contact with their parents; others are adolescents who
live at home but, for various reasons, choose to seek
therapy on their own. The clinic has had a policy of
keeping information about such issues as drug use and
teenage sexual behavior confidential; they assure their
clients that discussions about these issues will not be
disclosed to parents or juvenile justice personnel.
Recently, some parents and juvenile justice system workers
(probation officers) have criticized the clinic for keeping
this information confidential. You are meeting to discuss
the issues and determine whether the clinic should be
limiting their assurances of confidentiality to their
clients.

ROLES:

Dr. Clout: You are a psychologist who runs the clinic
in question. You strongly believe that therapy can only be
effective if the client knows that everything she/he says
during therapy will be kept in the strictest of confidence.
Without this guarantee, the client will be unable to trust
the therapist and unable to disclose his/her innermost fears
and secrets. Furthermore, you are certain that most of the
clients the clinic serves would not come to the clinic if
they knew that their illicit behavior would be reported to
their parents or to the probation officers. Therefore, if
confidentiality was limited, the important services being
provided by the clinic (such as information about safe sex,
drug abuse counseling, referrals to human service resources)
would not reach the community most in need.

Mr./Ms. Wright: You are a parent working for a parents
rights group, and are also involved in a Tough Love program
for keeping kids off drugs. You represent a group of
parents who are seriously concerned about the clinic's
policy of keeping information confidential which could harm
children. Recently, an adolescent girl who had been seen at
the clinic was found dead of a drug overdose in Hollywood.
Her parents feel that if the clinic had notified them of her
drug use, they might have been able to prevent this tragedy.
Furthermore, you feel that since the clients of the clinic
are minors, their parents should be asked for consent before
they are offered treatment of any kind.

Mr./Ms. Strict: You are a juvenile justice worker who is frustrated by your inability to significantly limit the gang activity and drug use in the community. You feel that the clinic, who has contact with many of the adolescents you are concerned about controlling, should be working with the juvenile justice system to help monitor and limit drug use.

Mr./Ms. Young: You are a teenager who has been a client at the clinic and have volunteered to offer your opinion about this matter. You have consulted with other clients at the center in order to better represent their position. You feel strongly that the clinic should be allowed to keep information about drug use and sexual behavior confidential. In fact, you are certain that most if not all of the adolescents who use the clinic would never set foot in the door again if their secrets were going to be exposed. In fact, since this inquiry has begun, the number of clients using the clinic has dropped dramatically.

NOTES

INSTRUCTIONAL FILMS

1. <u>Crime and Insanity</u>. (FI, 52 min., color, 1983) An NBC white paper in which Edwin Newman examines the issue of releasing people from mental hospitals following a determination that they are no longer dangerous.

2. <u>Involuntary Hospitalization of the Psychiatric Patient: Should it be Abolished?</u> (NMAC, 29 min., b & w, 1969) "Features a debate in which Dr. Masserman contends that there are certain clinical situations in which an individual must be hospitalized for psychiatric reasons against his will, whereas Dr. Szasz contends that psychiatry must be practiced on a purely contractual basis with the patient."

3. <u>Commitment Evaluation</u>. (ASC, 20 min.) Depicts a patient being evaluated for commitment to a psychiatric hospital, and raises issue of jail vs. therapeutic institutionalization.

4. <u>These People</u>. (Horizon House Instit., 28 min., color, 1976) "A case history on film of the response of citizens in Wilkes-Barr, PA, to the phasing-down of a nearby state hospital and the establishment of various kinds of community care facilities for the mentally ill and mentally retarded . . . the film presents the pros and cons . . . lots of solid, discussable material . . . all of it is highly commendable" (Mental Health Materials Center review).

5. <u>Obedience</u>. (NYU, 45 min., b & w, 1965) Presents Milgram's experiment on obedience to authority in which subjects were instructed to administer electric shocks of increasing severity to another person.

6. <u>Some of Your Best Friends</u>. (UCEMC-8266, 38 min., color, 1972) "Sympathetic documentary reveals the discrimination against homosexuals and shows some of the activities of the gay liberation movement. Includes candid interviews with male and female homosexuals, scenes from group meetings, demonstrations, and a gay parade. A homosexual lawyer amusingly recounts his entrapment by police and describes his subsequent trial."

LIST OF FILM DISTRIBUTORS

AACD - American Association for Counseling and Development,
Order Services Dept., 5999 Stevenson Ave.,
Alexandria, VA 22304

AIM - Association of Instructional Materials, 600 Madison
Avenue, New York, NY 10022

AMEDFL - American Educational Films, 132 Lasky Drive,
Beverly Hills, CA 90212

APGA - American Personnel and Guidance Association Film
Distribution Center, 1607 New Hampshire Ave., NW,
Washington, DC 10009

AVC - Audio-Visual Center, Indiana University, Bloomington,
Indiana 47401

AVNA - Audio Visual Narrative Arts, P.O Box 9, Pleasant-
ville, NY 10570

Carousel Films - 1501 Broadway, New York, NY 10036

CBSTV - Columbia Broadcasting System, 51 West 52nd St., New
York, NY 10019

CDI - Cambridge Documentary Films, P.O. Box 385, Cambridge,
MA 02139

CM - Concept Media, P.O. Box 19542, Irvine, CA 92714

CRM - Films, Del Mar, CA 92014

DOCUA - Document Associates, 211 East 43rd St., New York, NY
10023

EBEC - Encyclopedia Britannica Educational Corporation, 3712
Jarvis Ave., Skokie, IL 60076

EMC - Extension Media Center, University of California,
Berkeley, CA 94720

Filmakers Library - 290 West End Ave., New York, NY 10023

Films for the Humanities - Box 2053, Princeton, NJ 08540

FI or Films, Inc. - 1213 Wilmette Ave., Wilmette, IL 60091

FOCUSE - Focus Educational, Inc., 3 East 54th St., New York,
NY 10022

HAR or HR - Harper and Row, 10 East 53rd St., New York, NY
      10022

Herbert Krill - 789 West End Ave., PH 2, New York, NY 10025

Horizon House Institute - 1019 Stafford House, 5555
      Wissahickon Ave., Philadelphia, PA 19144

HRM - Human Relations Media (no address listed)

HSC - Health Science Consortium, 103 Laurel Ave.,
      Corroboro, NC 27510

IDEAL - Ideal School Supply Company, 1100 S. Lavergne Ave.,
      Oak Lawn, IL 60453

International Film Bureau - 332 S. Michigan Ave, Chicago, IL

ITVFP - International TV Film Production (no address listed)

IU -   Audio-Visual Center, Division of University
      Extension, Indiana University, Bloomington, IN 47401

JF -   Jason Films, 2621 Palisado Ave., Riverdale, NY 10463

J. Gary Mitchell Film Co. - 163 Tunstead Ave., San Anselmo,
      CA 94960

MEDCOM, INC - 1633 Broadway, New York, NY 10019

MGHF or McGraw-Hill Films - 330 West 42nd St., New York, NY
      10036

MIT - MIT Teleprograms, Inc., 420 Academy Dr., Northbrook,
      IL 60062

NAMH - National Association for Mental Health, Film Library,
      267 West 25th St., New York, NY

NFBC - National Film Board of Canada, 1251 Avenue of the
      Americas, 16th Floor, New York, NY 10020

NMAC - National Medical Audiovisual Center, 2111 Plaster
      Bridge Road, Atlanta, GA 30324

NET - NET Film Service, c/o AVC

NYU Film Library - New York University Film Library, 26
      Washington Place, New York, NY 10003

ODION - Odeon Films, 1610 Broadway, New York, NY 10019

PCR - Psychological Cinema Register, Pennsylvania State University, Audio-Visual Services, University Park, PA 16802

Peter M. Robeck & Company - 230 Park Ave., New York, NY 10017

PF - Polymorph Films, Inc., 118 South St., Boston, MA 02115

PFB - Pyramid Films, P.O. Box 1048, Santa Monica, CA 90406

PHPE - Phillips Petroleum Public Affairs, 16 B4 Phillips Bldg., Bartlesville, OK 74004

PSU - Penn State University, Audiovisual Services, 17 Willard Bldg., University Park, PA 16802

PSYCHD - Psychological Films, Distribution Center, 1215 East Chapman, Orange, CA 92669

PSYCHF - Psychological Films, 189 North Wheeler St., Orange, CA 92669

Psychological Films - 295 West 20th St., Santa Ana, CA 92706

PUBTEL - Public Television Library, 475 L'Enfant Plaza, SW, Washington, DC 20024

SF - Sterling Educational Films, 241 East 34th St., New York, NY 10016

SH - Stanfield House, P.O. Box 3208, Santa Monica, CA 90405

Research Press - Box 3177, Dept. J, Champaign, IL 61821

The Center for Cassette Studies - 8110 Webb Ave., North Hollywood, CA 91605

The Film Center - 189 N. Wheeler St., Orange, CA 92669

Time-Life Film or TL - 43 West 16th St., New York, NY 10011

TLM - Time-Life Multimedia, 100 Eisenhower Dr., P.O. Box 648, Paramus, NJ 07652

UA - United Artists Studios, 729 7th Ave., New York, NY 10019

UCEMC - University of California Extension Media Center, Film Distributor, 2223 Fulton St., Berkeley, CA 94720

USC - University of Southern California, Film and Video Distribution Center, School of Cinema-Television, University Park-MC2212, Los Angeles, CA 90089

USDA - U.S. Department of Agriculture (no address listed)

USNAC - U.S. National Audiovisual Center, General Services Administration, Washington, DC 20350

VACO - Veterans Administration Central Office (no address listed)

WILEYJ - John Wiley & Sons, 605 Third Ave, New York, NY 10016

Workshop Films - 4 Longfellow Rd., Cambridge, MA 02138